THE FALL OF HITLER'S THIRD
REICH

THE FALL OF HITLER'S THIRD
REICH
GERMANY'S DEFEAT IN EUROPE 1943–45

DAVID JORDAN

amber
BOOKS

First published in 2004

Published by
Amber Books Ltd
Bradley's Close
74–77 White Lion Street
London N1 9PF
United Kingdom
www.amberbooks.co.uk

ISBN: 1-904687-22-9

Project Editor: Michael Spilling
Copy Editor: Stephen Chumbley
Design: Graham Curd

Printed in Italy

PICTURE CREDITS

All photographs courtesy of TRH Pictures, except:
The U.S. National Archives: 9, 134, 145, 147;
POPPERFOTO: 72;
Ukrainian State Archive: 57, 64, 154, 158, 163, 167,
171, 182, 183.

Maps produced by Cartographica

Contents

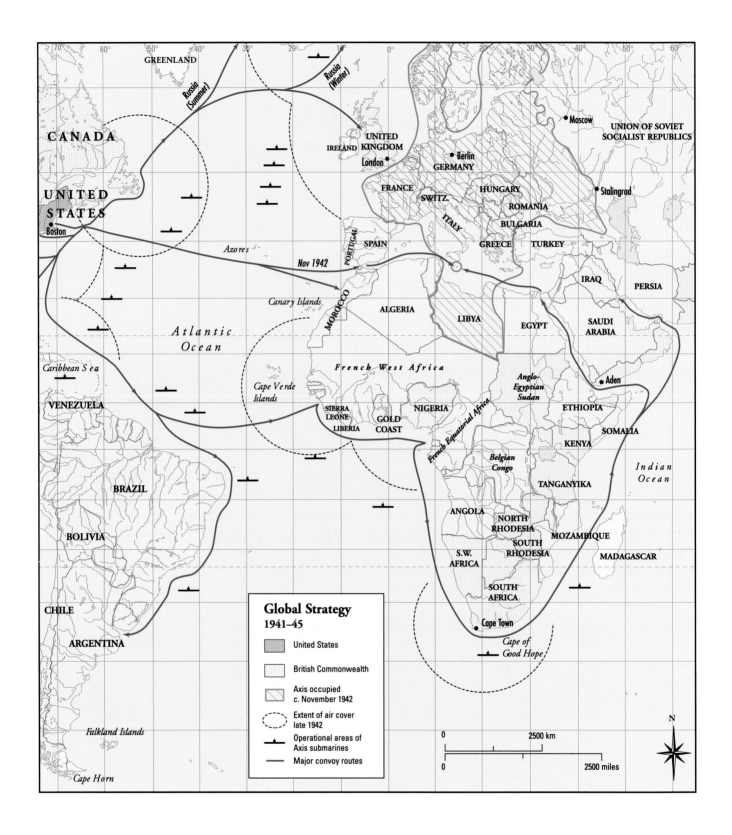

CANADA

GREENLAND

UNITED STATES

Boston

Russia (Summer)

Russia (Winter)

IRELAND

UNITED KINGDOM

London

Berlin

GERMANY

FRANCE

SWITZ.

HUNGARY

ROMANIA

BULGARIA

ITALY

GREECE

TURKEY

Moscow

UNION OF SOVIET SOCIALIST REPUBLICS

Stalingrad

IRAQ

PERSIA

Azores

Nov 1942

PORTUGAL

SPAIN

Canary Islands

MOROCCO

ALGERIA

LIBYA

EGYPT

SAUDI ARABIA

Atlantic Ocean

French West Africa

Aden

Cape Verde Islands

SIERRA LEONE

LIBERIA

GOLD COAST

NIGERIA

French Equatorial Africa

Anglo-Egyptian Sudan

ETHIOPIA

SOMALIA

KENYA

Caribbean Sea

VENEZUELA

Belgian Congo

TANGANYIKA

Indian Ocean

BRAZIL

ANGOLA

NORTH RHODESIA

SOUTH RHODESIA

MOZAMBIQUE

MADAGASCAR

BOLIVIA

S.W. AFRICA

CHILE

SOUTH AFRICA

ARGENTINA

Cape Town

Cape of Good Hope

Global Strategy
1941–45

United States

British Commonwealth

Axis occupied c. November 1942

Extent of air cover late 1942

Operational areas of Axis submarines

Major convoy routes

0   2500 km

0   2500 miles

Falkland Islands

Cape Horn

N

Introduction

As 1942 drew to a close, it was clear that the rise of the Third Reich had reached its apogee. After the stunning successes enjoyed in the first years of the war, German advances had at first been slowed, and then reversed. The Allied war effort had grown in strength during the year. The entry of the United States into the war meant that the weight of American industrial power could be harnessed in the fight against Fascism.

At the 'Arcadia' conference, held in Washington between December 1941 and January 1942 (their first summit as allies), President Roosevelt and Prime Minister Churchill had agreed that the main effort for the United States would be applied against Germany first, and then against Japan. Although it took time for the American armed forces to be available in strength, they had participated in their first combat in North Africa following the landings in French North Africa under the auspices of Operation Torch. Torch followed the British success at the second battle of El Alamein on 2 November 1942. El Alamein marked a turning point in British perceptions of the war – until that point, British forces had proved unable to inflict a meaningful defeat upon the Germans, and the victory by the Eighth Army raised morale considerably.

America Enters the Fray

American participation in Torch was controversial. It was proposed by Churchill at the 'Arcadia' conference, but opposed by the US Chiefs of Staff, who saw landings in North Africa as a diversion of effort that would prevent a quick assault against North West Europe. In February, General Dwight D. Eisenhower made clear that the best course of action for the United States was a build-up of American resources in Britain, followed by an invasion of France later that year. This was an over-optimistic assessment of what could be achieved in 1942, as Roosevelt was well aware. The President also felt that an early involvement of US troops in the European theatre of operations would be of considerable political advantage, both in reinforcing the 'Germany First' strategy, and demonstrating willing to the Soviet Union. As a result of these considerations, planning for a combined landing in North Africa got underway.

Opposite: The sea routes between the United States and Britain were of vital importance in supplying the Allies with men and munitions from North America. With its phenomenal industrial strength, the United States was the driving force behind the Allied war effort. Although Soviet industry was, in terms of military output, even more prolific, even the Red Army was dependent upon American factories for its trucks and jeeps. As the Soviets continued to push back the Wehrmacht *post-Stalingrad and inflict increasingly heavier casualties, the Anglo-American invasion of Europe became the prime focus for Allied strategy.*

The plan, now named 'Torch', called for three separate landings. The westernmost landing would be made by an all-American force near to Casablanca in Morocco; that in the centre would be carried out by American troops, while the Eastern Task Force would be mainly British, with a small US contingent. The landings took place before dawn on 8 November 1942, and met little resistance from the Vichy French forces. However, reinforcement of Tunisia by the Germans and Italians meant that Tunis could not be taken, and it became clear that it would not be until 1943 that the Allies would be able to launch a major effort to drive Axis forces from North Africa.

Defeat at Stalingrad

The German position was not only weakened in North Africa by the end of 1942, since events on the Eastern Front served to demonstrate that Hitler's notions of defeating the Soviet Union were perhaps over-optimistic. Grand plans for seizing Leningrad and the Caucasus oilfields had failed to come to fruition in 1942, and the German effort had been shifted to attacking Stalingrad, despite warnings from the German general staff that this represented a dangerous diversion to little strategic purpose. The German assault on Stalingrad was marked by savage street fighting as the advantage switched between the two sides. Although there were occasions when the Soviet situation appeared grim, the Germans simply could not break down resistance sufficiently to drive the Soviets from the city. Stalingrad's defence was the responsibility of Lieutenant-General Vasily Chuikov's Sixty-Second Army. Chuikov concluded that exploiting the constraints imposed on an army by fighting in a built-up area would make German co-ordination of their infantry, air power and armour – a hallmark of their successes to date – extremely difficult to attain. The battle started on 14 September 1942, beginning weeks of ferocious fighting.

While the battle raged, the Soviet high command had been busy preparing a counteroffensive. Over one million Soviet troops were gathered together to launch Operation Uranus, which was intended to encircle Stalingrad from north and south, cutting off the Sixth Army. The offensive began on 19 November and by the 23 November the Sixth Army was surrounded. Hitler refused to give permission for an attempt at withdrawal, and then forbade General Paulus to surrender. However, with his forces suffering attrition in the freezing conditions, Paulus met with Soviet emissaries on the 30 January 1943 to offer his surrender. Hundreds of thousands of men were marched into a captivity from which few would return.

The Battle of the Atlantic

One area of the war in which the Germans enjoyed a considerable advantage for much of 1942 was the conflict at sea. America's entry into the war provided a host of targets for U-boat commanders as the United States struggled to implement effective anti-submarine measures. From 12 January 1942, the U-boat fleet embarked upon what was known as the second 'Happy Time' as they operated with near-impunity off the east coast of America (the first 'Happy Time' had been while the British were struggling to address the threat posed by German submarines in mid-1940). The US Navy had serious difficulties in the first three months of the year, due to the lack of escorts and the lack of security measures employed by merchant shipping.

The German submarine arm enjoyed a further advantage in 1942. The British top-secret code-breaking station at Bletchley Park had succeeded in breaking the code for the

'Now this is not the end. It is not even the beginning of the end. But it is, perhaps, the end of the beginning.'

Winston Churchill 10 November 1942, after victory at Alamein

U-boat fleet, and had exploited this to enable convoys to be routed away from the submarines as soon as radio intercepts revealed where the U-boats were in the Atlantic. A modification to the German Enigma machine as part of a routine security improvement ordered by Admiral Karl Dönitz meant that Bletchley Park was rendered 'blind', and the vital information about where the U-boats were congregating could no longer be divined. By July 1942, the U-boats had begun to target convoys in mid-Atlantic again. However, by this point, the battle had begun to tip, imperceptibly, in favour of the Allies again. The Royal Navy at last began to receive enough ships and equipment for the anti-submarine role, while the British Coastal Command started to employ long-range aircraft such as the Liberator. After the capture of Enigma material from the U-559, Bletchley Park was able to crack the new German code by December. The Battle of the Atlantic was, therefore, in the balance by 1943, with the British Admiralty predicting that early 1943 would be the critical phase of the struggle.

Year of Transition

Consequently, 1942 was a year of transition. German defeats in North Africa and the Soviet Union suggested that tide was beginning to turn in favour of the Allies, an impression bolstered by American entry into the war. It would be wrong, however, to suggest that a final victory against the Third Reich seemed an obvious outcome at the time. Hitler was still in control of mainland Europe; Allied bombing raids were by no means devastating, and the Battle of the Atlantic was delicately poised. Rather than a decisive change, the events of 1942 marked the first cracks in the defences of Germany, cracks which would be forced wider apart in the next two and a half years until the façade of a thousand-year Reich was brought crashing to earth.

Above: British Prime Minister Winston Churchill, US President Franklin Delano Roosevelt and Soviet premier Joseph Stalin had the second of three tripartite meetings at the Yalta Conference in the Crimea, 4–11 February, 1944. During this conference, the Allied leaders discussed Europe's postwar reorganization. This included such issues as the re-establishment of the nations conquered and destroyed by Germany, as well as how a defeated Germany would be divided into zones of control.

The Desert War

After the defeat at El Alamein, and the Anglo-American landings under the auspices of Operation Torch, it was clear that the German position in North Africa was becoming increasingly perilous. While resistance to the Anglo-American landings had been sufficiently fierce to delay the Allied advance, German forces were simply not strong enough to hold the invaders off forever.

While the Allies advanced from the west, it was quite clear to all parties that the *Afrika Korps* was in full flight from the Alamein battlefield, even if the Germans were withdrawing in reasonable order. The nature of Montgomery's pursuit ensured that the retreat did not turn into a rout, but Montgomery's reason for being careful was based upon the notion that he would rather be fully prepared for the next round of battles, and not outrun his supply lines in the process of pursuit.

Although Montgomery's controversial decision has been the subject of considerable debate since, the simple fact is that such retrospective analysis cannot alter the history of events in North Africa. The Eighth Army advanced methodically, driving the Germans and Italians back towards Tunisia. Montgomery's forces reached Sirte on 25 December, and spent the next few weeks ensuring that their supply lines were secure before the next phase of the advance.

On 12 January 1943, aircraft from the Desert Air Force began a series of preliminary raids in support of an offensive south of Buerat. The advance, by XXX Corps, was steady rather than spectacular, covered by constant air support. Progress on the ground was slow, with minefields and difficult ground conditions making movement difficult. This prompted Montgomery to instruct 51st Highland Division to press on as quickly as possible, although this was hampered by the fact that the division had not been provided with sufficient transportation under the original plan, which had other units in greater need. This was overcome to some extent by moving by day and night.

On 19 January, the 51st Division entered Homs. German intelligence of British movements concerned Rommel to the extent that he decided that it was necessary to abandon his defensive line. In fact, Montgomery's intentions were not as Rommel had

Opposite: Grumman Martlet and Supermarine Seafire fighters await take-off from the aircraft carrier HMS Formidable, *off the North African coast. Although not obvious from this picture, many British aircraft were painted with American markings during the Torch landings, to make it easier for the recently arrived US troops to tell the difference between hostile and friendly aircraft.*

Above: British troops relax prior to a training exercise in Tunisia. The British provided the majority of the forces in the North African campaign, even after the arrival of American forces under the auspices of Operation Torch.

anticipated. He made his main thrust along the coast road, rather than inland, aiming for Tripoli. By 21 January, the prize of Tripoli was in sight, and British formations pressed on as quickly as possible. On the night of 22/23 January, Rommel decided that the position was hopeless, and abandoned the city, leaving only small rearguard forces to protect the withdrawal. As it was, the first British forces entered Tripoli on 23 January, and found there was no opposition.

At midday, Montgomery received the surrender of the city from the Italian vice-governor. Rommel's army had been driven out of Egypt, Cyrenaica, and nearly all of Libya and Tripolitania, but although the Axis position in North Africa was now critical, there was still a great deal of fighting to be done.

Fighting in Tunisia

The reverses suffered in January 1943 caused considerable uncertainty on the part of the Axis powers at the end of the month, since it was not clear what could be done to prevent the Allies from gaining ultimate victory. Rommel fell back on the defensive positions of the Mareth Line, as the last of his army withdrew from Libya, reaching Tunisia on 13 February. This did not mean that the Germans had given up, however, for the next day, they launched an assault against the inexperienced American II Corps. The Corps Intelligence Officer had warned that there was the possibility that the enemy would attack in strength against Gafsa, and air intelligence officers agreed with this assessment. As a result, Lieutenant-General Sir Kenneth Anderson, the commander of First Army, had instructed that Gafsa was not to be held against a major attack, and that the Americans should pull back and defend in the hills around Feriana.

The Germans had been planning for the assault for over a week. Rommel had assessed that the Allies might strike against the coast from their position at Gafsa, and concluded that the best counter was an attack launched through Gafsa, with the aim of attacking the Americans before they were prepared for further action. The attack would drive through Gafsa, then the American troops in open country beyond and in the hills to the west. There were a number of difficulties, however, since Rommel and Colonel-General Jürgen von Arnim endeavoured to persuade each other to release their mobile forces (a sign of the numerical problems faced by the Germans), but had failed in their efforts. Von Arnim would not release his mobile troops to support Rommel, since he was anxious to

Below: Battle-weary Afrika Korps *troops trudge through the desert between battles. The Germans suffered from a lack of motorised transport, and movement in daylight hours became increasingly dangerous as the British gained air superiority. After the campaign had ended, Rommel concluded that any army fighting under near-constant air attack would be unable to overcome its opponents.*

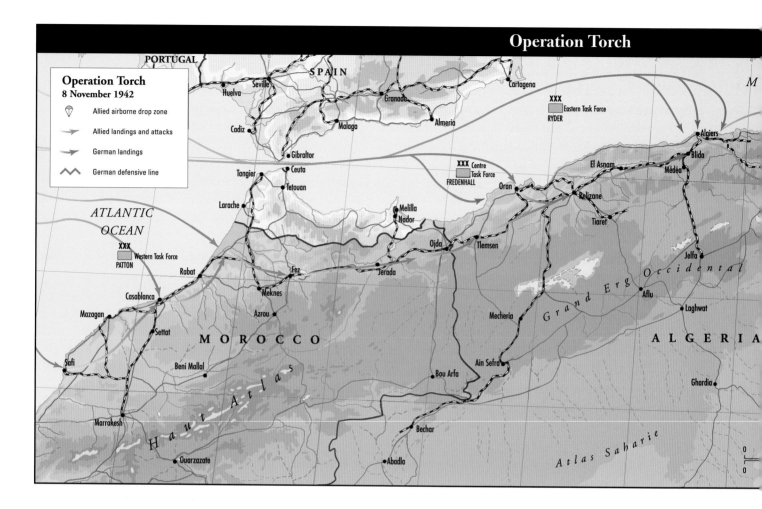

Operation Torch

Operation Torch
8 November 1942

- Allied airborne drop zone
- Allied landings and attacks
- German landings
- German defensive line

Above: Operation Torch was the first major Anglo-American operation of World War II, and saw four separate landing operations along the North African coast. A complication came in the form of the French troops defending Morocco and Algeria, since they were nominally opposed to the Allies as the result of the terms of the Vichy treaty. Although some resisted, most did nothing to oppose the landings, and the Allies made a swift advance until they came into contact with German forces in Tunisia.

launch an attack of his own through Faid to Sidi Bou Zid. Von Arnim's attack began first, just as predicted by US II Corps' intelligence, and went well. By 06:00 of the first morning, German troops were five miles west of the Faid Pass. American defensive efforts were not helped by a failure of communications which meant that their artillery's pre-planned defensive fireplan was not brought down on the enemy as intended. German air attacks supported the advance, and although the Americans did their best, they were unable to prevent German forces from linking north of Sidi Bou Zid by 10:00.

The success of the advance prompted Rommel to order that the attack on Gafsa should begin on 15 February, although the American and French troops there left for Feriana, in accordance with Anderson's instructions. A counter-attack by the American Combat Command C ran into difficulties and only just managed to withdraw, losing a battalion of tanks in the process. Combat Command A was left isolated, and although it was finally ordered to withdraw during the night of 16 February, some 1400 troops were captured during the course of the next day.

Anderson had meanwhile decided that US II Corps should hold Feriana, Kasserine and Sbeitla, without attempting any more counterattacks. This demanded several complicated movements for the units of First Army, but these were accomplished with little interference from the enemy. On 17 February, Anderson gave permission for Feriana and Sbeitla to be abandoned, and by the afternoon, Rommel's forces had entered the former, and also Thelepte, as well as Gafsa and Tozeur; Sbeitla and Sidi Bou Zid followed into German hands shortly afterwards. While the Germans held the initiative,

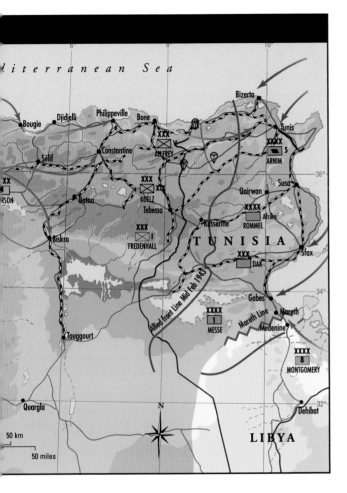

orders came from the Italian supreme command (which had overall responsibility for Axis forces in North Africa) ordering a move northwards, with the aim of attacking V Corps. Neither Rommel nor von Arnim agreed with the order. Von Arnim was concerned that the proposed move would in fact put his forces in contact with the enemy's reserves at the strongest point; Rommel, meanwhile, chose not to protest, but instead ordered the *Afrika Korps* Assault Group to capture the Kasserine Pass.

The Kasserine Pass

Following Rommel's instructions, a reconnaissance of the Kasserine Pass was carried out by German forces on 18 February, convincing the Americans that an attack there would soon be forthcoming. The commanding officer of the US 26th Infantry Regiment, Colonel Alexander N. Stark, was ordered to take control of a variety of units in the vicinity, to be known as Stark Force. The Germans attacked Stark Force on 19 February, with the aim of capturing and sealing the pass. An intense German effort thrust against the inexperienced American forces, and by mid-morning next day, the American defence began to collapse. A withdrawal to Djebel el Hamra was carried out, with considerable amounts of equipment left behind intact for the Germans to capture. In the face of these successes, the Allies were concerned about the position, and could not call on a great amount of air support as the weather was so poor as to prevent much flying.

A German advance on Thala and Djebel el Hamra on 21 February was blocked by Combat Command B at the latter location, but the British 26th Armoured Brigade was slowly pushed back to around four miles south of Thala. As the armoured brigade passed through the positions of the defending infantry, German tanks broke into the position, and only an *ad hoc* defence by the 17th/21st Lancers and two batteries of field guns firing over open sights as anti-tank weapons stopped the assault. The Germans withdrew at about 22:00, and an improvised defensive plan, including the grouping of British and American artillery into a single force, was drawn up. The situation appeared extremely dangerous, but in fact the pressure was about to be reduced. It seemed apparent to the Germans that they were not going to be able to break through, and by the afternoon of 22 February, Rommel made clear that he thought that there was little point in continuing the offensive. There were several reasons for these conclusions. First, Rommel was convinced that the losses sustained by the Allies had been heavy, and meant that they would be unable to take to the offensive for some time. Second, Rommel noted that the

'The total destruction or capture of all enemy forces in Tunisia, culminating in the surrender of 248,000 men, marks the triumphant end of the great enterprises set on foot at Alamein and by the invasion of North West Africa.'

Winston Churchill, 3 June 1943

DESERT AIR POWER

The use of air power proved critical to success in the desert campaign, and laid the foundations for Allied air operations in Italy and Normandy. Initially, the British found that the years of inter-service rivalry after World War I meant that air support for the Army was almost totally lacking, while the Army did not fully understand what could and could not be done with aircraft in support of land forces. This reached a nadir when the Army demanded that the RAF bomb individual tanks as they sped across the battlefield.

Fortunately, while the spirit of cooperation had been lacking at the most senior levels of the two services, the commanders in the desert campaign realized that air support was important, and developed a highly effective system. This required the RAF to gain control of the air, use fighter-bombers in support of Army operations and attack German supply lines. By the end of the desert war, the Allies had absolute air supremacy, enabling them to bring firepower to bear against key German targets in support of the advance of ground forces.

Kasserine area was unsuited to further mobile operations (particularly now the ground had been made more difficult by the weather); far better, he concluded to break off the offensive and turn attention to southern Tunisia for a blow against the Eighth Army. As a result, orders were given that the German forces should return to their start points. By the morning of 24 February, the Kasserine Pass was in Allied hands once more, after what had been a particularly fierce and bloody introduction for the Americans to what the Germans were truly capable of.

The Battle of Medenine
In the immediate aftermath of the Kasserine Pass, Rommel was given command of all Axis forces in Tunisia, but this new appointment came too late for him to prevent von Arnim's proposed attack northwards toward Medjez el Bab. Rommel expressed the view that von Arnim's plans were totally unrealistic, and was not surprised when the attacks ended in failure. Although over 2500 prisoners were taken in the attacks, the Germans lost over 70 of their tanks, which they could ill afford.

Map, page 18: The Battle of Kasserine Pass was the first clash between American and German troops. The inexperienced Americans were roughly handled by Rommel's forces, and for a time, the situation appeared critical. However, the defences held, and Rommel withdrew once it became clear that he would not achieve a breakthrough.

The offensive had another negative element in that it delayed preparations for Rommel's next planned attack, against Montgomery's position at Medenine. As it became clear that the Germans were building their strength in the area, Montgomery grew extremely concerned. Signals intercepted and decoded at Bletchley Park gave away Rommel's overall intentions, and information gathered from local reconnaissance patrols and prisoner interrogation made it clear that a major attack was in the offing. More men and equipment were rushed to the area, so that by early March, the British strength at Medenine had been more than quadrupled. The Germans seem to have been blissfully unaware of the increase in British strength, and when they finally attacked on 6 March, they were in for an unpleasant surprise.

The British defences had been carefully established, and rested upon two key components – a heavy defensive fireplan for the artillery, and the use of anti-tank guns located in the forward area. Anti-tank gun strength was bolstered by flying 100 of the new 17-pounder guns to North Africa, where they were fitted on to 25-pounder field gun carriages in the absence of carriages designed for the 17-pounder. When the Germans advanced, they were allowed to reach within 100 yards of the anti-tank guns, which then opened fire. The German tanks suffered heavy losses under the assault of the anti-tank guns, and matters were not helped by the heavy defensive artillery fire that made it almost impossible for the German infantry to advance. By 17:30, it was clear that there would be no breakthrough, and Rommel called off the attack.

The Mareth Line

Rommel's failure at Medenine convinced him that the time for German and Italian forces to abandon North Africa had come, and he determined to inform Hitler and Mussolini of this fact. Taking sick leave on 9 March, he flew to Italy, where he discovered that Mussolini had no appreciation of how dangerous the situation was. He continued his journey to Berlin, where Hitler demonstrated an even greater lack of awareness of the German situation, talking not of withdrawal, but of operations against Casablanca to throw the Allies out of Africa.

While the two dictators were demonstrating their lack of understanding of how grave the situation had become, Montgomery made plans to break through the German defensive positions on the Mareth Line, with a start date of 20 March.

Three days before the attack, US II Corps, now under the command of the inimitable Lieutenant-General George S. Patton, launched a supporting attack in the area of Gafsa. The attack began well, and Gafsa was taken without a fight as the enemy fell back; however, over the next three days, stubborn German defence prevented the Americans from moving to cut the coast road. On 23 March a German counter-attack in the El Guettar sector overran American forward positions before being thrown back. Although a relatively inconclusive engagement, the attack used up yet more of the German armoured reserve that could have been employed in the struggle for the Mareth Line.

Montgomery's attack began on 20 March as planned, using troops from X and XXX Corps, with 160,000 men, 600 tanks and over 1400 guns. The plan involved a main effort in the form of a frontal assault on the enemy defensive positions, but this made only a small dent in the Axis lines before being driven back by the end of 22 March. The second element of the attack, a flanking march by the New Zealand Corps against

Below: A flight of Hawker Hurricane IID fighter-bombers from the RAF patrol over the desert. The Hurricane IID was armed with two 40mm cannon for use against German armour, and proved extremely effective. However, the weight of additional armour protection and the guns had a drastic effect on the aircraft's top speed, making it vulnerable. Despite the success of the guns, the RAF moved on to using rocket projectiles when the fighting moved to mainland Europe.

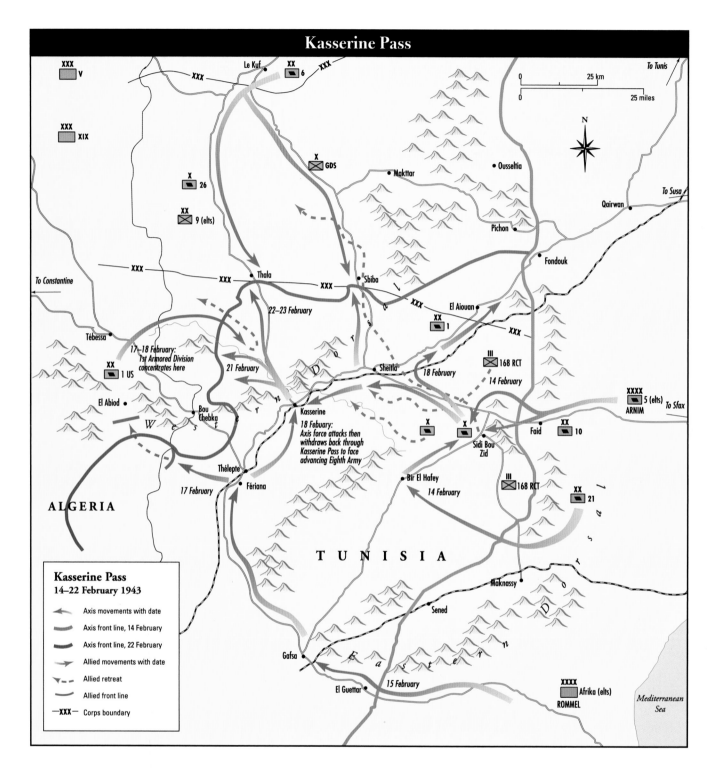

Kasserine Pass

Kasserine Pass
14–22 February 1943

← Axis movements with date
Axis front line, 14 February
Axis front line, 22 February
→ Allied movements with date
⤍ Allied retreat
Allied front line
—XXX— Corps boundary

El Hamma, initially enjoyed more success, but was then held up. After clearing the coastal approaches, the attack was stopped at the hill gap known, rather oddly, as Plum. The Plum Gap was reinforced by 21st Panzer Division and four infantry units brought down from the Mareth Line and it was soon clear that the New Zealanders would not be able to progress. As a result, Montgomery recast his plan, concentrating all his forces on the inland flank, where it appeared that a renewed attack might break through. X Corps and the 1st Armoured Division made a move inland to support the New Zealanders on

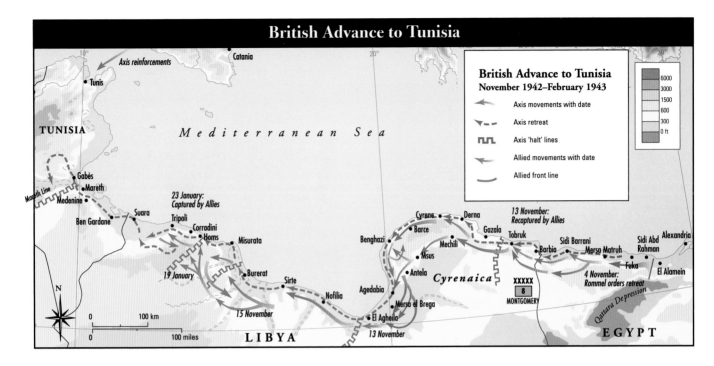

British Advance to Tunisia

British Advance to Tunisia
November 1942–February 1943

← Axis movements with date

∇ - - Axis retreat

ⅢⅢ Axis 'halt' lines

← Allied movements with date

‿ Allied front line

23 March, while 4th Indian Division was given the task of clearing the Hallouf Pass – taking this would reduce British supply lines by over 100 miles – then moving along the hills to the flank of the Mareth Line, presenting a new threat to the Axis forces.

The movement of the New Zealanders was detected by Axis reconnaissance, and further snippets of information about movement gleaned from observers located in the hills suggested that a major attack against the desert flank of their position was in the offing. This prompted von Arnim to instruct the Italian forces holding the Mareth Line to pull back; this in turn meant that the Plum Gap would only be held as long as it took for the non-mobile units in the Mareth Line to withdraw.

The attack began at 16:00 on 26 March, supported by heavy air cover and artillery. The 1st Armoured Division passed through the leading troops at about 18:00 and, advancing through the night, had reached the edge of El Hamma by dawn on 27 March. A German counter-attack checked the advance for 48 hours, giving most of the Mareth Line garrison the opportunity to retreat to the Wadi Akarit position. Montgomery now paused for a week to prepare for the next phase of the attack.

While the British were attacking, Patton's II Corps renewed their assault towards the coast and the Axis rear areas, attacking from El Guettar on 28 March. In a desire to act quickly, Patton was ordered to attack without waiting for the infantry to clear the German anti-tank gun positions, but after three days of fighting, the Americans had advanced no further. While the attack may not have taken much ground, it forced the diversion of 21st Panzer Division to this sector, reducing German armoured strength in the area of the Wadi Akarit.

A frontal attack at nightfall on 5 April by 4th Indian Division carried the ground ahead of it, with over 4000 prisoners being taken by dawn the next day, by which time the 50th and 51st Divisions had launched attacks of their own. While the 50th Division had been stopped, the 51st broke into the German lines. This offered the opportunity of a rapid exploitation by X Corps' armour, but there was a delay in moving the armour forward, which meant that the chance passed. Montgomery instead intended to put in a

Above: The British advance to Tunisia marked the end of an often painful campaign against the Germans. The advance began in earnest with the victory at El Alamein, with Montgomery pursuing the retreating Afrika Korps in a careful and methodical fashion that later came in for some criticism. Despite this, the Eighth Army pursued the Germans all the way to the Mareth Line, and then broke through, ready for the final push against Tunis.

Above: A British 5.5-inch gun fires as part of a night-time artillery barrage against the Mareth Line. Robust and reliable, the 5.5-inch gun was one of the mainstays of the Royal Artillery, and remained in use with the British Army for many years after the war.

decisive blow the next day, but when daylight came, it was clear that the enemy had simply slipped away. Without reinforcement, holding Wadi Akarit became more and more difficult, so the Axis troops began to withdraw to Enfidaville. As the Axis forces joined to defend the last remaining foothold in North Africa, plans were drawn up by the Allies to ensure victory.

The Final Act

By the last three weeks of the North African campaign, the growing numerical superiority of the Allies began to tell. While the Germans and Italians had 13 by now understrength divisions and 130 tanks, the British and Americans had 19 fully effective divisions, supported by over 1100 armoured vehicles. The Allies had three times as many artillery pieces as their opponents, and enjoyed almost complete dominance in the air. As ever, the key test for the Allies would be to translate this superiority on paper into actual supremacy on the field of battle.

For the Axis powers, retaining a foothold in North Africa was crucial, no matter how small the area occupied was in comparison with the territory held when the *Afrika Korps* was at the height of its power. Hitler and Mussolini understood that if they could hold on in Tunisia until the summer or autumn of 1942, they might be able to delay an Allied invasion of Europe until a time when amphibious operations would be made far more difficult by poor weather (also hindering the use of air support to ground troops). As a result, the Germans carried out a great deal of work aimed at improving the defences on high ground, with the aim of bogging down the Allied assault.

For the Allies, the best approach to Tunis was clearly through the Medjerda valley, by clearing the hills on either side of Medjez el Bab (a task which would be in the operating areas of First Army's V Corps and Patton's US II Corps). If this was achieved, it offered the prospect of opening a considerable gap for armour to exploit in a way that would not be possible elsewhere. As far as Montgomery's Eighth Army were concerned, their narrow front along the coastline gave possible access to Tunis or Cap Bon. However, since Sir Harold Alexander (Commander-in-Chief Middle East) was hoping to take the Tunisian ports quickly, the first option was far preferable – if the ports could be seized in short order, this would allow an invasion of Sicily to take place during the summer. As a result, he ordered Anderson's First Army to launch an attack on 22 April against the Axis forces between Medjez el Bab and Bou Arada, with US II Corps attacking in the direction of Bizerta. Eighth Army was to carry out a series of holding attacks around Enfidaville, with the aim of diverting attention from First Army in the days leading up to the offensive.

This instruction was complicated by the fact that Montgomery appears to have regarded giving primacy to First Army in this attack as an unacceptable step, denying Eighth Army the chance to win the final victory in the North African campaign. As a result, he proposed to carry out an attack by four divisions (three infantry and one armoured) which would aim to punch at least 20 miles into enemy lines – hardly the holding attack that Alexander had intended for Eighth Army. Montgomery's plan may have been inspired to some extent by a desire for his army to round off its North African

GENERAL GEORGE S. PATTON

George S. Patton was born in 1885, and graduated from West Point in 1909. Patton was appointed as an aide to General Pershing in the punitive expedition against Mexico in 1916, and was still serving as Pershing's aide when America entered World War I. He accompanied Pershing to France in May 1917. When in France, Patton transferred to the Tank Corps, and was promoted to command of the 304th Tank Brigade.

The end of the conflict saw the dissolution of the Tank Corps, which prompted Patton's return to the cavalry. In the interwar period, Patton's career progressed through the usual round of command and staff appointments, until, in July 1940, he was promoted to brigadier-general and assumed command of the 2nd Brigade, 2nd Armored Division at Fort Benning, Georgia. Promotion to major-general followed less than a year later, and he took command of his division. Patton was given command of the Army's newly formed Desert Training Center on 1 April 1942, before being assigned to the planning for Operation Torch. He was then appointed as commander of the Western Task Force during the invasion of North Africa, in which capacity he led the American forces that took French Morocco. Following the mauling of US II Corps at the Battle of Kasserine Pass on 19 February 1943, Patton was appointed to lead this formation, a role he held until the end of the desert conflict.

Right: The last phase of operations in North Africa came with the assault against the capital, Tunis. A series of attacks launched by Eighth Army to the southeast and the recently arrived invasion armies from Operation Torch met with fierce resistance, but the weight of numbers ranged against them began to tell on the Axis troops, who were forced to fall back towards Tunis.

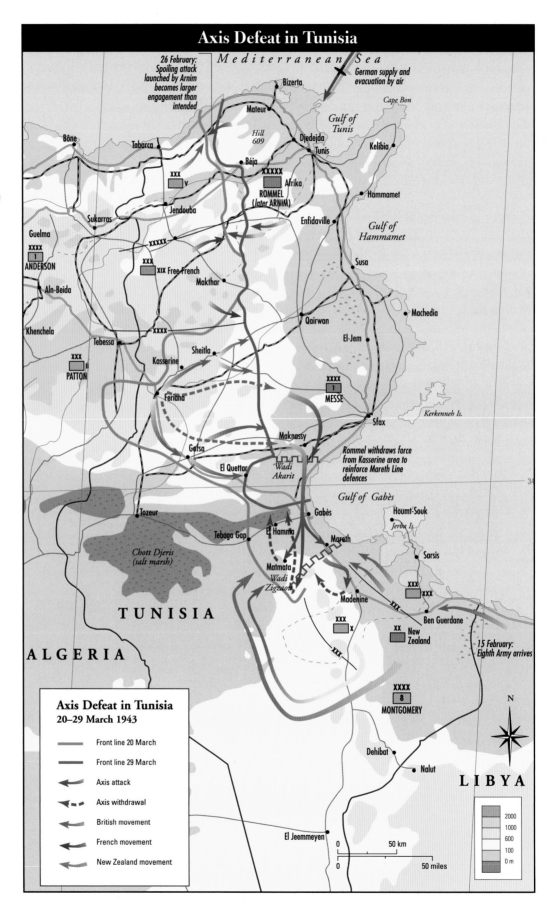

Axis Defeat in Tunisia

26 February: Spoiling attack launched by Arnim becomes larger engagement than intended

German supply and evacuation by air

Mediterranean Sea

Bizerta

Cape Bon

Mateur

Gulf of Tunis

Bône

Tabarca

Hill 609

Djedejda

Tunis

Kelibia

Béja

XXX V

XXXXX Afrika
ROMMEL (later ARNIM)

Hammamet

Sukarras

Jendouba

Enfidaville

Gulf of Hammamet

Guelma

XXXX 1 ANDERSON

XXXXX

XXX XIX Free French

Makthar

Susa

Aln-Beida

Qairwan

Machedia

Khenchela

El-Jem

Tebessa

XXXX

Sheitla

XXX II PATTON

Kasserine

XXXX 1 MESSE

Kerkenneh Is.

Feriana

Sfax

Maknassy

Rommel withdraws force from Kasserine area to reinforce Mareth Line defences

Gafsa

El Quettar

Wadi Akarit

Gulf of Gabès

Tozeur

Gabès

Houmt-Souk

Jerba Is.

Tebaga Gap

El Hamma

Mareth

Sarsis

Chott Djeris (salt marsh)

Matmata
Wadi Zigzaou

XXX XXX

Ben Guerdane

Madenine

XXX

TUNISIA

XXX X

XX New Zealand

15 February: Eighth Army arrives

ALGERIA

XXX

XXXX 8 MONTGOMERY

N

Dehibat

Nalut

LIBYA

Axis Defeat in Tunisia
20–29 March 1943

— Front line 20 March

— Front line 29 March

◄ Axis attack

◄- - Axis withdrawal

◄ British movement

◄ French movement

◄ New Zealand movement

2000
1000
600
100
0 m

0   50 km

0   50 miles

El Jeemmeyen

campaign in glorious fashion, but it would also deliver Cap Bon to the Allies before the enemy could turn it into a last redoubt. Alexander decided that he could afford to allow Montgomery to carry out the attack he proposed, but this had the unfortunate side effect of ensuring that resources were not concentrated within First Army area to the extent originally planned.

Bouncing the Enemy

Montgomery's plan was based upon the supreme confidence amongst his army as to what could be achieved against the Germans, and he made clear his intention to 'bounce' them out of the Enfidaville position. However, as intelligence was gained about the strength of enemy defences, he moderated his tone. A heavy attack would be launched, but without grandiose notions of a rapid advance. Unfortunately, this did not fully communicate itself to X Corps (Lieutenant-General Sir Brian Horrocks), and the plan worked out by the corps was rather optimistic. X Corps were under the mistaken impression that there were only around six enemy battalions facing them, when there were, in fact, 23. Although these units were below strength, they were still quite capable of putting up stiff resistance. Furthermore, only the 4th Indian Division had any preparation for fighting in the mountainous conditions facing them, with the 2nd New Zealand, 50th and 56th Divisions totally lacking the training required to be fully effective; worse still, the terrain was unsuitable for 7th Armoured Division's tanks, which meant that the employment of British armour would be hampered.

Below: German soldiers inspect the wreck of a crash-landed P-38 Lightning fighter. The Lightning was the most advanced fighter in front-line service with the US Army Air Force in 1942. While it was not as manoeuvrable as German and Italian fighters, the Lightning proved extremely effective, and came to be known as 'the fork-tailed devil' by German pilots.

Horrocks' plan called for 4th Indian and 2nd New Zealand Divisions to assault into the hills, cutting across the enemy's rear and heading for the coast. Once this was completed, Horrocks envisaged an advance that would gather in momentum as the enemy was defeated, aided by penetration from armoured units. A competent commander, Horrocks was well aware of the adage 'no plan survives first contact with the enemy', and made clear to his subordinates that the success of his scheme depended upon the strength of the enemy being as anticipated; as we have seen, it was not.

On the night of 19/20 April 1943, the assault began, as 4th Indian Division attacked. Enemy resistance was extremely fierce, and by daybreak, very little of the ground necessary for the next phase of the operation had been taken completely. Rather than breaking through into the enemy's rear area, the offensive had been brought to a near halt in the outer fringe of the Axis defence lines. This presented Horrocks with an uncomfortable choice – he could either try to press on, with the likelihood of significant casualties, or he could stay where he was, with a similar probability of casualties, but with greater opportunity of damaging the enemy as they counter-attacked. Whatever decision Horrocks reached meant that instead of the swift advance intended, a slower, attritional battle would develop instead.

During the course of the day, 50th Division took Enfidaville, but the rest of the corps could not make any decisive showing on the battlefield. Montgomery, therefore, sat down to refine his plan to address the situation now facing him, but it was clear that the main effort in the assault must now pass to First Army and US II Corps. The preliminary offensive on 18 April to put these formations into position for the offensive between Medjez el Bab and Bou Arada had made some gains. US II Corps was left facing the last enemy positions

Left: Tank crew from a Free French unit study map coordinates before moving off into the Tunisian desert, March 1943.

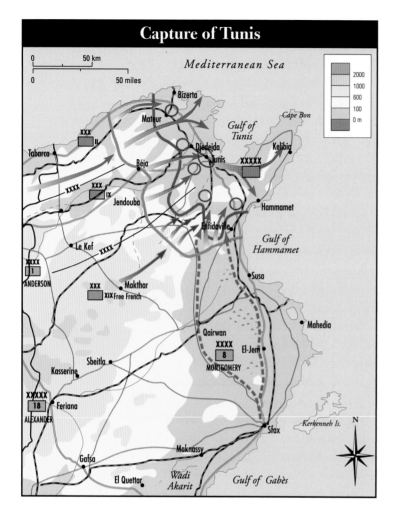

Capture of Tunis

Capture of Tunis
April–May 1943

————	Front line mid-April
————	Front line 3 May
◀–▪	Axis withdrawal
◀—	British movement
◀—	French movement
◯	Concentration of Axis surrenders 7–13 May

blocking the way to Bizerta, while First Army was faced with the possibility of breaking through the German defences if it could drive the enemy from the hills on either side of the river Medjerda. Further south, First Army faced the Goubellat plain, which was lightly held, and which offered good opportunities for exploitation as long as the enemy could be prevented from sealing the plain at its eastern end by withdrawing in strength to the broken ground between Kasr Tyr and Sebkret.

Alexander therefore had three key areas in his offensive, of which the most important was that for which British V Corps was responsible. If Longstop Hill and Peter's Corner were taken, then a direct approach on Tunis could be made. That this was most important was clear not only to Alexander, but to the Germans, who made plans for a series of attacks that aimed to disrupt the offensive. These attacks began on 20/21 April, on both V and IX Corps' fronts. The Germans became stuck in the positions of 1st and 4th Divisions, and their attack on 46th Division was particularly serious, since that formation was meant to launch the first assault of the offensive the next morning.

However, the preponderance of numbers began to tell on the Germans. Although their attack affected 46th Division, only one of that formation's brigades was late in joining the offensive on the morning of 22 April. All of V Corps was able to advance to its start line, while even in 4th Division's lines, where the German advance reached within half a mile of divisional headquarters, the attack was rebuffed. In brutal terms, a weakened attacking division ought to have stood little chance against two strong divisions with a brigade of tanks in support – and it did not. More than 30 German tanks were destroyed in the fighting, with British losses less than half that. The spoiling attacks, therefore, did not make a material difference to the British advance; they did, however, succeed in weakening the German mobile forces to a notable extent immediately before they were required to assist in the defence against an enemy offensive.

The British Advance

Although the German attacks were pushed back, this did not guarantee success for the attacking formations the next morning. As General Anderson had predicted, the anti-tank defences ahead of IX Corps proved particularly difficult, and prevented the corps from breaking through the German lines and heading to the north. In the crucial sector, that of V Corps' advance against the high ground around Peter's Corner, it was essential that Longstop Hill be captured, since if the Germans were allowed to remain in control of its peak, they would be able to fire upon both British and American forces.

The task of assaulting Longstop Hill was given to 78th Division, while 1st Division descended upon Guriet el Atach in the centre, and 4th Division secured the right flank at Peter's Corner. During the night of 22/23 April, British infantry seized the western slopes of Longstop Hill, but could not take the western summit. Early the next day, a battalion of the Argyll and Sutherland Highlanders continued the assault, in the face of fierce resistance. The battalion commanding officer was killed, and Major John Anderson took over; even though his force had been reduced to just over 40 men, they carried the summit and held it, a feat which won Anderson the Victoria Cross (he was killed in action in Italy later in 1943). Fighting on Longstop went on for three more days until the last Germans were cleared out.

Von Arnim realized that his position was becoming increasingly untenable, and sought to counter-attack, but although this started promisingly, it was thrown back by 30 April, with a notable cost in armour. Although the British and Americans were still advancing, it became evident that the general offensive was beginning to break down as individual formations undertook a variety of localized attacks. General Alexander decided that he needed to take decisive action to prevent the attack from stalling. The solution appeared to lie in ending Eighth Army's activities around Enfidaville, since it appeared that the operations here were unlikely to achieve anything of substance, and moving formations from Eighth Army to First Army.

In fact, Montgomery was reaching similar conclusions. Advised by Horrocks that while Eighth Army would break through in the end, there would be very little left of it afterwards, Montgomery offered 7th Armoured and 4th Indian Divisions, along with 201st Guards Brigade, to Alexander so that they could reinforce First Army.

The transfer of some of Montgomery's best troops to First Army did not escape the attention of the Germans, and while von Arnim knew what was coming (an assault in the

Opposite: The final push in Tunisia began on 6 May 1943, and was marked by far less resistance from the Axis forces than had been encountered previously. Tunis was entered the next day, and after five more days of fighting, the Axis forces surrendered.

Below: A formation of American troops march along a road in Algeria in a picture clearly staged for the camera. Resistance in Algeria and Morocco was relatively light, and the Allies made swift advances after the Torch landings; however, once they drew nearer to Tunisia, they encountered far stiffer opposition.

Right: General Eisenhower and other allied leaders on a reviewing stand, awaiting a march past by Allied troops. Lieutenant-General Sir Kenneth Anderson, the commander of British First Army, is standing directly behind Eisenhower, while General Sir Harold Alexander, the Commander-in-Chief Middle East, is to Anderson's right. The French officer standing next to Eisenhower is General Henri Giraud, the commander of French forces in North Africa.

Medjerda valley), there was little he could do to stop the offensive, such was the paucity of resources available to him in contrast to those possessed by the Allies. Alexander intended to launch the final blow against the Axis forces with a massive assault down the road from Medjez el Bab to Tunis on 6 May. This would be conducted along a relatively narrow frontage, before the attacking forces split, with half turning to the north to assist US II Corps in taking Bizerta, while the remainder would turn to the south to isolate the base of the Cap Bon peninsula. Once this was complete, the force would then round up the remaining enemy troops. Any Axis forces that sought to evacuate Tunisia would have to brave the Mediterranean, which was firmly under control of the Royal Navy. The final push began at 03:00 on 6 May 1943, and by 09:30 the 4th Indian Division had punched a large hole in the enemy defences, and just before 10:00, the lead elements of 7th Armoured Division began to drive through the gap created, but did so with rather more caution than was strictly necessary. Nonetheless, the next day saw the armoured cars of the 11th Hussars enter Tunis, followed by tanks and infantry who secured the city's capture. Meanwhile, US II Corps had reached Bizerta, and discovered that the Germans had left; by now the Axis forces had reached their limit. Mass surrenders began all along the line, and resistance broke into isolated pockets of men determined to continue the fight for a while longer.

On 12 May, von Arnim surrendered to 4th Indian Division, while the Italian commander, Field Marshal Messe, capitulated the next day. At 13:16 local time, General Alexander signalled London with a simple message:

'Sir, it is my duty to report that the Tunisian campaign is over. All enemy resistance has ceased. We are masters of the North African shores.'

The war in North Africa was over, the first theatre-wide defeat inflicted upon Hitler's Reich by the Western Allies.

The War In Italy

Once Axis forces had been defeated in North Africa, attention turned to invading Sicily as a prelude to a full invasion of the Italian mainland. Plans had been in place since early spring 1943, and some historians contend that the problems encountered by Eighth Army around Enfidaville were connected with the fact that Montgomery's attention was diverted between operations in North Africa and the need to plan for the assault on Sicily.

The origins of the plans stemmed from the Casablanca Conference of January 1943, at which Roosevelt and Churchill had discussed the next steps in Allied strategy. It was clear from the outset that there was disagreement between the two parties. The Americans wished to turn to an invasion of France, arguing that operations elsewhere were a pointless diversion from the ultimate goal of defeating the Germans. The British demurred. Conscious of the massive casualties sustained trying to defeat the Germans in France between 1914 and 1918, the British saw a campaign to knock Italy out of the war as being an extremely attractive alternative. Churchill, employing one of his favourite phrases, spoke of Italy as being the 'soft underbelly' of Europe, through which the Allies could drive into the heart of the continent. An invasion of Italy might also persuade neutral Turkey to join the war on the Allied side, a tempting prospect given the well-won reputation of Turkish troops, and their numbers.

Despite strenuous opposition from the US Army Chief of Staff, General George C. Marshall, Roosevelt was prepared to compromise with his ally. It was quite clear that the strength required to invade France was not yet near being achieved, yet to stop fighting until the requisite forces were in place for such an invasion was unacceptable for two reasons. First, the Allies would lose the momentum that they had managed to build during the latter stages of the North African campaign; second, to leave the burden of all fighting on land to the Soviet Union would be guaranteed to cause serious complaints from Stalin as the Germans were able to turn their full attention to the East once more.

As a result, it was agreed that the Allies would invade and occupy Sicily as a possible precursor to an invasion of Italy, although a decision on whether or not this course of action would be taken would be left until later. Eisenhower was appointed as supreme

Opposite: Two German paratroopers carry out observation of enemy positions from amongst the rubble of an Italian building. The Germans proved extremely adept at making strong points amongst the wreckage of buildings, nowhere more effectively than at Monte Cassino after the medieval monastery was reduced to rubble by air attack.

commander, despite the fact that American forces were in a minority in the Mediterranean theatre, but his deputies were all British – General Sir Harold Alexander, Air Chief Marshal Sir Arthur Tedder and Admiral of the Fleet Sir Andrew Cunningham. The plan, drawn up while the North African campaign was in its last stages, called for an attack on or around 10 July 1943. Montgomery's Eighth Army would land on the southeast corner of Sicily, while Patton's Seventh Army would land to the left of the British to protect the flank. With his flank secure, Montgomery would drive up the east coast of the island to Messina. The plan was not popular with American commanders, who suspected (rightly) that Montgomery was trying to relegate them to a supporting role, so that he could take the credit. Montgomery's general demeanour had not endeared him to the Americans, and the problems of command relationships that would later appear during the campaign in Northwest Europe originated from the plan for the Sicilian campaign.

The major concern for all parties, though, was not who gained the glory from the campaign, but whether the defenders of the island would fight. There were around 200,000 Italian troops, supported by 30,000 Germans. The Axis troops were commanded by General Alfredo Guzzoni, the commander of the Italian Sixth Army. Guzzoni was a competent general (not always a feature of the generals in Mussolini's army), but as insurance, the German troops maintained another chain of command that was headed by Field Marshal Albert Kesselring, the Commander-in-Chief South. While the Allies were confident that they could seize Sicily, there was very little idea of how fierce the resistance would be. That could only be discovered when the invasion was under way.

'Forward to Victory! Let us knock Italy out of the war!'

General Sir Bernard Montgomery, message to Eighth Army, 2 September 1943

Operation Husky

On 9 July 1943, 2500 ships and landing craft, carrying an invasion force of over 160,000 men drawn from the US Seventh and British Eighth Armies headed for Italian waters, with the aim of making the landing on Sicily in the largest amphibious operation mounted up to that time. The fleet steamed past Malta, a demonstration of just how important it had been that the island had held out against Axis air attacks, since had Malta fallen, the seas would have been completely covered by Italian and German air power, making the invasion impossible. As the day drew on, the invasion force was first gently buffeted by the wind, then thrown about with increasing violence as it rose in intensity. For a short while it appeared that General Eisenhower would have to call off the invasion, but after pondering the matter he decided that he would go ahead.

In Tunisia, a fleet of transport aircraft had been awaiting Eisenhower's decision; once it came, they lifted off, towing the gliders of the British 1st Airlanding Brigade towards Sicily. Unfortunately, they flew straight into the path of the storm, and chaos ensued as they reached Malta, with aircraft being driven off course while the gliders were tossed

about in the gale. The same fate befell another 200 transport aircraft carrying over 3000 US paratroops, and the airborne operation fell into confusion as aircraft wandered across the sky, unable to maintain their course in the teeth of the storm. This led to tragedy – while 40 of the glider tugs turned back, 69 released their gliders well short of the correct point, and the fragile transport craft fell into the sea, causing many fatalities among the airborne troops. While the American paratroops remained in transport aircraft until the dropping zone, they fared little better – the navigational problems caused by the weather meant that very few of the transports dropped their cargo in the correct place. Only 200 men landed in reasonably close proximity to their objectives, and such was the confusion that the American airborne commander, General James M. Gavin, was for some time convinced that he had been dropped into mainland Italy by mistake. The only positive note about the confused air landings was that the enemy had been fearfully confused as well. There were so many reports of paratroops and glider landings that the Germans

Above: German troops participate in a training exercise near Salerno, prior to the Allied invasion of Italy. The tank is a Panzer Mk IV, which remained an important type until the end of the war, although it came to be overshadowed by the later Panther and Tiger tanks.

Right: The invasion of Sicily (Operation Husky) was preceded by appalling weather, which lulled the defending Italian troops into believing that the Allies would not contemplate an invasion until the sea conditions were better. The landings went well, although the airborne element ran into serious difficulties, with many troops landing miles away from their drop zones.

and Italians were initially convinced that Sicily had been invaded by at least 20,000 and possibly even 30,000 airborne soldiers – in fact, there were just over 4500.

Mercifully for the invasion, the wind dropped away overnight, and as the invasion fleet approached the beaches it was clear that the landings could go ahead as planned, although the US Seventh Army, due to land on the west of Sicily, were some way behind schedule as a result of the weather conditions. Eighth Army were on time, and discovered very little opposition as they came ashore. The Italians defending the invasion area had surmised that any attempt at making a landing in the weather they were experiencing would be lunacy, so relaxed once the Allied transport aircraft had left. The first assaulting troops landed without opposition, and stormed up the beaches to seize the coastal defences. As it became clear what was happening, some desultory Italian artillery fire was experienced, but this was suppressed by naval gunfire support provided by six British battleships sitting offshore ready to deal with any such eventuality.

It was not long before the advanced elements of the forces ashore in eastern Sicily were moving inland – by 08:00, the town of Cassibile was in the hands of the British 5th Division, making the arrival of XIII Corps and elements of XXX Corps rather easier than might otherwise have been the case if the defenders remained in place. The Americans did not enjoy similar fortune. The defenders in western Sicily were alive to the fact that an invasion was under way, and opened fire on the invasion craft as soon as they fell within range of the coastal gun batteries. These were engaged and neutralized by naval gunfire, and the Americans went ashore with relative ease. At Licata, American soldiers found an abandoned command post, and as they entered it, heard the telephone ringing. An Italian-speaking war correspondent accompanying the troops, Michael Chinigo, answered it. An Italian officer anxiously enquired whether it was true that the Americans had landed. Chinigo informed the officer (in Italian) that the story was ridiculous. Satisfied, the Italian rang off.

By mid-morning, the invading forces were firmly ashore, and their leading elements were pushing inland, aided by the fact that the American airborne troops had overcome the problem of not landing in the right place. A number of *ad hoc* groupings of paratroops who had met up with one another as they tried to reach their intended drop zones set about causing havoc behind the Italian lines. This greatly aided the forces moving inshore from the beaches, since the flow of reserves to the invasion area was hampered by the activities of the paratroops.

The British airborne formations also tried to make the best of a poor situation. Only about 100 of the 1500 men who were supposed to have landed made it onto the island,

Invasion of Sicily
10 July–17 August 1943

→ Allied landings with dates

→ Axis counterattacks

— Allied front line 11 July

— Allied front line 15 July

— Allied front line 23 July

- - - Axis retreat line

- - - Axis retreat line

- - - Axis retreat line

◄- - Axis retreat route

⊕ Airfields constructed by Allies

▽ Allied airborne landings

Invasion of Sicily

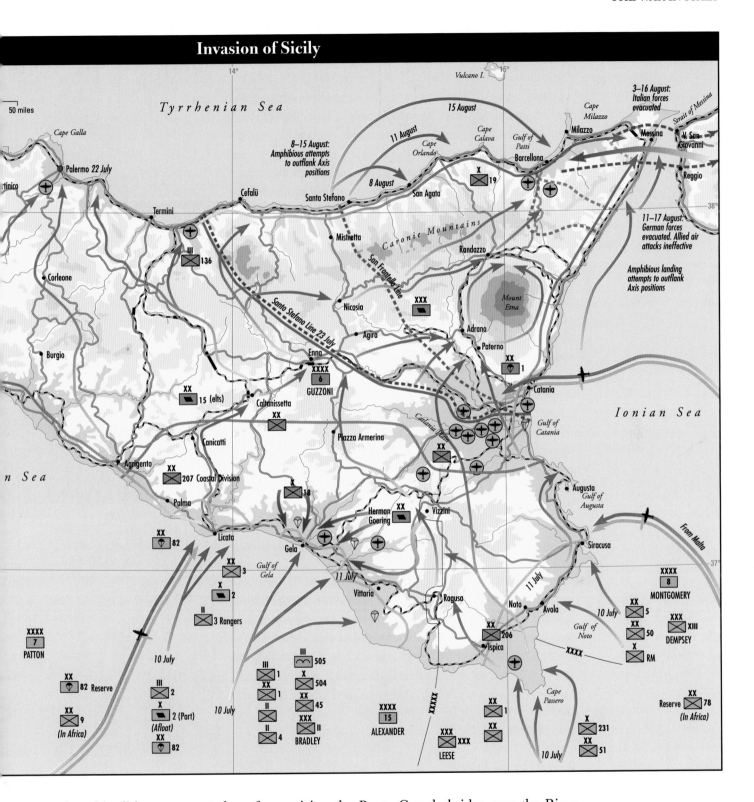

but this did not prevent them from seizing the Ponte Grande bridge over the River Cavadonna. The Italians made numerous attempts to dislodge the airlanding brigade's survivors, but it was not until late in the afternoon of 10 July that they finally succeeded. By this point, only 15 of the British troops were left, and seven of them were killed in the Italian assault. Undaunted, the eight survivors split into two groups – two men took up positions on a nearby hill and prevented the Italians from moving by sniping at them at

Right: British troops make their way through the wreckage of an Italian building. The leading man is armed with a Thompson sub-machine gun, while his colleagues are all equipped with Lee Enfield .303-inch rifles. In urban areas, the compact size of the Thompson, coupled with its rate of fire, made it a popular weapon.

Map, page 38: The invasion of Italy began smoothly, with little opposition provided by defending Italian troops in the very south, but the Germans put up fierce resistance, particularly around Salerno. After some hard fighting, the beachhead was firmly established by the end of September, and the Allies moved northwards, towards the German defensive positions around Cassino.

every opportunity, while the remaining six made their way back to the invasion area, in the hope of finding friendly troops. This they did, and promptly led a mobile column from 5th Division to the bridge, from which the Italians were removed in short order. This opened the way for an advance into Syracuse, marking the first major success of the campaign.

The Americans ran into some difficulties around Gela, particularly after the German Hermann Göring Division entered the fray. Disruption to communications meant that the Germans were unable to coordinate with the Italians, and this perhaps hampered their activities. While the Germans caused problems for the Americans, they could not break through to attack the landing beaches, and as night fell, it was clear that the Allies were safely ashore in some numbers.

The second day of the Sicily campaign demonstrated that the battle to take the island would not be easy, as the Germans and Italians began to show a more coordinated response to the attack. An assault by 60 German tanks came within two miles of the beaches, and all unloading operations had to stop as every man in the area grabbed his weapon and ran to defensive positions. The tanks were slowly forced back, at which point ships standing offshore began to fire in support of the troops, now that the danger of fratricide from their shells was removed. Powerful though the German tanks were, they were no match for the broadside from a ship, and pulled back as quickly as they could.

There was also tragedy when aircraft bringing reinforcements to the American sector were engaged by anti-aircraft fire after they had been mistaken for German bombers. Twenty-three were shot down and another 37 badly damaged; over 200 men were killed. The following day, the Germans made an airdrop of their own, landing reinforcements at Catania. This marked the start of a major German reinforcement of the island; while the troops were arriving, the Allies continued their advance.

The Drive on Palermo

For the rest of July, the two Allied armies pushed forward, with the rivalry between Patton and Montgomery increasing as they moved further north. This was most notable when British XXX Corps was held up near Lentini, prompting Montgomery to order a change of direction around the base of Mount Etna, to enable an assault on Messina from the west. To achieve this manoeuvre, XXX Corps' commander, General Sir Oliver Leese, had to use Route 124, a road running from Vizzini to Caltagirone. The road was in the American sector, but Montgomery sent Leese up the route without bothering to inform

the Americans of the fact that his troops would be joining them. This led to a situation where both American and British units, who had been told that they would be working independently of one another, found themselves attacking the same objective, namely the town of Enna. Despite initial confusion, all went well.

However, Montgomery's action irritated Patton, not least since it meant that the role of the Americans in providing flank protection became more important, and denied them the chance to participate in taking Messina. Patton was not as angry as he might have

Invasion of Southern Italy

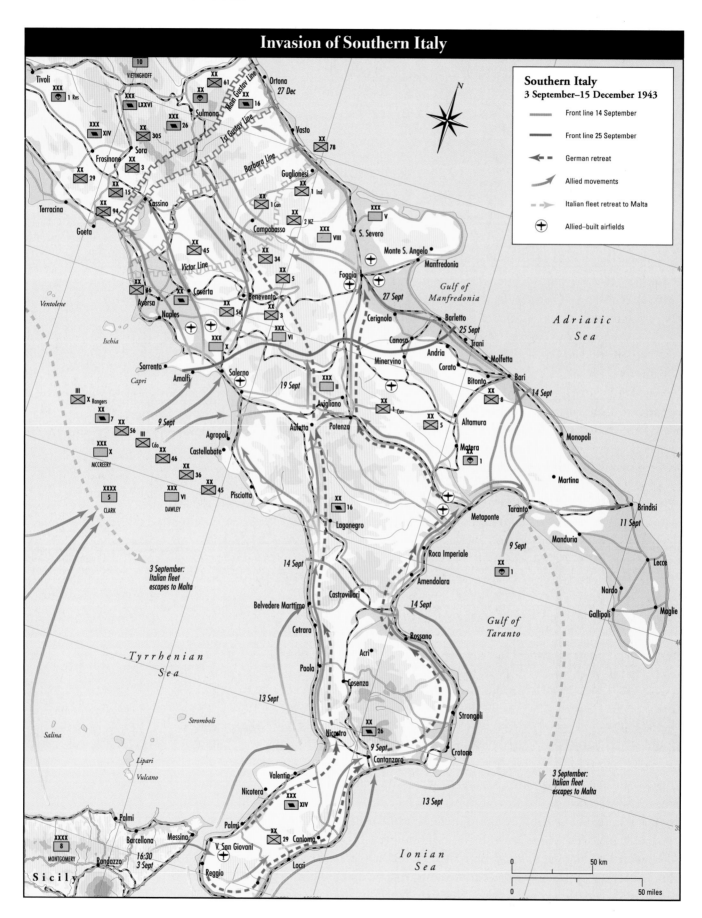

Southern Italy
3 September–15 December 1943

- Front line 14 September
- Front line 25 September
- German retreat
- Allied movements
- Italian fleet retreat to Malta
- Allied–built airfields

Tivoli

VIETINGHOFF

1 Res

LXXVI

XIV

61

Ortona
27 Dec

Sulmona

16

26

305

Sora

Frosinone

3

29

15

Cassino

94

Terracina

Goeta

1st Gustav Line

Main Gustav Line

Barbara Line

Vasto

78

Guglionesi

1 Ind

Campobasso

1 Can

2 NZ

45

Victor Line

34

VIII

S. Severo

V

Monte S. Angelo

Manfredonia

5

Caserta

46

Foggia

27 Sept

Gulf of
Manfredonia

Aversa

Naples

56

3

Cerignola

Barletto

25 Sept

Canosa

Adriatic
Sea

Sorrento

Amalfi

Salerno

19 Sept

VI

X

II

Minervino

Andria

Corato

Trani

Molfetta

Bari

14 Sept

Capri

Ventolene

Ischia

III

X Rangers

7

56

III

Cdo

X

MCCREERY

46

36

VI

DAWLEY

45

5

CLARK

Agropoli

Castellabate

Pisciotta

Aviagliano

Potenza

Auletta

1 Can

16

Lagonegro

9 Sept

Bitonta

8

Altamura

5

Matera

1

Martina

Monopoli

Taranto

Metaponte

9 Sept

1

Manduria

Brindisi

11 Sept

Lecce

Nardo

Maglie

Gallipoli

Roca Imperiale

Amendolara

3 September:
Italian fleet
escapes to Malta

14 Sept

Castrovillari

14 Sept

Gulf of
Taranto

Belvedere Marttimo

Cetrara

Paola

Acri

Rossano

Cosenza

Tyrrhenian
Sea

13 Sept

Stromboli

Strongoli

Salina

Lipari

Vulcano

Nicastro

26

9 Sept

Cantanzaro

Crotone

3 September:
Italian fleet
escapes to Malta

Valentia

Nicotera

XIV

13 Sept

Ionian
Sea

Palmi

Barcellona

Messina

8

MONTGOMERY

Randazzo

16:30
3 Sept

Palmi

V. San Giovanni

29

Canloma

Reggio

Locri

Sicily

0   50 km

0   50 miles

been, however, since he was already considering taking Palermo, the island's largest city. After personally asking General Alexander to order him to take Palermo (although the request verged on being a demand), Patton was more content. The US 2nd Armoured and 3rd Infantry Divisions were tasked to drive on the city, and after covering 100 miles in four days entered Palermo on 22 July. There had been very little resistance on the way, and the only enemy troops the Americans encountered in Palermo were Italians who were simply waiting to surrender. The Germans in the city had abandoned it some days before, sabotaging the harbour by scuttling over 40 ships, but US Army engineers had it working at over half capacity within a week, a remarkable achievement.

Patton's drive on Palermo now left him in a position to advance on Messina, and he determined that he should arrive there before the British, informing his subordinates that the pride of the US Army was at stake. The task of advancing on Messina would be much more taxing than taking Palermo, since the terrain through which Seventh Army had to pass was mountainous, and the roads could easily be blocked by the Germans. The advance, therefore, was slow, and stalled at Troina, where a whole US division and heavy air attacks were needed to clear out the defending Germans on 6 August. Spurred on by Patton's advance, Montgomery also drove his troops forward. By the middle of the month, both British and American units were on the outskirts of Messina; on 17 August, an American patrol entered the city, to be joined a little later by British armour. The city was deserted, since the Germans had pulled back across the Strait of Messina to the mainland.

It transpired that Kesselring had taken the decision that the position in Sicily would be untenable in the end, and that the island was not worth sacrificing a large number of Germans for. As early as 8 August, he gave orders for an evacuation, and by the time that Messina fell, 40,000 troops and their equipment had been withdrawn successfully. Although the Allies had failed to stop the Germans from escaping, they had succeeded in their primary aim – after 38 days of fighting, Sicily was in Allied hands. Attention could now turn to Italy itself; not least because of a dramatic development during the course of the Sicilian campaign – Mussolini had been deposed.

The End of Mussolini

By the middle of July, it seemed obvious that the Anglo-American invasion of Sicily would succeed, and discontent with Mussolini mounted. Anger was increased when an Allied bombing raid on Rome on 9 July destroyed not only the railway marshalling yards that were the target, but killed and wounded 4000 civilians. It seemed clear that such disasters would continue as long as the war went on. The only obstacle to ending the

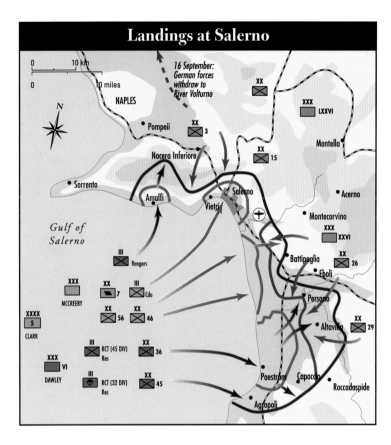

Landings at Salerno
9–16 September 1943

▬▬▬	German front line 14 Sept.
▬▬▬	Allied front line 11 Sept.
▬▬▬	Allied front line 9 Sept.
◀──	German movements
──▶	British movements
──▶	U.S. movement

Above: The landings at Salerno were met by particularly heavy opposition from the Germans. A build-up of reinforcements and the provision of greater air support reduced the pressure on the Allies, and by the end of the month they were able to move out from the Salerno area.

'The dominant aim should be to kill Germans and make Italians kill Germans on the largest scale possible in this theatre.'

Winston Churchill, 5 September 1943

conflict seemed to be Mussolini, so the Grand Council of the Fascist Party did something that would have been unimaginable with the German Nazi Party – it held a meeting, decided that the leader was taking them to ruin, and voted to replace him. Mussolini was taken into captivity in a state of utter amazement, while a new government, headed by Field Marshal Pietro Badoglio, made less-than-convincing announcements that Italy would remain allied to the Germans.

Hitler was certain that this step meant that the Italians would soon surrender, and gave orders that Mussolini should be rescued from wherever he was being held, a mission that was later carried out by commandos landing in gliders, who recovered the Italian dictator and took him to Berlin. He also told his generals to prepare to disarm the Italian Army, to prevent the defection of the country to the Allied cause. Hitler was right to be suspicious. Mussolini was deposed on 25 July; on the 26th, Badoglio announced that Italy remained an unshakeable ally of Germany; and on the 31st he sent emissaries to meet with the Allies to negotiate peace.

Excited by these developments, the Allies started to negotiate, and to plan for an invasion of the mainland. The invasion was planned with the complicity of the new government, who were anxious to ensure that the Germans could not simply remove them and install a government of their own. It was agreed that the Allies would land at Salerno on 9 September, just a few hours after the Italians would announce that they had surrendered. Anticipating this, the Germans made plans to sacrifice most of Italy, and retire to hold a line in the north of the country running from Pisa to Rimini.

MUSSOLINI

Mussolini's early life gave little clue that he would go on to lead his country for 21 years. A rebellious youth, Mussolini was often in trouble, and continued his penchant for upsetting the authorities by becoming editor of a socialist newspaper. He broke with the socialists over the issue of Italian entry into World War I, giving the conflict his full backing. He enlisted and reached the rank of sergeant by the end of the war. Mussolini then returned to political activism, but this time at the head of his own movement, the Fascists.

He achieved power in 1922, and secured his position through a mixture of populism and ruthlessness. Mussolini attempted to make Italy a significant European power, seeking new colonies in Africa. This culminated in the conquest of Abyssinia in 1936. By this point, Hitler's similar views had provided Mussolini with a notable ally, but one who was soon to dominate the Italo-German relationship.

Italy entered the war only after the fall of France, and endured a series of military reverses, often requiring assistance from the Germans to prevent humiliation. The Allied invasion of Italy led to Mussolini being deposed in September 1943. Rescued from imprisonment by a daring German commando raid, he was installed as the puppet leader of German-held northern Italy. When the German position collapsed, Mussolini's time had run out – he was captured by partisans and executed, a humiliating end for a man who had cast himself as the father of a great Italian nation.

The Italian Campaign

The invasion of Italy began with a landing by Eighth Army on the 'toe' of the country on the morning of the Italian surrender. The only Italian troops they encountered offered to assist with the unloading of their landing craft. A few hours later, Lieutenant-General Mark Clark's US Fifth Army (which contained British troops as well as Americans) came ashore at Salerno, where they were to face much harder opposition in the form of the Germans. To complete the invasion, the British 1st Airborne Division was landed at Taranto and captured the port.

The eight German divisions under Kesselring's command could be expected to put up stiff resistance, and they did. Counter-attacks began on 11 September, and dislodged British formations from the Molina Pass the next day. The attacks were of such ferocity that serious consideration was given to abandoning the beachhead in the southern sector, although this was dismissed when the Royal Navy provided gunfire support that prevented further German gains, even though the enemy had come to within a mile of the beaches by the time they were forced to stop. Reinforcements were brought in over the course of the next few days, and between 13 and 16 September, the fighting was notably fierce. The construction of landing strips in the beachhead meant that air support could be provided to the hard-pressed troops, and the situation began to ease. Meanwhile, the British 1st Airborne Division had captured Taranto, and once reinforced began to move out towards the other Allied troops. The link-up of the Eighth Army, 1st Airborne Division and Fifth Army took place on 20 September, by which time the beachhead was well established as the Germans were pushed back.

The Allies began to advance on Naples, and the Germans were forced to fall back. On 1 October, the Allies reached the city and entered it unopposed. Alexander ordered that armour from both the Fifth and Eighth Armies should pursue the enemy. By 5 October, the Allies were on the River Volturno. Some newspapers made optimistic assessments of

Above: In a picture that appears to have been posed especially for the camera, two German soldiers discuss the situation before them during the Italian campaign.

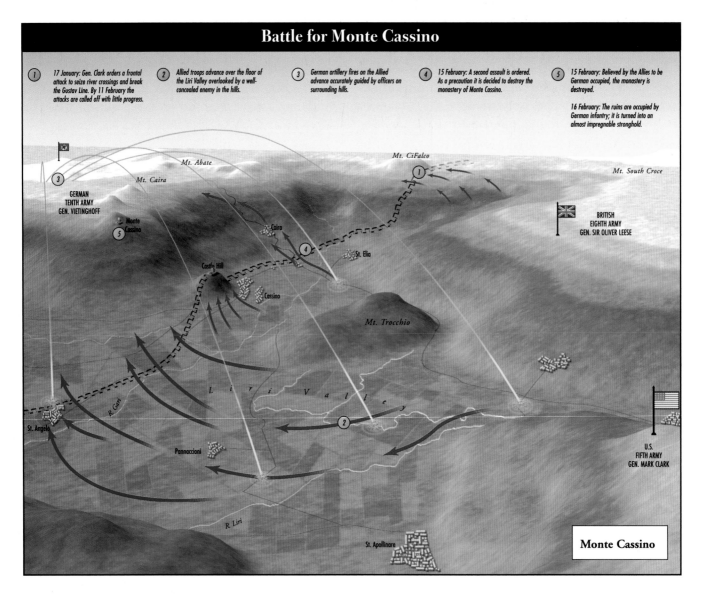

Battle for Monte Cassino

① **17 January:** Gen. Clark orders a frontal attack to seize river crossings and break the Gustav Line. By 11 February the attacks are called off with little progress.

② Allied troops advance over the floor of the Liri Valley overlooked by a well-concealed enemy in the hills.

③ German artillery fires on the Allied advance accurately guided by officers on surrounding hills.

④ **15 February:** A second assault is ordered. As a precaution it is decided to destroy the monastery of Monte Cassino.

⑤ **15 February:** Believed by the Allies to be German occupied, the monastery is destroyed.

16 February: The ruins are occupied by German infantry; it is turned into an almost impregnable stronghold.

Mt. Abate

Mt. CiFalco

Mt. South Croce

Mt. Caira

GERMAN
TENTH ARMY
GEN. VIETINGHOFF

Monte Cassino

Caira

St. Elia

BRITISH
EIGHTH ARMY
GEN. SIR OLIVER LEESE

Castle Hill

Cassino

Mt. Trocchio

L i r i   V a l l e y

R. Gari

U.S.
FIFTH ARMY
GEN. MARK CLARK

St. Angelo

Pannaccioni

R. Liri

St. Apollinare

Monte Cassino

Above: The battle of Monte Cassino was crucial to the progress of the Italian campaign, since if the Allies did not break through, the route to Rome would be blocked. An attritional battle developed, and it was only after the fourth major assault by Allied troops that a breakthrough was achieved.

how soon it would be before Allied troops entered Rome – but their guesses were wildly inaccurate as the Allies had to face the reality of the situation on the ground.

The Germans had a number of advantages in defending their positions in addition to the high quality of their troops. The narrow mountain passes which had to be traversed as the Allies progressed northwards were relatively simple to defend, and this slowed down the advance considerably, along with careful demolition of bridges and communications links as the Germans withdrew. A further obstacle to the advance came with heavy rainfall early in October, about a month before it was normally due. The precipitation caused landslides and waterlogged the ground, making a swift advance impossible. Kesselring used the opportunity to prepare for a fighting withdrawal to a new defensive position some 15 miles north of the Volturno, which was carried out on 16 October. This defensive position, the Gustav Line, was to present a major obstacle to Allied efforts, since it had to be breached before any advance on Rome could be contemplated. Alexander, reporting on the situation to Churchill, expressed the view that the advance on Rome would be difficult and something of a 'slogging match' as the Allies attempted to break through the German positions.

Alexander's plan for the Gustav Line was to start with an assault along a 10-mile front by the British 46th Division near Minturno. The 46th Division went into battle on 4 January 1944, and managed to take some ground overlooking the German positions, giving it an advantage. Hard fighting continued across the line for several days, and it was not until 17 January that the British managed to establish a bridgehead across the mouth of the River Garigliano, and it took a further 10 days of struggle for this to expand to include Monte Juga. An American attempt to cross the river ended in disaster with most of the US 36th Division being lost in the attempt. Overall, while the Allies made some ground, the defenders still held the advantage.

Anzio and Cassino

On 22 January 1944, a landing was made at Anzio, due south of Rome, with the aim of cutting the German lines of communication between the Italian capital and Cassino. Some 36,000 men were landed and captured the port intact, aided by the fact that a large number of the troops who would have been defending it had been moved to the Gustav Line. This was followed by the bitter struggle for Cassino, which depending upon the preferred nomenclature was the site of one long battle, or four shorter ones. The fighting was intense and was arguably the nearest that the Western Allies came to fighting a World War I-style battle where manoeuvre was all but impossible. Cassino had to be taken, or the advance northwards would be halted. The task of taking it would be very difficult indeed, since the town had numerous fortifications, and was overlooked by a hill on which sat the famed medieval monastery, potentially a perfect defensive location.

Below: The Anzio landings were made on 22 January 1944, with the aim of cutting German lines of communication between Rome and the position at Monte Cassino. The landing was successful, helped by the fact that many of the troops who would normally have been defending the area had been moved to bolster the defences elsewhere in Italy. Fierce German counter-attacks nearly dislodged the Anglo-American landing force, and it took until May for the Allies to break out from the beachhead.

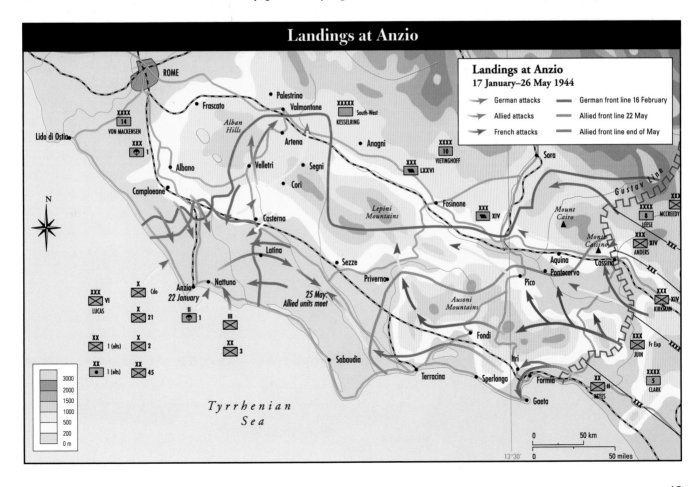

The first fighting at Cassino occurred between January and February 1944 as the Allies launched their attack into the teeth of the German defences. The Germans could not be dislodged, and the attack swiftly came to a halt. This set the pattern for the next month as the Allies made numerous attempts to advance, but found the sheer face of Monte Cassino an almost impossible obstacle to overcome. Ground was traded between the two sides on a regular basis, until the Allies tried a different tack.

On 15 March, a massive aerial bombardment was launched against Cassino, in an attempt to shatter the German defences. The historic monastery was destroyed in the process (every building in the town was either demolished or damaged in the raid), and it

Below: Armed with an MG42 machine gun, two German paratroopers man a defensive position in the ruins of the monastery at Monte Cassino.

appeared that the way for an advance was now clear. However, the Germans simply moved from their well-made defensive positions into the ruins of the monastery, and became even harder to dislodge. Once again, bitter fighting occurred, with regular trading of small patches of ground. A third attempt to take Monte Cassino failed after a week, and a fourth attempt was made in early May 1944.

On this occasion, the better weather and the fact that the Allies had massed an overwhelming number of troops meant that they were able to carry the hill. The monastery fell to the Polish II Corps on 18 May, and once this was in Allied hands, the Gustav Line had been unlocked. This finally meant that the Allied advance on Rome could continue, after five months of savage fighting – hardly the swift advance to the Italian capital that had been predicted by excited journalists when news of the Italian surrender came through eight months before. The landings at Anzio met with similar problems. As at Salerno, the Germans made determined efforts to reach the beaches and drive the Allies back into the sea. On 19 February, the Germans came perilously close to doing just that, and they were driven off with some difficulty. Further attacks followed, but did not imperil the Allied position. Nevertheless, a stalemate persisted at Anzio until 23 May, when the Allies broke out from the beachhead.

Within two days, US 1st Armoured and 3rd Infantry Divisions had joined with the US II Corps, which was pushing forward to Rome. General Clark had decided that his army was to have the glory of taking Rome, and duly entered it on 4 June 1944, much to the irritation of the British, Polish and French troops who thought that their efforts at breaking through at Cassino (thus making the advance on Rome possible) at least merited equal publicity; as well as making himself unpopular with the troops, Clark was disobeying Alexander's orders that his main effort should be to ensure the capture of Valmontone.

On to the Gothic Line

The capture of Rome did not mean that the campaign in Italy was at an end, since there was still much fighting to do to dislodge the Germans from the north of the country. Several units were withdrawn to support the Normandy campaign, which made Alexander's task more difficult. He now had to break through the last German defensive line (the Gothic Line) just to the south of the Lombardy plains. Success here would give access to Austria and the Balkans, and was a prize that Kesselring was anxious to deny the Allies.

The Allied offensive began on 25 August. Eighth Army, now commanded by Lieutenant-General Sir Oliver Leese after Montgomery's departure for 21st Army Group in Normandy, carried out the attack, and progressed well to begin with. Unfortunately, the weather intervened once more, and coupled with supply problems, the offensive slowed. Throughout September, a series of attacks along the length of the Gothic Line gained some ground, but nothing of significance. As the offensive slowed, Kesselring redeployed his forces to meet the threat now posed by Fifth Army's approach from the west, and the advance here was brought to a near halt.

By early November, a stalemate had been reached again. The campaign could not be restarted until the spring, and yet more Allied forces were removed from the theatre and sent to the Western Front. Many of the units in Eighth Army left as well, detailed to assist with the restoration of order to Greece after the German withdrawal and the outbreak of civil war there.

Maps, following pages: Once Cassino had been taken, the Allies had to fight their way northwards, against heavy German opposition. After the break-out from Anzio, the Allies were able to make a major push towards Rome, although General Clark's decision to take the city (on 4 June 1944) was fiercely criticized for his perceived wish to put personal vanity ahead of the Allied effort against Valmontone. Once Rome fell, the Germans continued to put up steady resistance, and the campaign ground to a halt in November 1944. The Allies restarted their campaign in April 1945, and the by now seriously weakened German troops fell back. The execution of Mussolini by partisans may have been of no military significance, but symbolized the hopelessness of the Axis position. On 25 April, a surrender was agreed, and the Italian campaign was brought to an end on 2 May 1945.

Liberation of Rome

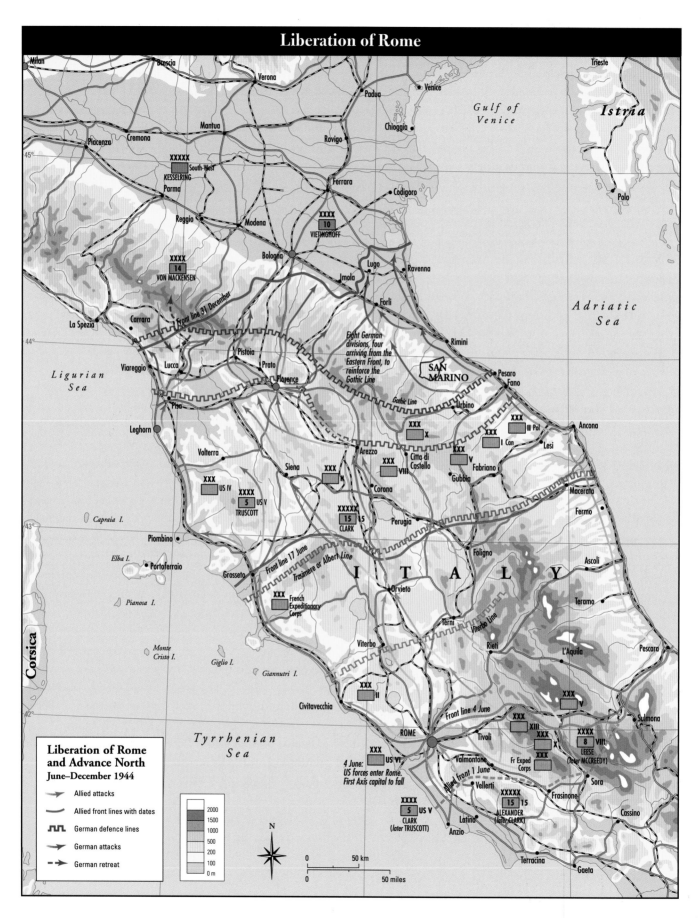

Liberation of Rome and Advance North
June–December 1944

- → Allied attacks
- ⌒ Allied front lines with dates
- ⎍⎍⎍ German defence lines
- → German attacks
- ⇢ German retreat

2000
1500
1000
500
200
100
0 m

N

0 ___ 50 km
0 ___ 50 miles

The End in Italy

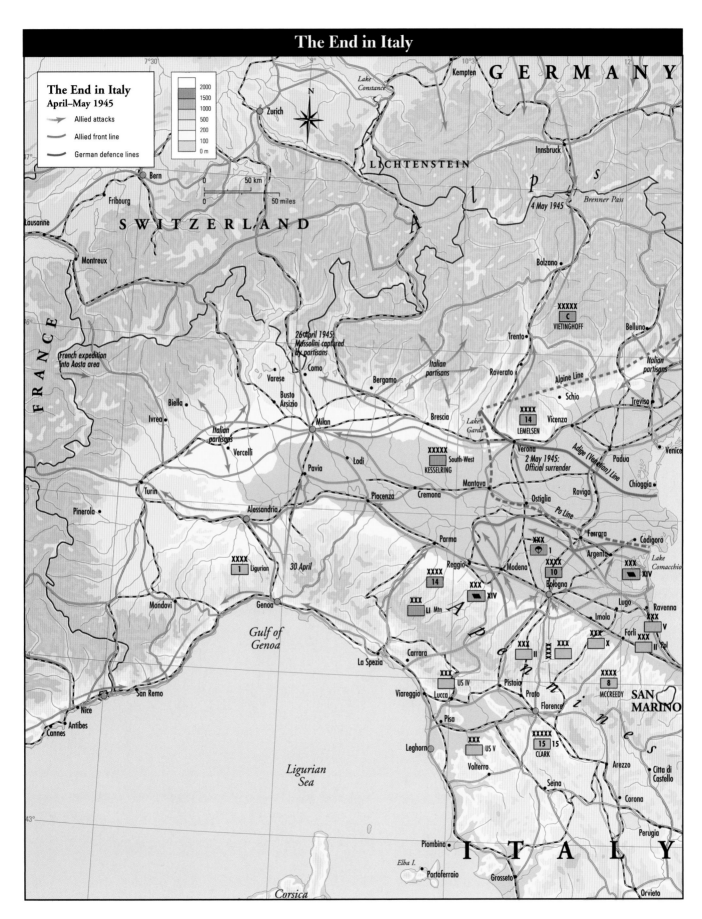

The End in Italy
April–May 1945

→ Allied attacks
⌒ Allied front line
⌒ German defence lines

GERMANY

Kempten

Lake Constance

N

Zurich

Innsbruck

LICHTENSTEIN

Bolzano

Bern

Brenner Pass

4 May 1945

Fribourg

A   l   p   s

Lausanne

SWITZERLAND

XXXXX
C
VIETINGHOFF

Belluno

Italian partisans

Trento

Montreux

French expedition into Aosta area

26 April 1945:
Mussolini captured by partisans

Varese

Como

Bergamo

Italian partisans

Rovereto

Alpine Line

Schio

Italian partisans

Treviso

FRANCE

Biella

Busto Arsizio

Brescia

XXXX
14
LEMELSEN

Vicenza

Ivrea

Milan

Lake Garda

Verona

Padua

Venice

Italian partisans

Vercelli

Lodi

XXXXX
South-West
KESSELRING

2 May 1945:
Official surrender

Adige (Venetian) Line

Pavia

Mantova

Rovigo

Chioggia

Turin

Piacenza

Cremona

Ostiglia

Po Line

Pinerola

Alessandria

Parma

Ferrara

Codigoro

XXX
1

Argenta

Lake Comacchio

XXXX
1   Ligurian

30 April

Reggio

Modena

XXXX
10

XXX
XIV

Mondovi

Genoa

XXXX
14

XXX
XIV

Bologna

Lugo

Ravenna

XXX
LI   Mtn

A

Imola

Forlì

XXX   V

Gulf of Genoa

Carrara

La Spezia

XXX
II

XXXX

XXX

X

XXX   II Pol

XXX
US IV

Pistoia

p

XXX

Viareggio

Lucca

Prato

XXXX
8
MCCREEDY

SAN MARINO

San Remo

Pisa

Florence

e

Nice

n

Antibes

Cannes

Leghorn

XXX
US V

Volterra

XXXXX
15   15
CLARK

Arezzo

Città di Castello

n

Ligurian Sea

Seina

Corona

i

Perugia

Piombino

I T A L Y

Elba I.

n

Portoferraio

Grosseto

e

Corsica

Orvieto

s

47

The Final Phase

While the Italian front was in limbo during the winter, the Allies replaced those units that had been sent elsewhere so that they began 1945 with a strength of over 600,000 men. In addition, supplies of ammunition, armoured vehicles and tracked amphibious vehicles were sent to the theatre, the latter a particularly welcome addition for a campaign that was beset with frequently waterlogged ground impassable to conventional vehicles. On 9 April 1945, the Allies resumed the offensive, with Fifth and Eighth Armies heading towards Bologna. The Germans, worn down and considerably weaker than before, were unable to hold the advance back, despite fierce resistance at the outset.

Kesselring had been injured in a car accident, and it was left to his successor, General Heinrich von Vietinghoff, to recognize that the position was becoming near untenable. He requested permission to fall back to the line of the River Po, but as was common by 1945, Hitler peremptorily rejected this. Vietinghoff ignored the nonsensical order, and told his men to withdraw. This sparked the collapse of the German position. British paratroops took Milan and Genoa, while a band of partisans found Mussolini and his mistress near Lake Como.

Nominally reinstalled as Italian dictator by Hitler after the rescue mission by German commandos, Mussolini had been little more than a puppet of the Germans ever since. This mattered not a jot to the partisans, who executed Mussolini, his mistress and other members of his entourage, and then displayed the corpses hanging upside down in the town square.

Lake Garda, Verona, Trieste and Turin all fell next, and the Germans were on the brink of surrender. Negotiations between the head of the SS in Italy and the US Office of Strategic Services had begun as early as February, but Hitler's obstinate refusal to accept the idea of capitulation meant that nothing had happened in this regard. Finally, despairing of the *Führer*, the German commanders decided that they would ignore him on this subject again. Proper negotiations began, and on 25 April 1945, orders were given for German and Italian Fascist forces to surrender at 12:00 noon on 2 May. The war in Italy was over.

Opposite: An American soldier, armed with an M1 Garand rifle, takes careful aim from his position in a ruined house in Cisterna. Cisterna fell on 25 May 1944, as the American VI Corps drove the defending Axis troops from the town.

The Russians Advance

The German failure to overcome the USSR by 1943 meant that factors other than just martial skill and good fortune came into play on the Eastern Front. In a total war, the ability of one side to out-produce the other could be of huge significance, particularly if this could be coupled with a vast source of manpower for the front line. The Soviet Union had both the capacity to out-produce the Germans, and the men and women who could make full use of that equipment at the front.

Soviet industrial potency was one of Stalin's major achievements, even though the cost in human terms during the 1930s had been horrific as those suspected of not cooperating had been purged; sometimes even those who had given wholehearted support to Stalin's vision found themselves arrested and consigned to the *Gulag* or execution. The reason for Stalin's drive towards mass industrialization had been simple – he knew that one of the primary causes of Russia's failure in World War I had been the appalling lack of material required to fight a modern war. Some Russian troops had found themselves equipped with a derivative of the Winchester Repeating Rifle more commonly seen in the American West since the middle part of the nineteenth century; they had been the lucky ones, since many soldiers had been forced to acquire their weapons by taking them from dead or wounded colleagues. Stalin had been determined that the USSR should never again find itself in a similar position, and this was one of the key factors in his ambitious plans for industrialization of a nation that had previously been considered as backward.

Opposite: A Soviet propaganda poster exhorts the population to greater efforts in the fight against the Nazis. The Soviet Communist Party made considerable use of such posters, and it was natural that the skills of the artists would be turned to encouraging the populace in warlike endeavours, drawing on sentiments of patriotism and idealism to convey their message.

'Feeding Mars'

Industrialization was carefully thought out, with the creation of huge industrial complexes deep in the Soviet interior, as exemplified by the city of Magnitogorsk. In 1928 it had 25 inhabitants; by 1932 there were 250,000 people living there to support the industrial city that had risen from the barren land. The location of such complexes, involving the relocation of thousands upon thousands of workers, had been carefully chosen – far to the east of the Urals, in Siberia or Central Asia, well out of range of attack by any likely enemy. While this was the case for heavy industry, light industry had not

Above: Soviet troops go into action riding on the rear deck of a T-34 tank. The Red Army regularly used tanks as a means of transporting troops up to the front line, with the 'tank riders' dismounting just before contact was made with the enemy.

been in as happy a position in 1941, since much of that sector was well within the compass of an invading enemy. As a result, the State Defence Committee ordered a mass exodus of factories and workers, evacuating industries to the heartland of the USSR. While this caused considerable disruption during 1941, by 1942 production had begun to increase dramatically.

As an illustration of just how impressive the manufacturing achievement of the USSR was, the simple fact that Russian factories produced around twice as much war material as German industry in 1942, despite the fact that Soviet industry had access to only around a third of the steel and coal supplies available to Hitler that year, serves as a telling example. The reason for this lay in careful development of industrial capacity, so that a factory that produced tractors as its main business would also turn out some tanks; when war came, the ratio of tank to tractor production was reversed, so that a rapid build-up in Red Army tank strength could be guaranteed. While production for agriculture would inevitably fall considerably, it did not disappear entirely, enabling a balance to be struck between feeding the front line with armaments and feeding the nation as a whole.

As a consequence of Stalin's vision, Soviet industry was able to produce nearly 240 million tons of munitions in 1942, a dramatic increase on the 1940 figures – and even more impressive when the disruption caused by evacuating industry is taken into account. The overall output from Soviet industry was prodigious. Between 1943 and 1945, over 80,000 aircraft, 73,000 armoured vehicles and 324,000 artillery pieces had been made; as an example, the Ilyushin Il-2 'Sturmovik' attack aircraft was built to the tune of 36,000 examples, making it the most heavily produced aircraft in history (a figure which is almost certainly never to be beaten).

While it would be ridiculous to claim that industrial output was all that was required to defeat Hitler on the Eastern Front, the ability to produce almost unimaginable amounts of war material, coupled with the massive strength of the Soviet armed forces, needs to be appreciated when making any assessment of the fighting that took place from 1943 onwards – the sheer scale of men, machines and other equipment involved is difficult to grasp, but without industrial capacity, victory on the Eastern Front would have been impossible to achieve.

The Precursors to the 1943 Campaigns

Following the success of Soviet operations around Stalingrad and the crushing of the German Sixth Army, the Russians continued with their offensive operations, continued to advance, eager to exploit their success. On 29 January 1943, Operation Gallop was launched, with General Vatutin's Sixth and First Guards Armies attacking along the entire German front, with considerable success. The front collapsed rapidly, and the Soviets pushed deep into the German rear area. Vatutin's main effort began two days later, with troops moving in support of the Voronezh Front's attack towards Kharkov, which had also begun on 29 January. This too had punched a huge gap in German lines. Although the Germans recovered their poise to a considerable degree and put up stiff resistance, they were unable to stop the onward march of the Soviet forces, until by 14 February, they were in danger of being surrounded in front of Kharkov itself. German commanders were uncertain of how best to defend against the possibility of disaster, and were not aided by Hitler's insistence that the city be defended to the last man. As a consequence, German resistance became fragmented, and after particularly heavy street fighting on 15 and 16 February, Kharkov was retaken.

This freed Vatutin to reorganize his plans for his forces, and he aimed to seize crossings over the river Dnieper, although this move was risky – it would stretch the overextended Soviet forces over a much wider area than originally planned, making it difficult to ensure that supplies could be maintained. Stalin was concerned by the possible dangers, but granted permission for the plan to be enacted. While Vatutin moved on towards the Dnieper, the newly created Central Front, under General Rokossovsky, began operations towards Smolensk, with the aim of encircling German Army Group Centre. Although the attack began well, the need for Rokossovsky to employ men and armour

Map, page 55: Success at Stalingrad marked a turning point for the Soviets, although it took time before the victory was fully exploited. After the Soviets had retaken Kharkov, the Germans appreciated that they were in for much hard fighting. Although the Russians had sustained huge casualties, they were still capable of offensive action, and were beginning to inflict serious damage upon the Germans.

T-34 – THE BEST TANK OF THE WAR?

The T-34 is one of the legendary weapons of World War II, and small numbers still remain in use even 60 years after the end of the conflict. The T-34 went into production in 1940, and struck an effective balance between armour protection, speed and armament, using a 76.2mm (2.9in) high-velocity gun. The tank was kept a closely guarded secret and proved an unpleasant surprise for the Germans in 1941.

By 1943, as the tide of the war in the East turned in favour of the USSR, the T-34 was the mainstay of the Soviet armoured formations, and was undergoing continual improvement. In 1944, a larger, 85mm (3.3in) gun was fitted to the vehicle, ensuring that it remained capable of dealing with all but the heaviest of German tanks. As well as being a thoroughly capable tank, the T-34 was available in huge numbers, enabling Soviet tank forces to dominate the battlefield.

Third Battle of Kharkov

Battle of Kharkov
29 January–20 February 1943

Soviet front line 29 January
Soviet front line 9 February
Soviet front line 20 February
Soviet advance to 9 February
Soviet advance to 20 February
Soviet withdrawal
German counter-attack
German withdrawal

Above: The Third Battle of Kharkov came as the Soviets were anxious to exploit their success at Stalingrad. A Soviet offensive forced the Germans back all along the line, and the Voronezh Front drove towards Kharkov.

redeployed from around Stalingrad represented a risk – if they could not reach the front in time, the attack would fail. The poor weather and the effect this had on the rather limited transport network meant that the reinforcements were not available for the proposed start date of the Central Front's offensive, which had to be put back by 10 days to 25 February. By this time, it was clear that operations by the Soviet Western and Kalinin Fronts would not be able to achieve success, and the fact that Central Front's offensive was meant to be carried out in conjunction with these two fronts meant that the scope of Rokossovsky's operations had to be recast so that they were less ambitious.

However, the Germans had managed to hurry troops to the area, and this meant that they were able to counter-attack. By early March, Rokossovsky had been forced to switch to the defensive in positions north of Kursk.

Fourth Battle of Kharkov

The initial successes of the Soviet offensive caused considerable concern to Field Marshal Erich von Manstein, the commander of Army Group Don. Manstein was well aware that the length of front under his control was too great for the forces available to him, and the need to shorten the line was pressing. He therefore managed to persuade Hitler, after much argument, that he should withdraw from the salient around Rostov and the Donbas area to a better position on the River Mius. Even this withdrawal was insufficient to meet the threat posed by Vatutin's advance, and Manstein decided that the position was on the verge of becoming untenable. The Dnieper crossings were in serious danger, and if the railway junction at Dnepropetrovsk were taken as part of the drive to the Dnieper, Army Group Don would be cut off without supplies.

Manstein's solution was one of the most daring moves of the entire war in any theatre. Rather than pull back to protect his supply lines from the onrushing Soviet forces, he chose instead to launch a counter-attack. Although this plan was dangerous, Manstein assessed that the enemy would, by now, have become worn down by the high tempo of operations in recent weeks, not least because their supply chain would be far more fragile than it had been at the outset. The offensive began on 20 February, with an attack by the SS Panzer Corps against Vatutin's Sixth Army. Over the course of the next few days, the Germans made rapid progress against the Russians, who were poorly positioned to meet what was an almost entirely unexpected counter-attack. By 25 February, Vatutin's forces were exhausted, and he went over to the defensive, enabling Manstein to launch the second phase of his campaign.

A drive into the left flank of the Voronezh Front began in the first week of March, and the Germans closed in on Kharkov once more, until by 10/11 March the city was on the point of falling into German hands once more. After a few more days' fighting, Kharkov was firmly under German control, and Manstein's daring had averted disaster. The counter-attack came to a halt as the arrival of additional Soviet troops stabilized the front just prior to the spring thaw that brought operations to a

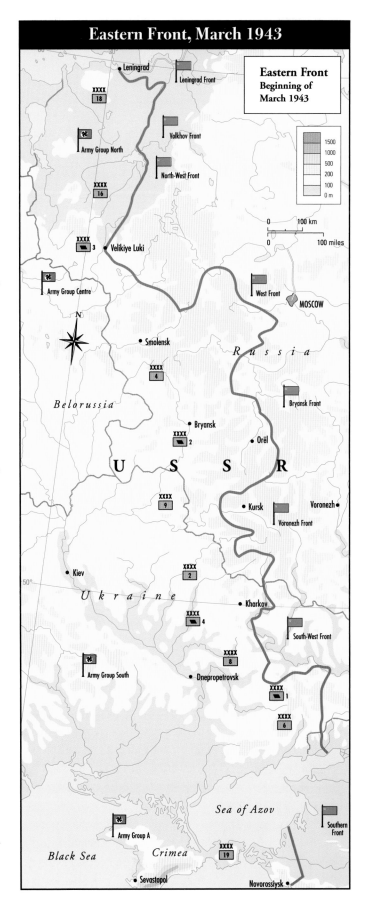

Eastern Front, March 1943

Eastern Front
Beginning of
March 1943

halt for the time being. Despite the brilliance of Manstein's counter-attack, the Germans could not be said to have been in an enviable position by April 1943, since they had suffered huge losses. Three German armies had been annihilated in the fighting between November 1942 and the halt in late March 1943. While the Russians had also suffered grievously, they were far better positioned to bring newly formed units into the line.

A further negative factor for the Germans, and one which they were to come to appreciate over the next few months was that the Red Army began to put into practice a number of the key lessons learned in the first 18 months of the war. Stalin finally recognized that he could take credit for the success of operations without controlling them totally, and his mistrust for his generals, so high in the 1930s, dissipated as they began to deliver success. As a result, Stalin abandoned the monolithic command structure centred around him, and turned the high command into something more than just a glorified staff which would implement his every wish. While Stalin remained firmly in control, he made some significant changes that brought the generals firmly back into the planning process.

General Georgy Zhukhov was appointed as Stalin's deputy, making him the most powerful Soviet general, while Colonel-General Aleksander Vasilevsky was handed the role of chief of staff at the high command. These changes were followed by a total reorganization of the Red Army's command structure. Previously, political officers appointed to ensure that the army acted with the utmost loyalty had taken an undue part in planning. Since the overwhelming majority of these officers had no idea about how to organize a battle, they were a considerable obstacle to effective operations, demanding unrealistic goals for operations with the implication that commanders who did not accede to these demands would be removed. Zhukhov made sure that this was overturned at once, and the political officers, while still deeply involved in planning, did

Above: A Soviet sniper takes aim from his position at the foot of a ruined building. The fact that the man has not made any effort to camouflage his position suggests that this may be a propaganda photograph, rather than an image from actual fighting.

Opposite: Two partisans, seen operating around Leningrad in the summer of 1943. The picture demonstrates how the partisans drew their forces from all age groups, presenting the Germans with a massive security problem as they attempted to quell resistance.

Right: The retaking of Kharkov by the Soviets left the German Army Group Don under serious threat, prompting Field Marshal Manstein to launch a daring counter-attack. He assaulted the Soviets on 20 February 1943, forcing the Russians back over the River Donets. Kharkov fell into German hands again, bringing the 1942–43 winter campaigns to an end, as both sides were exhausted.

Opposite: The end of Manstein's counter-offensive left a significant salient in the Russian lines, centred on the town of Kursk. Hitler decided that this offered an opportunity to destroy the two Soviet fronts (Central and Voronezh) that held the area, and set in train plans for what was to become the biggest tank battle in history at Kursk.

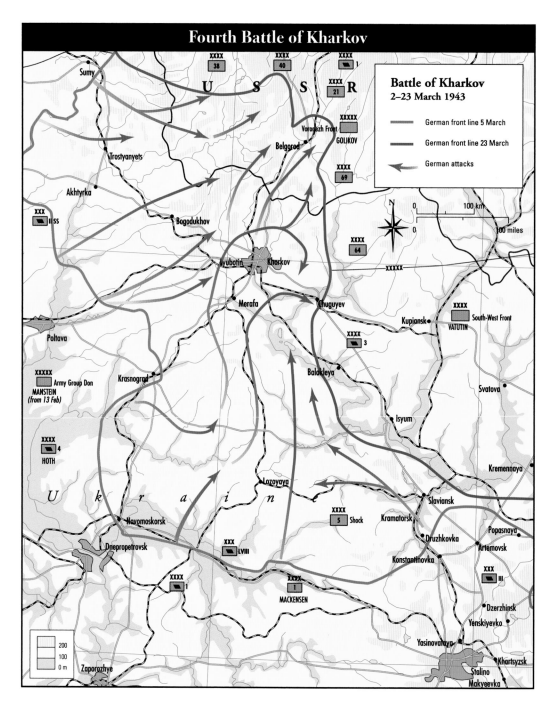

not have the authority to overrule Red Army officers. The sum of these developments was to leave the Germans facing an enemy that was improving its equipment, strategy and tactics with a much better command structure than before, a problem that would become all too apparent once the effects of the spring thaw lifted and the operations of summer 1943 began.

On to Kursk

The end of Manstein's counter-offensive against Kharkov left the Soviets holding a significant salient, centred on the town of Kursk. In another of his optimistic visions, Hitler concluded that this offered his troops the ideal opportunity to destroy the two

Soviet army fronts (Central and Voronezh) holding the area. This did not take account of the fact that the Soviets would recover from the demands made upon them by the post-Stalingrad operations, and Hitler only made matters worse by his insistence upon a course of action that he proclaimed would deliver the decisive blow for which he was aiming.

Hitler was convinced that many of the problems that had confronted his troops since Stalingrad had been caused by the lack of armour capable of dealing with the Soviet T-34. However, there was hope, since the Germans had developed two new tanks, namely the Panzer Mark V (better known as the Panther) and the large Tiger tank. Hitler argued that these armoured vehicles were the key to the offensive. If enough of them were made available to his forces around the Kursk salient, success would follow. To aid matters further, he pointed to the fact that more self-propelled guns, an integral part of German offensive tactics in that they supported the advance of the infantry, were coming off the production lines. The validity of these thoughts was questionable, but Hitler would not be dissuaded from his intended course.

This failed to take into account the fact that while Panthers, Tigers and self-propelled guns were indeed coming off the production line, they were not being produced in anything like the numbers to guarantee success against the Soviets. This prompted Hitler to postpone his planned offensive until enough were available, a move loaded with risk. By delaying the attack he granted the Soviets more time to recover from the winter's fighting and to increase their strength. This in turn meant that it would be more difficult to make a breakthrough, even with the new weapons in which Hitler invested so much faith.

The German generals were less than impressed with the idea of an offensive when Hitler presented it to them in early May 1943. Not unreasonably, they queried whether the resources for such a venture would be available, and they made clear their concerns about Hitler's decision to postpone the attack while waiting for new tanks. The generals made it very clear that the Soviets were almost certainly going to build far stronger defences around Kursk, given that it was an obvious weak spot in

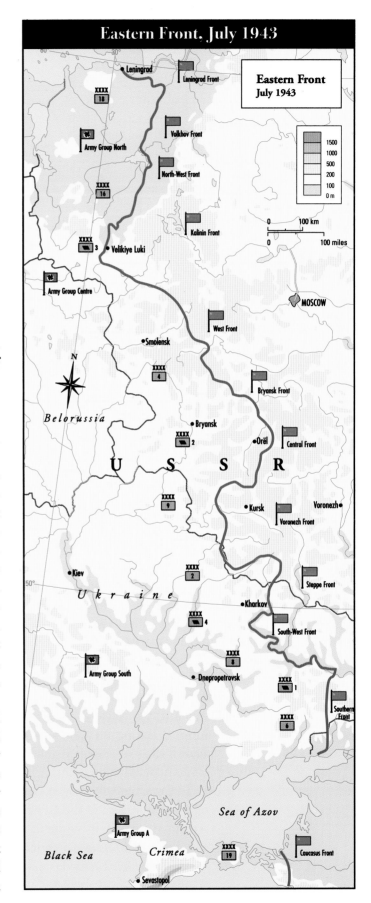

Above: Soldiers from the SS Totenkopf Division make their way towards the front lines at Kursk, July 1943. Massive troop concentrations were to fight a savage battle that saw huge losses on both sides – but these were losses that the Soviets could absorb, and which the Germans could not.

their line, and that every day that passed to allow German forces to grow stronger was a day in which the Soviets did the same. Not for the first time, nor for the last, Hitler simply refused to listen. He was presented with a number of alternative options, designed to maintain the German position, but was fixed upon his own idea. General Heinz Guderian, the inspector-general of Panzer forces, presented bitter opposition to the idea of any offensive in Russia, be it around Kursk or anywhere else.

Guderian was well aware that the Axis position in North Africa was on the verge of total collapse, and that the majority of the troops still in Tunisia would inevitably be captured and unavailable for redeployment. He also suggested that once North Africa was lost, the Allies would turn their attention to opening a second front in Western Europe, leaving the Germans facing the unwelcome prospect of a war on two fronts against allies who seemed able to conjure up massive amounts of equipment, despite the losses inflicted upon them.

To Guderian, this dangerous strategic situation suggested that any attempt to go on the offensive in Russia would be absurd. Rather than squander large amounts of Germany's armoured strength in another attritional battle in the East, Guderian argued, the Panther and Tiger tanks upon which Hitler was pinning so much hope should be kept for facing the invasion forces in the West. He contended that the logical conclusion was that German troops in the USSR should adopt a defensive posture, and not gamble on offensive action at all. Hitler listened to Guderian's views and then ignored them totally, pressing on with the plan, and committing the Germans to another major attritional battle.

To make matters worse for the Germans, Soviet intelligence-gathering capabilities were improving. Unlike in June 1941 when the German attack had come as an almost complete surprise, by May 1943, the Soviets were much better at divining German intentions. Indeed, it is possible that Zhukhov had enough information to suggest that Kursk would be the venue for the next German offensives before some of Hitler's generals were aware of the fact. Unsurprisingly, Zhukhov made sure that his troops would be prepared for the assault that would follow.

Operation Citadel

As part of Zhukhov's preparations, troops were brought in from other fronts to defend the salient, while plans were made to follow up a German attack with a huge counter-offensive along the entire southern part of the front. By early July, the Germans had concentrated nearly 3000 tanks and assault guns around the salient, but while this force was being built up, the Soviets quietly prepared a series of strong defensive positions. Seven defence lines were constructed between April and July, while Zhukhov moved reserves opposite the largest German troop concentrations to ensure that they could not have a decisive effect when thrown into battle against the Soviet lines. As well as the seven major defensive positions, the Russians set up a further line of defence well behind the salient, to deal with the possibility of a German breakthrough.

As a result, a huge force stood directly opposite the Germans by the start of July. There were nearly one million men and 3300 tanks in position, while another 380,000 men and 600 tanks were held in reserve. While these figures seem incredible, they do not represent the entire strength of the Soviet position – the 1.38 million men and 3900 tanks

'[Hitler's] interest in anything technological led him to exaggerate the effect of armament. For example, he imagined himself to be able with the help of a few battalions of self-propelled artillery or Tiger tanks to redress situations where only the engagement of several divisions held out any hope of success.'

Field Marshal Erich von Manstein

SOVIET HEAVY TANKS

In addition to medium tanks such as the T-34, the Soviets developed a number of heavier vehicles that were designed to take on enemy tanks, as well as to provide support to the infantry. The first of these was the T-35, which, despite its designation, was produced several years before the T-34. The T-35 proved slow and difficult to manoeuvre; when they faced the Germans in 1941, they proved very vulnerable.

The T-35 was followed by the more successful KV-1. This was used as an assault tank, designed to lead the attack and break through German lines, whereupon the more mobile T-34s would exploit the success. The KV-1 was much better than the T-35, and was developed into the KV-85, with an 85mm (3.3in) gun as its main armament, and the KV-152, armed with a 152mm (5.9in) howitzer. While the KV-1 and KV-85 were a handful for German defences, they were succeeded in production by the IS series of heavy tanks, which first entered service in mid-1943. The IS-2, introduced in early 1944, was the most notable, armed with a massive 122mm (4.8in) gun that could defeat any German tanks it encountered. It remained the most powerful tank in the world for a decade after the end of the war.

Below: By early July 1943, the Germans had 3000 tanks and assault guns around the Kursk salient. The Soviets, aware of an impending attack, prepared incredibly strong defensive positions. Nearly two million Soviet troops and 5000 tanks faced the Germans, setting the scene for one of the largest battles in military history.

represented just the tactical level defences against and assault. The operational line behind the salient had a further 500,000 men and another 1500 tanks available to it, ready for deployment where required. To make matters worse for the Germans, the Red Air Force (strictly Frontal Aviation) was present in large numbers to provide direct air support against the attack.

As a result, Hitler's decisive offensive was to begin with the attacking forces heavily outnumbered by their opponents. These sat in strong defensive positions that would take huge effort to overcome, and they had massive reserves to come to their aid if required, or to exploit the developing situation on the battlefield – a recipe for potential disaster, rather than the decisive victory that Hitler insisted would follow.

The Clash of Battle

Army Group South carried out a number of preparatory operations on 4 July to secure the starting positions for Operation Citadel, with the attack itself due to begin at 04:30 the next morning. At this point, the German guns opened fire all along the Central Front, while aircraft joined in the bombardment on the Voronezh Front. Shortly after 05:00, the first reports of tank and infantry attacks were made by Soviet front line positions. Fourth Panzer Army committed 700 armoured vehicles to the assault against the Soviet Sixth

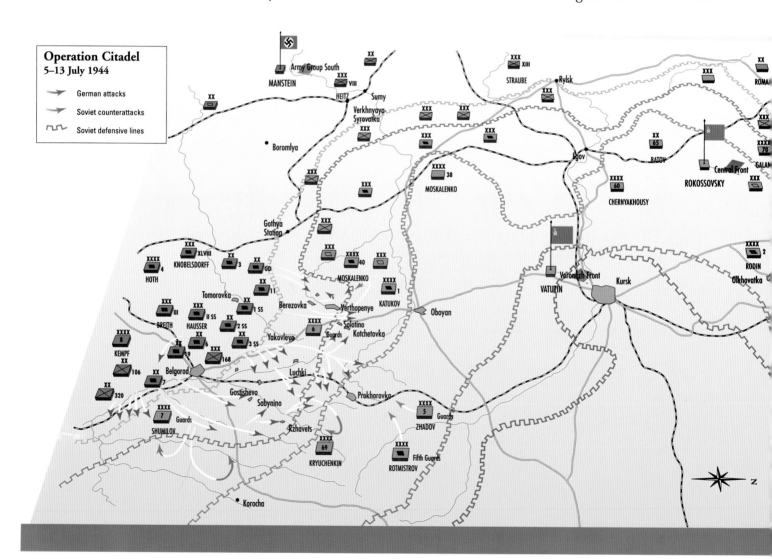

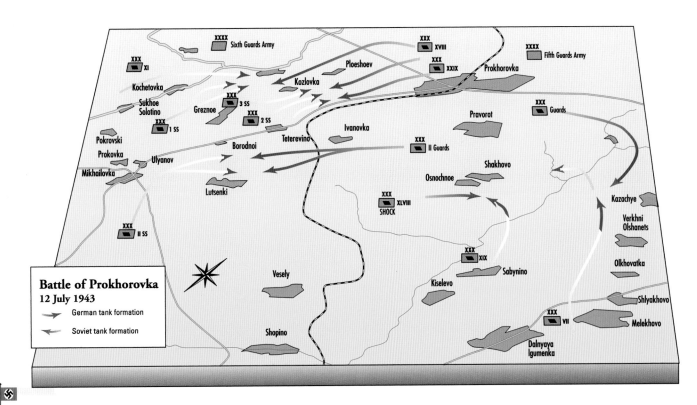

Battle of Prokhorovka
12 July 1943

→ German tank formation
→ Soviet tank formation

Army Group Centre
KLUGE

Guards Army, with tanks packed 40 or 50 per kilometre of line in most sectors, rising to as many as 100 per kilometre elsewhere.

The Germans managed to gain ground to a depth of four to six miles, and Rokossovsky secured agreement from Stalin that the Twenty-Seventh Army would be sent forward to assist. However, when it became clear that the situation on the Voronezh Front was even more serious than that facing Central Front, Stalin withdrew his offer and sent the forces there instead. By 18:00 on 6 July, both sides were pouring men and material into the battle, with the armour of both sides moving on a scale never seen before or since, moving in formations up to 200 strong on both sides of the front. Some 4000 Soviet and 3000 German tanks and assault guns were now on the verge of entering the battle, which continued with ever greater ferocity; the Soviet high command estimated that nearly 600 German tanks were destroyed or disabled on the first day of the fighting.

Attack was followed by counter-attack, and the Germans managed to make a number of gains, so that by the morning of 7 July they were threatening the high ground near Olkhovatka, which gave command of the battlefield. Rokossovsky promptly reinforced the approaches to Olkhovatka, and fighting of rarely paralleled intensity broke out as the Germans tried to attack against anti-tank guns, mines, armour and artillery, with both sides suffering fearful losses as they went. By 10 July, the Germans were regrouping after the first five days of combat, and it was clear that the climax of the battle

Above: By nightfall on the first day of Kursk, the Germans had managed to advance around seven miles. By 11 July, II SS Panzer Corps had reached Prokhorovka, a small village that swiftly became the location of the largest tank battle in history. The Soviet commander, General Vatutin had concluded that the Germans would attack at Prokhorovka, and reinforced his positions there. The end result was an enormous battle on 12 July, in which over 1000 tanks participated. After 36 hours' fighting, the Germans were brought to a halt.

Above: Soviet assault troops leave their trenches. The man on his knees is armed with a PPSh 41 sub-machine gun, a robust weapon with a 71-round drum and which was built in huge numbers during the war. The man behind him is equipped with a Tokarev self-loading rifle, one of the first such designs to be employed by a major army.

was approaching. Despite having made a penetration of nearly 20 miles towards Oboyan, the Germans had been unable to break through to the necessary depth, and were about to shift the axis of their attack towards Prokhorovka, a small village which had a railway junction as its most notable feature. Within 24 hours, it had become the site of the largest tank battle the world has ever seen.

Climax

In response to the German moves and the increased threat to Prokhorovka, armour and troops were moved to strengthen the Voronezh Front, being placed in blocking positions. If the Germans could break through here, they would be in a position to unhinge the Soviet defences. General Vatutin saw the threat as an opportunity, however. He was well aware that the Germans had suffered massive losses in the course of the battle so far, and felt that if the Germans were to attack against Prokhorovka, they would have to move units from their flanks to support the attack. This reduction in strength on the flanks appeared to offer an ideal opportunity to counter-attack, with the aim of encircling the German forces.

At dawn on 11 July, the Germans attacked Prokhorovka and Oboyan, with a massive battle taking place between Fifth Guards Tank Army and three SS divisions. The battle for Prokhorovka was in the balance by nightfall, and the Soviet relief attack to the north against the Orel bulge was timely, but the main struggle took place at the village itself. Fifth Guards Tank Army was sent into the fray once more, counter-attacking vigorously. Yet again, the battle was fierce with huge casualties on both sides. The Germans had lost more than 300 tanks (including 70 Tigers), while around 50 per cent of the Fifth Guards Tank Army had been destroyed. Yet despite the heavy losses, the Soviets had achieved their aim. The German attacks had been halted, while the Russians still had reserves in hand to use if required.

The Germans continued probing attacks for three more days, but it was clear that they were not going to be able to break through at Prokhorovka, nor were they going to be able to bypass it. By this point, the battle was over, since developments elsewhere had seized Hitler's attention.

On 10 July, an Anglo-American invasion force landed in Sicily, with the obvious implication that Italy would be next to be invaded. Hitler feared that the Italians would capitulate as soon as the Allies invaded, and decided that he had no alternative but to reinforce his units in the West, at the expense of Operation Citadel.

Hitler gave orders for the transfer of a number of units to the Western Front. In a number of instances, the units that were to head west found their transfer was complicated by the need to extricate themselves from the battle before they could obey their instructions. With the reduction of strength that this move entailed, the Germans had no option but to carry out a fighting withdrawal and head back to their start points of 5 July. To all intents and purposes, the Battle of Kursk was over.

Aftermath

As the northern element of the German attack at Kursk ground to a halt the Soviet Western Front (General Sokolovsky) launched Operation Kutuzov, an attack against Second Panzer Army. The German forces were distracted by their own offensive, and taken by surprise. Their defences were quickly overrun, and as it became obvious that Soviet units would soon be in a position to cut the lines of communication of General Walther Model's Ninth Army, the Germans were forced to defend vigorously before finally checking the attack. This was not the end of the fighting, however.

Operation Kutuzov was quickly followed by an offensive towards Orël by General Popov's Bryansk Front. Orël was the key road and rail junction in the region, and, as was always the case, the prospect of losing such a key communications point was a major concern to the Germans. After a week's fighting, the Soviets took Orël, and continued their advance; by the middle of August, the German positions on the northern shoulder of the Kursk Salient became untenable, and had to be abandoned.

The Germans fell back to prepared defensive positions some 75 miles away to the west, having failed in their objectives for the northern shoulder of the offensive against Kursk. A similar dismal result was to befall the Germans in the southern sector as the Steppe Front (General Koniev) and Vatutin's Voronezh Front launched their own offensive (Operation Polkovodets Rumyantsev), with the aim of destroying the southern shoulder of the salient as a precursor to an advance towards Belgorod and Kharkov.

When Operation Rumyantsev began on 3 August, the Germans were again taken by surprise. They had correctly assessed that both the Steppe and Voronezh Fronts had taken heavy losses during the fighting at Kursk, but totally underestimated the Russians' ability to bring replacements into the line. As a result, they had not prepared to meet an enemy attack, and were taken completely by surprise when the blow fell upon them. The offensive thus enjoyed considerable early success. By nightfall on the second day, Belgorod was back in Soviet hands. This success allowed an advance towards Bogodukhov and Kharkov, with a German counter-attack proving futile. The Soviets

'Whenever I think of this attack, my stomach turns over.'

Adolf Hitler on Operation Citadel to General Heinz Guderian, May 1943

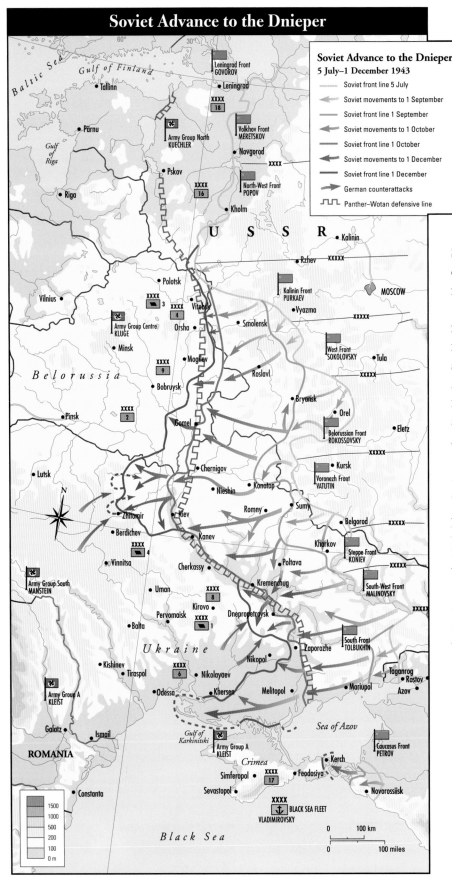

Soviet Advance to the Dnieper

Soviet Advance to the Dnieper
5 July–1 December 1943

- Soviet front line 5 July
- Soviet movements to 1 September
- Soviet front line 1 September
- Soviet movements to 1 October
- Soviet front line 1 October
- Soviet movements to 1 December
- Soviet front line 1 December
- German counterattacks
- Panther–Wotan defensive line

advanced inexorably upon Kharkov, which changed hands for the fourth – and final – time in the war on 21 August.

As Operation Rumyantsev progressed, Rokossovsky's Central Front launched an offensive of its own from its positions around Kursk. Central Front acted as a link between the two offensives to the north and south of its positions. Alongside this attack the Southwest and South Fronts began offensives of their own against Army Group South. As a result, by the middle of September 1943, Army Group South had been forced back across the Dnieper. The first bridgehead across the river was secured by a Soviet advance party on 23 September, with the main force reaching the river along a frontage stretching from Gomel to Zaporozhye.

The offensive continued, and by 25 October, the Soviet advance had cut off German forces in the Crimea. Another German counter-attack battered some of the Soviet advanced forces around Krivoi Rog, but this was not enough to prevent the Russians advancing on Kiev. The offensive here began on 3 November, and the city was back in Soviet hands within 48 hours. As Christmas approached, the Germans were left holding just a few small sections of the western bank of the Dnieper, hoping to hold on until the Soviet offensive had exhausted itself. Initial signs that the Russians had lost momentum were misleading, though – they had no intention of slackening off their pace for the remainder of 1943, and were to bring further disaster upon the Germans before the year was out.

Left: A German non-commissioned officer carries two land mines. He is armed with a single hand grenade and probably a pistol for personal protection. The Germans made considerable use of mines on all fronts, with the aim of destroying Soviet tanks and attacking formations, thus reducing the enemy's forces to more manageable proportions.

Opposite: The events following Kursk came as a massive blow to German forces on the Eastern Front. The Soviets followed up their success at Kursk with Operation Rumyantsev in early August 1943, in which the Germans found themselves outnumbered by nearly 3:1, facing nearly 700,000 Russians. The Soviets advanced quickly over the coming months as they drove on to the Dnieper, and as the year drew to a close, Soviet troops lined the river banks, waiting to make their next move against an increasingly stretched enemy.

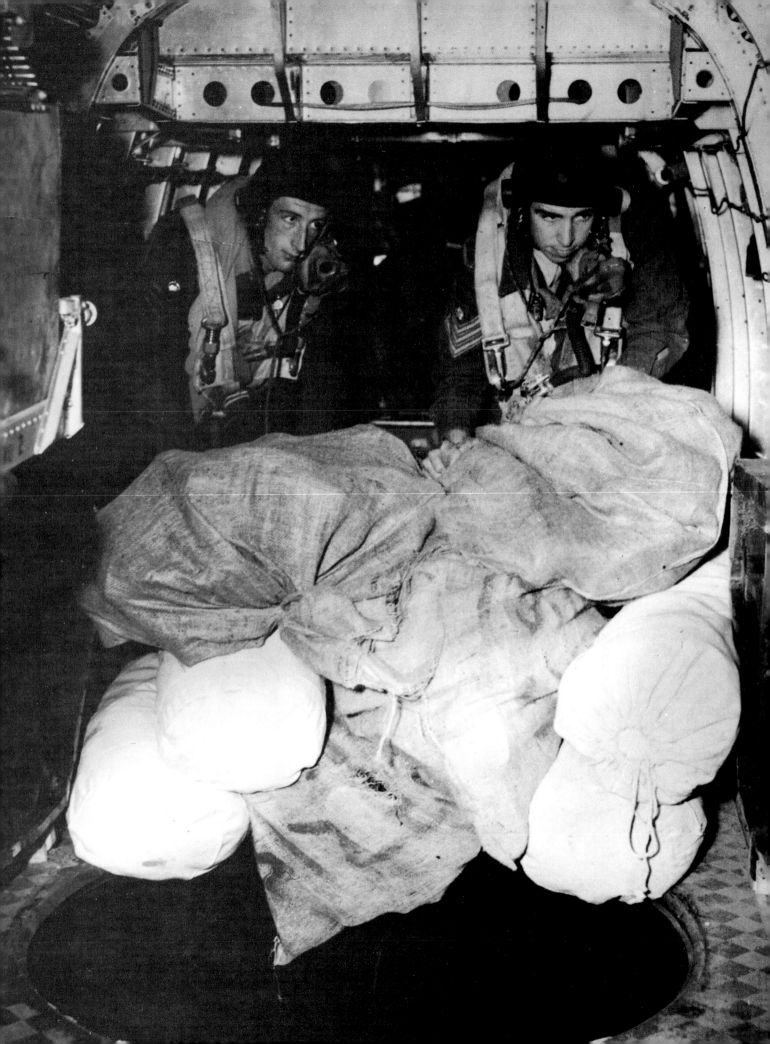

The Balkans

For much of the war, the Balkan theatre saw little in the way of conventional fighting. However, there were substantial numbers of resistance fighters at work in Yugoslavia, Greece and Albania, all aiming to overthrow German occupation. The Balkan area was also notable for the fact that Hitler's minor allies were to be found there, in the form of Bulgaria, Romania and Hungary, although each had a different perspective on their relationship with Hitler and with each other. These subtleties were not appreciated by the Soviets, who regarded them simply as allies of the Nazis, and therefore to be defeated.

If the Germans thought that they would have an easy time in Yugoslavia after their rapid victory there in 1941, they were swiftly disabused of this notion. Unbeknown to them, a leading member of the pre-war Yugoslav Communist Party, Josip Broz, was determined that the country should rise against the Nazi invaders. At the time, Broz was living in Zagreb under the name of Babiç. Although the new puppet government of Croatia was attempting to round up all communist activists, Broz had considerable practice at avoiding the authorities. The previous government had spent some time attempting to locate, with a similar lack of success, a 'Comrade Tito', the *nom de guerre* by which Broz would become known for the rest of his life.

The Yugoslav Partisans

The invasion of the USSR prompted Tito to issue a call for a national revolt against the 'Fascist hordes', issued on 4 July 1941. The partisan war began almost immediately, with acts of sabotage across the country, most notably in Serbia and Montenegro; in the latter, the Italian occupying forces were routed. The German response to the uprising came in the form of reprisals in which thousands of people were killed; this only encouraged more to join the Partisans.

Tito expected that the conflict to liberate Yugoslavia would be a long and difficult one, and he was quite correct. The task was complicated considerably by the presence of another resistance group, the Çetniks, headed by a former army officer, Draça Mihailoviç.

Opposite: Two RAF aircrew prepare to drop supplies to Yugoslav Partisans. The RAF established a number of 'special duties' squadrons to carry out supply runs to underground organizations and to drop liaison officers into occupied territories to advise and assist the resistance in their struggle against the Nazis.

Yugoslavia, 1943

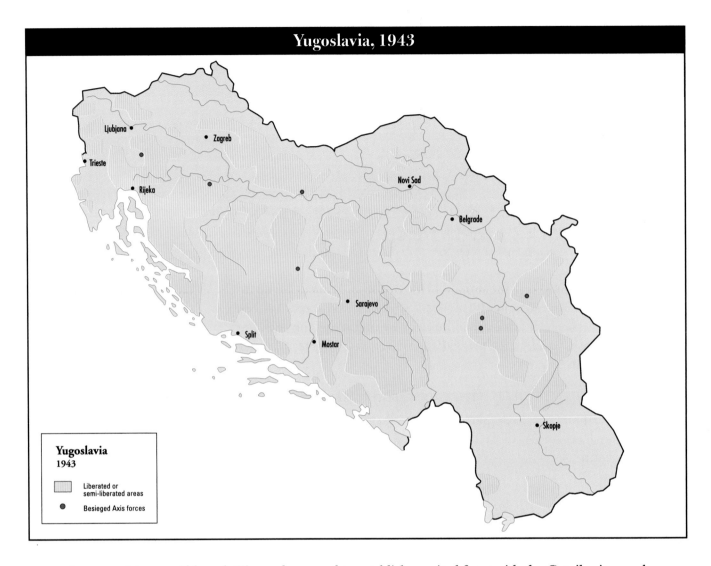

Yugoslavia
1943

Liberated or
semi-liberated areas

Besieged Axis forces

Above: The nature of the countryside in Yugoslavia meant that it was impossible for the Germans to control all of the country. This allowed Tito's Partisans to run large parts of Yugoslavia themselves as 'liberated areas'. While German offensives meant that the amount of territory held by Tito's forces fluctuated, the Partisans always managed to remain a viable combat force, and never lost great swathes of territory.

Although Tito endeavoured to establish a united front with the Çetniks, it soon became clear that this was an unlikely alliance. Mihailoviç was an ardent royalist, aiming for the restoration of the *status quo*, while Tito hoped to see the establishment of a communist state after the Germans had left. The Çetniks had the advantage to begin with, in that a British liaison officer was sent to support them. The liaison officer arrived before a second meeting between Tito and Mihailoviç, but was excluded from the talks, leaving him poorly informed about the Partisans. The negotiations between the two sides collapsed, and it became clear that the Çetniks saw the Partisans as being their principal enemies ahead of the Germans. This led to a situation in which the Çetniks began to work alongside the Germans and Italians, with the aim of destroying Tito's movement.

German Offensives

Owing to the nature of Yugoslavia's terrain, it was extremely difficult for the Germans and Italians to control all the territory in the country. This meant that it was possible for the Partisans to control large swathes of territory, running them as liberated areas with their own administrative structures.

The Germans were determined to crush the Partisans, and launched a series of offensives, beginning in Serbia in September 1941 and lasting until December. The

Partisans were driven back from much of the territory under their control, falling back on the liberated town of Foča in Bosnia. The Germans followed this offensive with a second, beginning on 15 January 1942, and this drove Tito's forces out of Foča by 10 May as they advanced across the countryside. The Partisans fell back again across the high ground around Mount Kozara, which the Germans found impossible to take. Their offensive then merged into a third assault, beginning in April, prompting Tito to lead his forces out of eastern Bosnia and nearer to Croatia. The retreat started on 24 June 1942, and was to cover 150 miles before it was complete. Unlike conventional military retreats, this withdrawal was marked by considerable success, since the Partisans captured the towns of Jajce and Bihać as they went. By capturing Bihać, the Partisans gained control of a large amount of liberated territory, in which Tito was able to hold a political congress, the Anti-Fascist Council for the National Liberation of Yugoslavia. The council arranged elections and laid down a manifesto for the future direction of the Partisan movement. This had a positive effect on Partisan morale, and raised their profile in the West.

The Četniks had enjoyed all the support of the British and Americans up to mid-1942, receiving liaison officers in mid-1941. The Četniks had ensured that relatively little information about the Partisans reached London, by controlling the radio transmissions of the liaison team. The Allies, including the Soviets, had already recognized the right of the exiled royalist government to return, and Mihailoviç was a member of their cabinet; not aiding the Četniks or sending increased support to their rivals would be politically difficult. All of this militated against Allied help being sent to Tito, but by the end of 1942, enough information had reached London to provide a better picture of how successful the Partisans had been. It also became clear that the Četniks were collaborating with the Germans and Italians in many areas, while in others they were largely inactive. These factors were particularly relevant to Allied considerations by the end of 1942, since planning for the invasion of Sicily and then, possibly, Italy was well under way. It was quite evident that it would be beneficial if Axis forces could be tied down in Yugoslavia by increased Partisan activity, denying the enemy the opportunity to

Below: German paratroops take up positions during the raid on Tito's headquarters at Drvar. They were unsuccessful in their aim of killing or capturing the Partisan leader, who managed to escape. Several days of bitter fighting left most of the paratroops who had led the raid dead or wounded, with nothing to show for their sacrifice.

Above: German soldiers guard Partisan prisoners, taken during one of the Axis offensives against Tito's organization. Despite making massive efforts to destroy the Partisans, the Germans never quite succeeded in achieving their goals, leaving large areas of Yugoslavia under Tito's control.

redeploy a number of divisions to the new battlefront. However, while it was clear that the Partisans were a major force in Yugoslavia, the decision over what, if any, help should be despatched was still being made when the Germans launched yet another assault in January 1943, in response to a decision by Hitler that the danger of the Allies invading the Balkans was such that the Partisans' constant interference with communications and supply routes had to be stopped. The Germans employed over 150,000 troops in five divisions, while the Italians employed three divisions of their own. In addition, some 18,000 Çetniks and troops loyal to the puppet regime in Croatia were used. The German and Croatian troops attacked from the north and east, while the Italians approached from the west and south. Tito ordered a retreat to east Bosnia, with the intention of crossing into the mountains of Montenegro. To achieve this, the Partisans had to pass through enemy territory across the River Neretva, where 12,000 Çetniks were waiting for them.

As the Partisans reached the Neretva, fierce fighting broke out as they encountered Çetnik and Italian forces. The Partisans inflicted severe damage on the Italians, and utterly routed the Çetniks to the extent that they were never able to reconstitute themselves as a major force. Tito's forces successfully crossed the river, and headed into Montenegro, pursuing what was left of the Çetnik forces at they went.

The Germans were far from impressed at the results of the offensive, blaming the Italians and the Çetniks for the failure. A fifth offensive was planned, and began in the third week of May 1943. Just as the offensive began, the first Allied liaison officers arrived, in time to witness the capabilities of the Partisans first hand. The Germans attacked with the support of an Italian division, along with Bulgarian troops and elements of the Çetniks, a total of some 120,000 men. The Germans managed to trap Tito's forces in the Montenegrin mountains. Tito decided to attempt a break-out, and used his 3rd Division to hold the Germans off while the 1st, 2nd and 7th Partisan Divisions fought their way out. The battle was particularly hard, since the Germans had correctly assessed where Tito would try to break out – but they were unable to stop him. By the middle of July, the Partisans had evaded the German attempt to encircle and destroy them, but had lost 8000 fighters in the process.

Changing Fortunes

The loss of 8000 men was a blow to Tito, but the liaison officers had been convinced that the Partisans were a viable organization and worthy of support. As a result, a full British military mission under the command of Brigadier Fitzroy Maclean was sent to Tito's headquarters in September 1943. This was a particularly auspicious month for the Partisans, since as well as the arrival of the British mission, Italy surrendered. Although the Germans maintained their position in the north of Italy, this had a major effect in Yugoslavia. The Partisans took the opportunity to round up 10 Italian divisions, relieving them of their equipment; a proportion of the Italian troops decided that they wished to fight alongside the Partisans, and three Italian Partisan divisions were set up as a result.

The Partisans were able to liberate territory under Italian control, creating further problems for the Germans, who had to try to fill the vacuum left by the capitulation of their allies. The Partisans took advantage of the situation to increase the size of their army by 80,000.

In addition, the arrival of British support meant that there was a steady flow of medical supplies and other equipment; in addition, it was possible to evacuate wounded Partisans to North Africa and other Allied-held territory, thus removing a major logistics burden from the Partisans, who did not have to ferry their wounded with them as they moved across the countryside.

TITO

Born Josip Broz in 1892, Tito had been a prominent communist activist in the years prior to the German invasion of Yugoslavia (and it was during these activities that his alias of Tito was created). His influence over the Partisan movement was incalculable, since he appreciated that victory over the Germans would not be achieved in a short time.

Tito established political structures within the Partisan movement, and held a national assembly in 1942, to demonstrate that the Germans did not have control of all of the country. Although the Western Allies initially supported the Çetnik movement as the resistance to the Germans, they switched their allegiance to Tito's far more effective Partisans in 1944.

As the military situation throughout Europe deteriorated for the Germans, the Partisans made more and more gains, taking Belgrade on 20 October 1944, supported by the Red Army. Tito became president of Yugoslavia in the aftermath of the war, and remained fiercely independent of Stalin, refusing to become a mere satellite of the USSR. When Tito died in 1980, it marked the start of the disintegration of Yugoslavia, which many argue was held together solely by the strength of his leadership.

Soviet Advance into Romania and Hungary

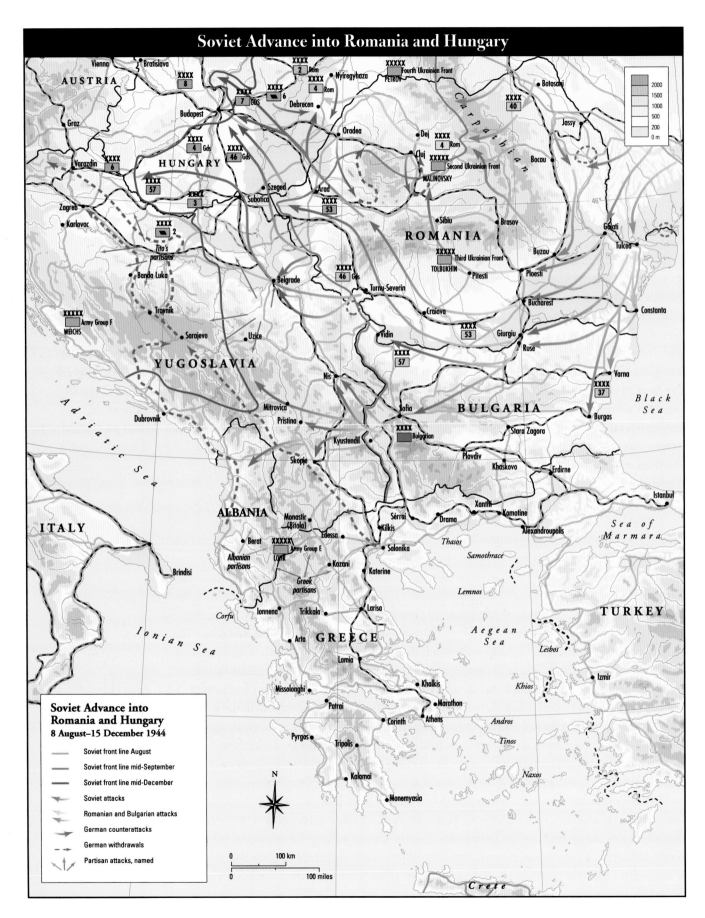

Soviet Advance into Romania and Hungary
8 August–15 December 1944

Soviet front line August

Soviet front line mid-September

Soviet front line mid-December

Soviet attacks

Romanian and Bulgarian attacks

German counterattacks

German withdrawals

Partisan attacks, named

0   100 km

0   100 miles

N

The Final Offensives

By the end of 1943, Tito had an army 300,000 strong, controlling around two-thirds of Yugoslavia. Once again, Hitler decided that the threat posed by the Partisans had to be addressed, but the approach taken to the sixth offensive was very different. Rather than trying to destroy the Partisans through one major operation against their main body, the Germans instead launched attacks in several parts of the country, aiming to overwhelm individual Partisan groups by sheer weight of numbers. Although the Germans made some gains, the whole campaign began to peter out in mid-January 1944, by which time it was clear that World War II was entering a decisive phase. The Russians were advancing all along the Eastern Front, while the campaign in Italy had seen Allied landings at Anzio. It was quite clear that the German position in Romania would soon be under threat, and Hitler determined to remove the Partisans with a final effort.

The seventh offensive was duly launched in April 1944, with fighting in a variety of locations. All of these skirmishes were overshadowed by a daring German airborne assault on Tito's headquarters at Drvar in Bosnia. Early in the morning of 25 May, the headquarters complex was attacked by German bombers, the precursor to a glider assault. The glider-borne troops established firm defensive positions, while paratroops and more gliders were dropped in. Tito's escort held the Germans off, and help was sent for. Tito took the opportunity to escape, but fierce fighting raged through the town for the next two days as the Germans sought to capture their now departed quarry. When German infantry arrived in Drvar, they found that only one-sixth of the airborne troops had survived the operation. By this time, Tito had been flown out of Yugoslavia to Italy, before moving to the island of Vis where he set up a new headquarters. Although the Germans obtained some propaganda value from the raid, displaying captured uniforms, papers and equipment, this could not hide the fact that their plan had failed.

Hitler's focus now turned away from the Balkans to France, since the Allied landings in Normandy occurred just days after the abortive attempt to kill or capture Tito. As the pressure on the Germans increased in the West, the Russians made their presence felt as they advanced on Romania.

Romania

By early August 1944, Soviet offensives in the north and centre of the Eastern Front were going well, and planning for an attack into Romania was begun as soon as it was clear that no redeployment of forces to support other attacks would be required. The plan that emerged called for 2nd Ukrainian Front to attack German and Romanian defences to the north west of Iasi, and once a break-in had been achieved, the exploitation forces would cross the River Prut behind the German Sixth Army (now reconstituted after the original Sixth Army had been lost at Stalingrad). The 3rd Ukrainian Front would make an attack at Bendery, breaking through enemy lines to allow it to link up with 2nd Ukrainian Front. This would allow the Soviets to encircle all German forces in the Kishinev area, while the other forces would head south towards Bucharest and the oilfields at Ploesti.

The offensive began on 20 August 1944. The attack at Bendery was held up by two German divisions, but in the northern sector, only Romanian forces stood in the way of the advance. Many of the Romanian troops did not have any desire to support the Germans, and many units offered nothing more than token resistance before they retreated or surrendered. Despite this, the Germans were initially convinced that the Soviet threat was not particularly serious, and planned to fall back on to a ridge to the

Opposite: As the Soviet armies advanced through 1944, it was natural that they would turn their attention to the Balkans, seeking to deal with Germany's allies in Romania, Hungary and Bulgaria. Bulgaria and Romania were not eager to fight the Soviets, and detached themselves from Hitler with alacrity and changed sides. This did not prevent the Russians from invading both countries and destroying the German formations still there, while Hungary proved a difficult battleground, particularly the attempt to seize Budapest.

Above: Soviet troops, riding on T-34 tanks, enter Bucharest on 31 August 1944. The Romanian population had grown increasingly weary of the alliance with Germany, and the Nazi attempt to assassinate the king (to prevent him from capitulating) alienated them even more; however, the arrival of Russian troops was met with concern and ambivalence, as can be seen in the less than ecstatic welcome being given to these soldiers.

south of Iasi where a defensive line (the Trajan Line) had been erected. However, it soon became clear that the Soviets were doing better than anticipated, and their armour seized the high ground behind Iasi without any resistance. This undermined the German plan, and the German commander, General Hans Friessner, was forced to order a withdrawal to the Prut. The following morning saw the 3rd Ukrainian Front make a breakthrough at Bendery, and the danger of encirclement rose rapidly for the German forces.

As the Russian advance continued, it was clear that the Romanian front had all but collapsed. This precipitated a political crisis in Bucharest. King Carol II took the opportunity to sack his government, and made clear his intention to seek an armistice with the Allies. The German response was to send 6000 SS troops to the capital, where they discovered that the Romanians were quite happy to turn their guns on their supposed allies and put up vigorous resistance.

Friessner came to the conclusion that the situation was so desperate that the only chance of maintaining the German position in Romania was to remove the king. He promptly ordered an assassination attempt against Carol II on 24 August, led by dive bombers attacking the royal palace. The dive bombers failed in their task of killing the monarch, but managed to kill or injure many civilians. The attempt to kill their king and the casualties caused by the bombing only served to turn the Romanians against their erstwhile allies – Romania declared war on Germany the next day.

Friessner now faced complete disaster, so ordered all units under his command to retreat to Hungary, then to block the mountain passes in the Carpathians and

Transylvanian Alps as they went. This was far more complex than it sounded, since Sixth Army was now trapped in two pockets on the eastern bank of the Prut, making withdrawal unlikely. As the other German forces pulled back into Bulgaria, their movements caused concern in Sofia. Bulgaria was a member of the Axis, but had not declared war on the USSR. The government feared that allowing German troops to make use of their territory would be considered a hostile act by Moscow, so Bulgarian troops set about disarming the Germans as soon as they entered the country, sending the Germans to internment camps. While the Bulgarians were trying to ameliorate the effect of their alliance with Germany, the Soviets were busy completing their advance – Ploesti fell into their hands on 30 August, and Bucharest the next day.

As Soviet forces started occupying Romanian territory, the Fourth Guards Tank Army was sent to destroy the remains of the German Sixth Army, which was now attempting to escape from the pockets into which it had been forced by the fighting. The Russians had air superiority, and were able to make considerable use of their aircraft to hamper movement of German convoys. By 26 August, what was left of Sixth Army managed to break through a series of Soviet cut-off positions, opening a narrow corridor to the Prut. This was the only possible escape route for the Germans, and as thousands of men tried to gain the relatively safety of the river as a preliminary to withdrawing across it, they found that the Soviets had concentrated their artillery and armour against the corridor in a bid to prevent their escape.

The results were predictable. Heavy Soviet fire caused huge numbers of casualties, and forced the surviving Germans to plunge into the Prut with the aim of swimming to the west bank. Unfortunately for the Germans, they discovered that what they thought was the bank was in fact an island in the middle of the watercourse. Some Germans attempted to swim from here to the west bank, only to find that the Fourth Guards Tank Army was waiting for them. The Soviets attempted to secure the surrender of the remnants of the German force by sending emissaries to negotiate; however, as command and control had completely broken down amongst the Germans, they did not receive a response. As a result, the island was shelled, forcing the Germans to leave the island for the waters once more. Thousands were killed as they attempted to cross, and most of the others were taken prisoner. When the shelling ended, it was clear that Sixth Army had been completely destroyed in the fighting. Out of a strength of 275,000, the army had lost at least 125,000 dead by the start of September, with another 150,000 captured.

Bulgaria

The Soviets were now in a position to exploit the Romanian transport network and turned their attention to Bulgaria. Despite the best efforts of the Bulgarians to stay out of the war with Russia, this proved impossible. Attempts to negotiate with the Soviets failed, and although the Bulgarian government proclaimed that it was no longer at war with the Western Allies, the Russians could not be convinced. They announced that Bulgaria was a possible refuge for retreating Germans, and that this could not be tolerated; on 5 September 1944, they declared war.

The 3rd Ukrainian Front crossed the border on 8 September, and this prompted the Bulgarians into a new step – the next day, they announced that they were now at war with Germany, fighting alongside the Soviets, in one of the swiftest defections in military history. The effective surrenders of Romania and Bulgaria left the Russians with a front that was 425 miles long, stretching from the Hungarian border to the Aegean Sea.

'The proposal to save the Balkans from communism could never have been made good by a "soft underbelly" invasion, for Churchill himself had already cleared the way for the success of Tito … [who] had been firmly ensconced in Yugoslavia with British aid long before Italy itself was conquered.'

General Albert C. Wedemeyer

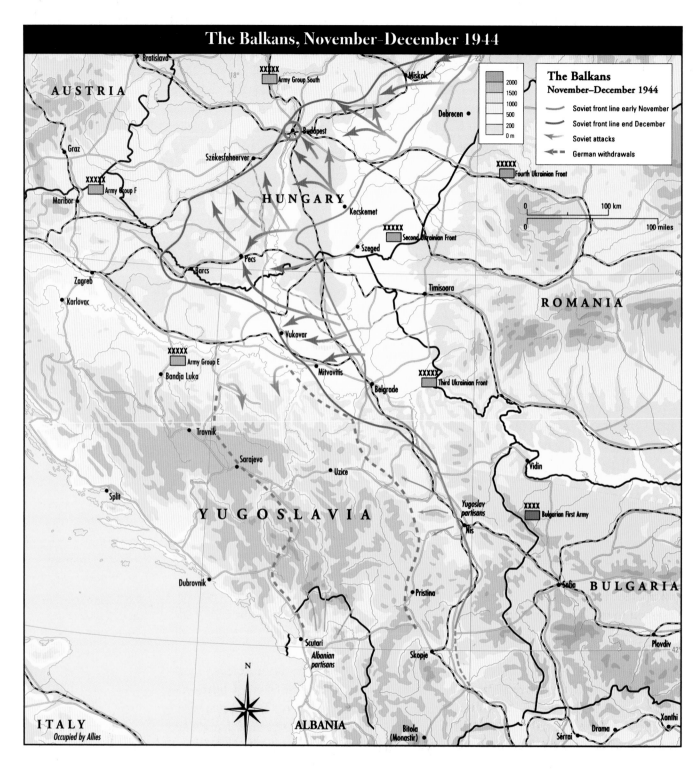

The Balkans, November–December 1944

The Germans were now forced to reorganize to meet the threat posed along this immense extent of front, and it was obvious that one of the solutions to the problem was to withdraw from Greece. The decision to do this was helped, oddly, by the failure of an Allied plan to assist Tito's Partisans to push into Serbia so that they might link up with the Red Army. Air attacks against communications links, aimed at blocking the routes by which German forces might leave Greece and southern Yugoslavia so as to block the Partisans, caused confusion when the Partisans failed to make anything like the progress

Left: Bulgarian troops set up defensive positions, awaiting the arrival of Soviet units. The machine gun is a World War I vintage Schwarzlose MG05, originally made for the Austro-Hungarian Army. Although old by 1944, it was tough and reliable, and still a viable combat weapon.

Opposite: The Soviet advances during mid- to late 1944 succeeded in driving the Germans from most of their positions in the Balkans. Belgrade was liberated on 31 August 1944, although fighting with German units remaining in Yugoslavia continued until the very end of the war, while the advance in Hungary culminated with the encirclement, and then capture, of Budapest after several weeks of hard fighting.

anticipated. Hitler and his generals reached the conclusion that the air attacks must be designed to trap German units in Greece, so that they could not be redeployed.

Hungary

Events in Romania led to considerable concern in Hungary as to the future. Romania and Bulgaria had been fierce rivals in the interwar period, with a number of territorial disputes arising from the Versailles settlements causing tension. The threat now presented by the Russians persuaded the Hungarian Army that it should launch an attack into Romania, which it did on 5 September 1944. The Soviets responded by turning more of their units towards Hungary. This in turn prompted panic in Budapest, and on 7 September, the government announced that unless the Germans sent the equivalent of five Panzer divisions to defend the country, the Hungarian government would be forced to act in its own interests, a clear indication that following a path similar to Romania and Bulgaria was imminent. Sufficient German forces were available to meet the demand from those pulling back from Romania. Hitler was concerned that the Hungarians would be unconvinced by the level of support that they were receiving if the Germans fell back any further, and ordered a halt to the retreat. This would have left the

*Above: A jubilant
Bulgarian leads the
celebrations welcoming
the Red Army into the
outskirts of Sofia. The
Bulgarians had become
increasingly
uncomfortable with their
alliance with the
Germans, and although
they had not been at war
with the USSR, this had
not prevented the
Russians from declaring
war; rapid political
manoeuvring saw the
Bulgarians denounce
their allies and declare
war upon them within a
matter of days in
September 1944.*

Germans in a highly disadvantageous position, and representations that withdrawal to a line some 40 miles west of the Muresul (as had been planned) would be far more sensible were accepted. The relative slowness of the Soviet moves towards the border (caused by increasing reliability problems with trucks and armour that needed attention after hard going over the previous weeks) meant that this vacillation was not as immediately problematic as it might have been.

As 2nd Ukrainian Front made its way forward, orders reached it from the high command that it was to carry out three separate attacks – one was to target Budapest, the second Debrecen and Miskolc, while the third was to head for Debrecen as well. The plan was too ambitious, since the Russians were having supply difficulties (Romanian railways were of a totally different gauge to Soviet rail lines, forcing greater reliance upon lorries). The second of the planned attacks, by Sixth Guards Tank Army from Oradea to Debrecen, began on 6 October, but was checked by the Germans, who then counter-attacked. A massive tank battle saw three Soviet corps cut off and destroyed, but although this was a dramatic success, it could not be regarded as anything other than a postponement of ultimate Soviet success.

On the day that the counter-attack at Debrecen began (10 October), other elements of the Red Army came within 10 miles of Belgrade, and as it became clear that the position there was untenable, the decision to evacuate the Yugoslav capital was taken; by this time, the folly of leaving German troops in Greece for a moment longer had been recognized, and the Germans began to withdraw from the country.

Greece

For nearly three years, the Germans had been confronted by a Greek resistance movement made up of communist and pro-royalist groupings, each subdivided into groups and factions. The movement was complicated by the fact that all of these groups greatly mistrusted one another. While there may have been mistrust amongst the pro-communist and pro-royalist factions towards other members of their group, there was outright enmity between the two generic factions. The only thing more certain than the fact that the Greek royalists and communists detested one another to the point of open hostilities being likely was that their hatred of the Germans would be sufficient to prevent them from embarking upon a civil war before the German occupation ended. As the Germans retreated, the situation collapsed as royalists and communists turned on one another.

On 12 October 1944, British troops landed in Greece, with the intention of assisting the exiled government to return to power. They found themselves present at the start of a bitter civil war. Although Greece was completely liberated by 4 November 1944, fighting would continue for some years as the two sides struggled to gain the upper hand until the royalists triumphed in 1948.

Budapest and Vienna

The increased risk of Soviet intervention in Hungary had alarmed the government in Budapest considerably, prompting its demand for at least five Panzer divisions to assist

Left: An Albanian farmer looks on as a British soldier searches a German prisoner. While taking control in Albania was a smooth operation, the British occupation of Greece faced far more difficulties from the warring Greek factions than it did from the Germans, most of whom had been withdrawn before the British landed.

Battle of Budapest and Vienna

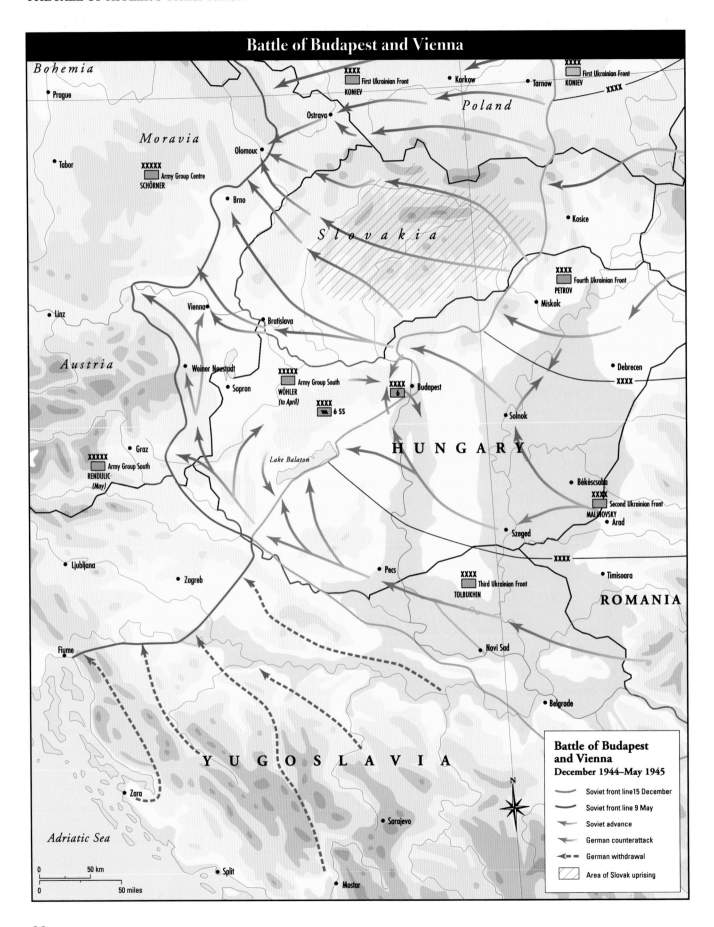

Bohemia

• Prague

Moravia

• Tabor

• Olomouc

XXXXX
Army Group Centre
SCHÖRNER

• Brno

Slovakia

• Kosice

XXXX
First Ukrainian Front
KONIEV

• Karkow

• Tarnow

XXXX
First Ukrainian Front
KONIEV

Poland

XXXX

• Ostrava

XXXX
Fourth Ukrainian Front
PETROV

• Miskolc

Vienna •

• Bratislava

Austria

• Linz

• Weiner Neustadt

• Sopron

XXXXX
Army Group South
WÖHLER
(to April)

XXXX
6 SS

XXXX
6
• Budapest

• Debrecen

XXXX

• Solnok

H U N G A R Y

• Graz

XXXXX
Army Group South
RENDULIC
(May)

Lake Balaton

• Békéscsaba

XXXX
Second Ukrainian Front
MALINOVSKY

• Arad

• Ljubljana

• Zagreb

• Szeged

XXXX

• Pecs

XXXX
Third Ukrainian Front
TOLBUKHIN

• Timisoara

R O M A N I A

• Fiume

• Novi Sad

Y U G O S L A V I A

• Belgrade

• Zara

• Sarajevo

Adriatic Sea

0	50 km
0	50 miles

• Split

• Mostar

N

Battle of Budapest and Vienna
December 1944–May 1945

— Soviet front line 15 December

— Soviet front line 9 May

→ Soviet advance

← German counterattack

◄--- German withdrawal

▨ Area of Slovak uprising

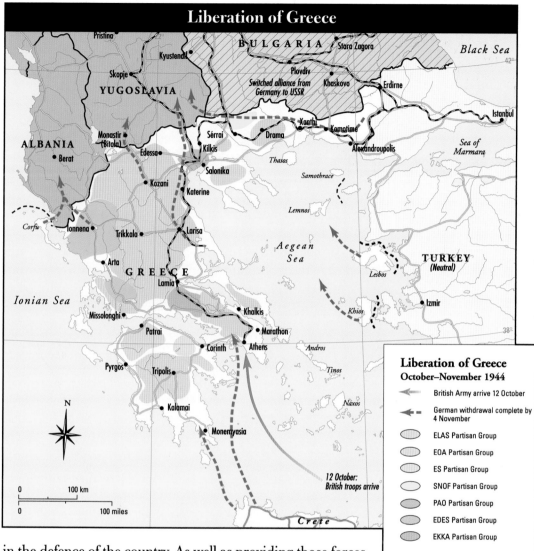

Liberation of Greece

Liberation of Greece
October–November 1944

→ British Army arrive 12 October

◄- - German withdrawal complete by 4 November

ELAS Partisan Group
EOA Partisan Group
ES Partisan Group
SNOF Partisan Group
PAO Partisan Group
EDES Partisan Group
EKKA Partisan Group

Left: The liberation of Greece was assisted by the German decision to withdraw from the country once it became clear that the forces there could be cut off by the Soviet invasion of Yugoslavia. The British landed in Greece on 12 October 1944, and advanced quickly through the country after the fleeing Germans, and then into Albania. Greece rapidly descended into a four-year-long civil war as rival royalist and communist factions sought to establish the country's government now that the Germans had left.

Opposite: The Soviet attack against Budapest began on 6 October 1944, and the twin cities of Buda and Pest were encircled on 24 December. The layout of Pest meant that it was easy to defend, and it took until 12 January 1945 until the Germans were dislodged from the city. Buda was equally difficult to take, and the Russians were forced to advance street by street until the Germans surrendered on 13 February. The Russians then moved on to Vienna, which fell on 13 April 1945 after a week's fierce fighting.

in the defence of the country. As well as providing those forces, Hitler tried to encourage the Hungarian leader, Admiral Horthy, by promising to give Hungary those parts of Romania that it claimed as its territory. This was popular with the Hungarian population in general, since nationalist sentiments towards the Romanians were high. Horthy was not convinced, however, wondering exactly how Hitler proposed to overturn the disasters that were now enveloping his forces. Horthy opened secret negotiations with the Russians, prior to the offensive of 6 October 1944. While the attack against Debrecen ran into serious difficulties, the Soviet approach to Budapest was easier. Within three days, Soviet forces were less than 70 miles away from Budapest, causing panic in the capital.

Horthy's lack of resolution in dealing with the Russians persuaded Hitler that a change in leadership was required in Budapest, and a team of SS commandos, led by Otto Skorzeny, kidnapped Horthy's son in an attempt to stiffen the Hungarian leader's resolve. Horthy stepped down instead, and the pro-Nazi Ferenc Szálasi was installed in his place on 16 October. Although German success in slowing the Soviet advance may have demonstrated that the Germans were not beaten yet, it did not mark anything like a turning point. The Russian advance resumed, and by the end of the month, Russian tanks were within 50 miles of Budapest.

General Malinovsky asked for five days to prepare his 2nd Ukrainian Front for the attack against Budapest, but was ordered to attack immediately by Stalin. The assault moved slowly, being joined by 3rd Ukrainian Front as it went. The twin cities were duly surrounded by Christmas 1944, as 2nd and 3rd Ukrainian Fronts linked up.

The Russians dealt with Pest first, but the layout of the city – large, easily fortified factories and streets that were difficult for tanks to operate in – meant that the task of an attacking force was extremely difficult. As it became clear that moving down the streets of the city was to invite certain death, the Russians took a brutally simple approach. They advanced one building at a time, blasting the defenders out with artillery and tank fire, with bitter hand-to-hand fighting characterizing the attack. Finally, on 12 January 1945, Soviet forces reached the city's racecourse. This had been used to fly supplies in to the Germans, and its loss meant that the defenders could not hold out for much longer, and they surrendered on 18 January. Buda was equally difficult to take, since its topography meant that the streets were narrow passages up cliffs and hills, hard going for any attacker. The Soviets pushed in to the city from 20 January, but although many of the Hungarian troops defending the city either surrendered or defected, the Hungarian Arrow Cross youth movement provided hundreds of fanatical boys willing to fight against the Soviet attackers. This opposition, in which youths used their knowledge of the city to outflank the Russians, sniping at them or launching small-scale attacks, forced the Russians to adopt another methodical approach. The Soviets brought up assault guns, and forced their way through the streets by the simple expedient of destroying any building that stood in their way. By 12 February, it was clear that resistance was hopeless, and around 16,000 German troops attempted to break out. They were trapped in the Lipotmezo valley the next day and annihilated on 14 February. By this time, Buda had fallen. The German escape attempt meant that organized resistance collapsed, and the remaining defenders surrendered at 10:00 on 13 February 1945.

By 23 March, the Germans had taken up positions to the west of Lake Balaton, but it was clear that they were in serious difficulties, and 3rd Ukrainian Front took the key road junction in the Bakony Forest. This meant that the Germans would be forced to move along the shore of the lake to withdraw, and left them in danger of imminent encirclement. It became clear to General Hermann Balck (commanding the once-more rebuilt Sixth Army) that his troops were beginning to lose their will to

GENERAL DRAÇA MIHAILOVIÇ

Mihailoviç was a Yugoslav Army officer, in charge of the Operations Bureau of the General Staff when the Germans invaded in 1941. He left Belgrade for Serbia after the defeat, and established the Çetniks, a small resistance group that immediately gained recognition in Britain and then the USSR and America. However, it soon became clear that the Çetniks were far more opposed to communism than to Nazism, and this prompted the collapse of efforts to link Tito's Partisans and the Çetnik movement in 1941.

Fighting between the two parties left the Partisans victorious, and Mihailoviç decided to alter his strategy. He abandoned fighting the Germans in the hope that they would destroy Tito and the Partisans, and this soon evolved into a policy of collaboration with the Nazis. By careful management of the information sent back to London, Mihailoviç managed to conceal this fact for a while; once the Allies discovered his collaboration, they switched their support to Tito. Devoid of support, Mihailoviç was unable to sustain operations, and his treachery guaranteed that he had no place in the post-war government; instead, he was tried for treason and executed in 1946.

Left: Partisans crowd around the corpses of dead Çetniks. The Çetniks and Partisans loathed one another, and the picture demonstrates the depth of feeling of the Partisans. This contempt was in many ways understandable, since the Çetniks had collaborated with the Germans in an attempt to ensure the destruction of the Partisans, abandoning their supposed role as a resistance organization seeking to free Yugoslavia.

fight, and wished to withdraw as quickly as possible to avoid being encircled. Balck reported this to Berlin, causing consternation, but his comments were accurate. The Russians launched the final phase of their operations in Hungary on 24 March, and within the space of four days had reached the Austrian border, with the Hungarian troops under German command beginning to desert. The Russians reached Vienna on 7 April, and although fighting continued for the next six days, there was little danger of the battle turning into another Stalingrad or Budapest. Resistance in the rest of Austria continued until early May, when the majority of German forces surrendered not to the Russians, but to Patton's US Third Army, which had entered Austria some days before.

The Last Act

The last major activity in the Balkans came in Yugoslavia. The Soviets entered the country on 11 October 1944, and their arrival prompted the collapse of German resistance in Belgrade. As the Partisans and the Red Army approached, the Germans carried out a fighting withdrawal, the futility of remaining in the city to be wiped out being obvious. By the end of 1944, Serbia, Montenegro, Macedonia and much of Bosnia had been liberated, with the Germans on the back foot everywhere else in the country.

The dramatic changes in Yugoslavia were demonstrated on 7 March 1945, when Tito formed a provisional government, in which he included some members of the exiled royalist administration (although he was to leave them there for as short a time as possible before replacing them). The final act in the Balkans came, appropriately enough, on 8 May 1945, when Zagreb was liberated at around the time that the full German surrender was signed. A few isolated pockets of German resistance continued to fight for another week, but were overcome. The war in the Balkans was over.

The War At Sea

From late 1942, the war at sea against Germany was dominated by the struggle against the U-boats, with relatively little in the way of surface action taking place. The struggle beneath the waves of the Atlantic was crucial to the outcome of the war, and the bland alphanumeric descriptions of some convoys across the ocean now stand alongside more familiar names of battles as a testament to the defeat of the Third Reich in this environment.

On 19 December 1942, convoy ONS154, made up of 45 ships escorted by Royal Navy Escort Group C1, set sail. The escort group was inexperienced, and had not been given the opportunity to work up on an exercise before leaving. In addition to this, in an attempt to direct the convoy away from appalling weather in the North Atlantic, the convoy was given a course that took it straight into the jaws of two U-boat groups totalling 20 boats. The first sighting of ONS154 was made by *U-154* on 26 December, and the first attack came that night, when *U-356* made two runs through the convoy sinking four ships. *U-356* was sunk by the escorts, but this was to be their only success. The following day, *U-225* sank a tanker, then on the 28th, a total of 13 U-boats closed in on the convoy. At least five got amongst the ships, and within the space of two hours, nine vessels had been sent to the bottom. Relief came on 31 December, with the arrival of the destroyer HMS *Fame,* but it was quite clear that the Germans had won this particular battle – 14 ships had been sunk for the loss of just one U-boat.

As the climax of the battle of ONS154 was being reached, convoy TM1 set sail from Trinidad, heading for Gibraltar. It consisted of nine oil tankers, and was protected by the rather weak escort of four ships. Bletchley Park's signals intercepts located a group of six submarines patrolling between the Azores and Madeira, clearly lying in wait for convoys such as TM1. The U-boat group was unaware of the convoy's approach, but *U-514* spotted it on 3 January 1943.

Late that evening, *U-125* attacked and fatally damaged the tanker *British Vigilance,* and although contact with the convoy was lost as *U-125* made good its escape, an inspired piece of planning by Admiral Dönitz meant that TM1 was not allowed to evade the

Opposite: The crew of a Royal Navy destroyer watch the explosion of a depth charge rolled from the stern of the vessel on top of a suspected U-boat contact. The seaman bending forwards in the foreground of the picture is preparing another depth charge for use.

clutches of the submarines. Another group of U-boats was placed across the last known course of TM1 just in case the convoy was continuing in the same direction. It was. On 8 January, *U-381* made contact, and four more submarines were sent to join in. That night, *U-436* sank two tankers before being damaged by the escorts, *U-552* crippled two more ships and an hour later, *U-442* sank another. Over the next three days, the pack managed to sink 77 per cent of the convoy, along with another vessel sailing independently, but which was unlucky enough to blunder into the way of the pack.

Casablanca

The events of ONS154 and TM1 gave Churchill and Roosevelt much to discuss when they met at Casablanca on 14 January 1943, in the pleasing afterglow of Operation Torch. Although the landings in North Africa had been an outstanding success, there was little doubt that the Battle of the Atlantic was going less well.

The conference went smoothly, and it was agreed, to the irritation of the Anglophobe Admiral Ernest King (the US Navy Chief of Staff), that the Atlantic should be reinforced. Churchill told Roosevelt that to win the battle, 65 escorts, a dozen escort aircraft carriers and as many B-24 Liberators (to be used as long-range anti-submarine aircraft) as possible were required. While agreement was reached, it took time to deploy these resources, and the struggle between the convoys and the submarines remained of major concern.

There were some good points for the Allies in early 1943, since appalling weather in the Atlantic meant that the U-boats found it extremely difficult to locate convoys. Worldwide shipping losses were reduced to 261,000 tons. While the loss of TM1 was a serious blow, only one North Atlantic convoy – HX222 – was attacked, and lost only one ship. This respite was short-lived, however, since on 29 January, convoy HX224 was sighted and once a wolf pack of submarines had been formed over the course of the next three days, three ships were sunk. In return, a Coastal Command Flying Fortress sank *U-265*. A survivor from

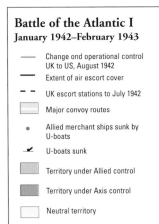

Battle of the Atlantic I
January 1942–February 1943

——— Change and operational control UK to US, August 1942

——— Extent of air escort cover

— — UK escort stations to July 1942

▨ Major convoy routes

• Allied merchant ships sunk by U-boats

↗ U-boats sunk

▨ Territory under Allied control

▨ Territory under Axis control

▢ Neutral territory

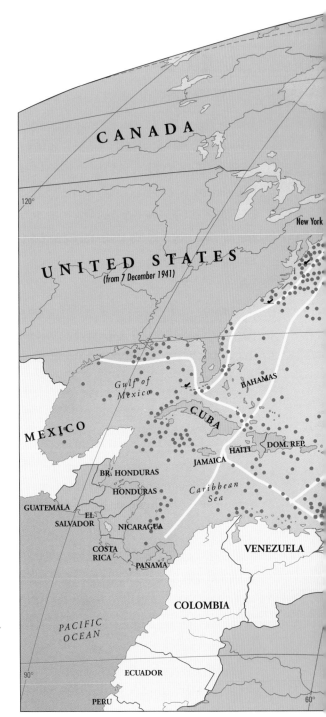

one of the merchantmen was rescued by a U-boat, and revealed that another convoy, SC118, was following on the same route. As a result of this a pack of 20 U-boats was formed for use against SC118.

On the morning of 4 February, the wolf pack closed in. The first action came when the destroyer *Vimy*, under Lieutenant-Commander Richard Stannard VC, sank *U-187*. By

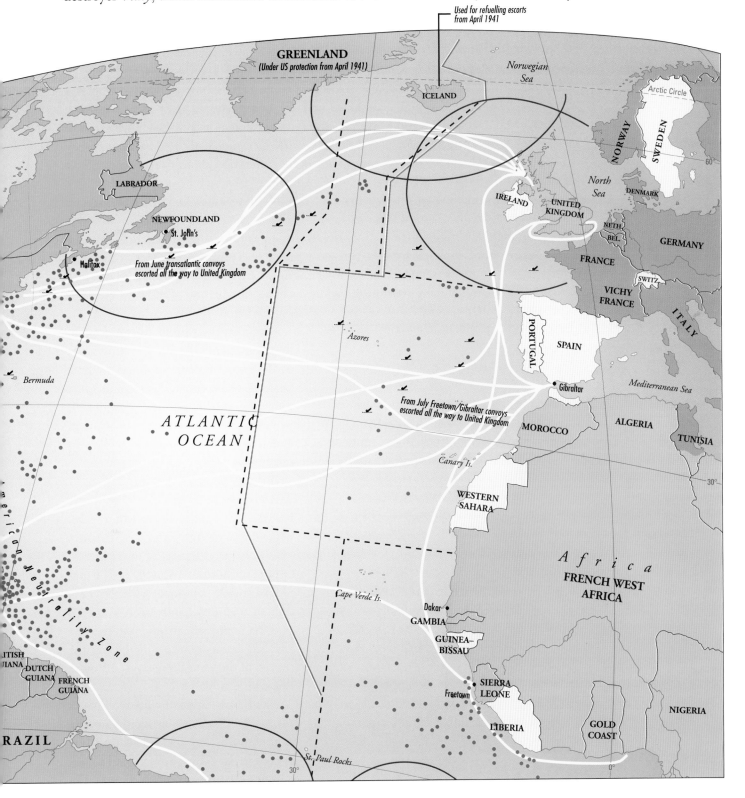

the afternoon five U-boats were in contact with the convoy. While heavy air cover prevented attacks on the 5th, on 6/7 February, the U-boats struck, *U-402* sinking six ships in four hours. Air cover returned at daylight, and a Fortress from 220 Squadron sank *U-624*, while *U-609* was sunk by the Free French corvette *Lobelia*. However, on the night of the 7th, *U-402* sank a seventh victim. When the battle was broken off on 9 February, SC118 had lost 13 ships, while three U-boats had been sunk and another four seriously damaged. This was one of the hardest fights of the battle so far.

For Admiral Sir Max Horton, the worrying aspect of the battle was that the losses had been inflicted despite an unusually large escort (including five destroyers). However, while the British were worrying over the losses to SC118, Admiral Dönitz – who was appointed head of the German Navy at the end of January – was equally concerned with the losses and damage inflicted upon his submarines. While it may not have appeared to be the case at the time, it was obvious that while the Germans had the upper hand, they were not having things all their own way, and were concerned about the possible effects of effective Allied convoying.

For the Allies, matters got worse when convoy ON166 was attacked by 21 U-boats on 21 February. The initial attack went badly – *U-225* was sunk, then next day, *U-606* was also lost, mainly as a result of an incorrectly sealed conning tower hatch. The crew managed to get the submarine to the surface, where it was rammed by the USCG cutter *Campbell*. The submarine stayed afloat long enough for the survivors to stand on deck eating sausage and drinking champagne while awaiting rescue; one of the crew, perhaps emboldened by the drink, took the opportunity to punch the unpopular first lieutenant. Despite the experience of the escort group, 14 ships, or 22.2 per cent of the convoy, were sunk. Only the skill of the escorts prevented a worse fate from befalling the convoy, and it was evident that the battle was reaching a peak.

The Height of Battle

For the Allies, the crisis point came with attacks on four successive convoys – SC121, HX228, SC122 and HX229. On the night of 6/7 March, *U-566* and *U-230* made contact with SC121, sinking one merchantman. A Force 10 gale the next day caused contact to be lost, but it was soon regained. Over the course of the next three days, 12 more ships were sunk.

The havoc caused by the wolf packs led to HX228 being ordered to evade to the south, but the instruction was intercepted by the Germans and a pack sent in against this convoy as well. On

SUBMARINE TECHNOLOGY

Perhaps the most critical element of the Battle of the Atlantic was technological development, particularly in the area of anti-submarine warfare. When the war broke out, the British relied almost entirely upon ASDIC (or sonar) to detect submerged U-boats, but had failed to appreciate that the Germans preferred to attack on the surface at night, and would only fire their torpedoes from beneath the waves if there was no other alternative. This was overcome by the use of radar mounted on escort vessels, while the employment of patrol aircraft forced the Germans to submerge for long periods to avoid being depth-charged.

This led to experiments to improve the endurance of a submarine operating underwater, and led most notably to the *Schnorchel* (Snorkel), a device which, as the name suggests, allowed the submarine to take on air for the operation of its diesel engines while beneath the waves. Although this proved a reasonably effective means of improving the submarine's endurance, the Germans were not satisfied, and began development of closed-cycle engines that could operate without the need for *Schnorchel*. However, the war ended before these could be brought into full service.

10 March, HX228 was spotted by *U-336*. HX228, unlike SC121, was exceptionally well escorted by four destroyers, five corvettes and the American Carrier Support Group TU 24.4.1 (also known as Escort Group 6). This contained the escort carrier USS *Bogue* and two destroyers. The weather prevented *Bogue* from flying her aircraft to begin with, which meant that she could not play a part in the convoy's defence.

The battle began when *U-336* was located and driven off. *U-444* remained in contact and guided in *U-221* which sank two ships. Within a few hours, *U-336* (again), *U-86*, *U-406* and *U-757* had also joined in, sinking two more ships. One of the victims was the *Brant County*, carrying munitions. The explosion that ripped the merchantman apart also damaged *U-757*. It was at this point that the battle turned against the U-boats. HMS *Harvester* sighted *U-444* on the surface and attacked. The submarine submerged, but was forced to surface by depth charge attack and *Harvester* rammed her. As the two hit, the submarine scraped along *Harvester*'s keel, and became wedged under the propellers. *U-444* broke free, and remained afloat, only to be rammed again and sunk by the French corvette *Aconit*.

During the morning, *Harvester*'s damaged propellers stopped, *U-432* spotted the stricken ship, and sank her. *Aconit* saw the smoke from the sinking *Harvester,* and hurried to the scene.

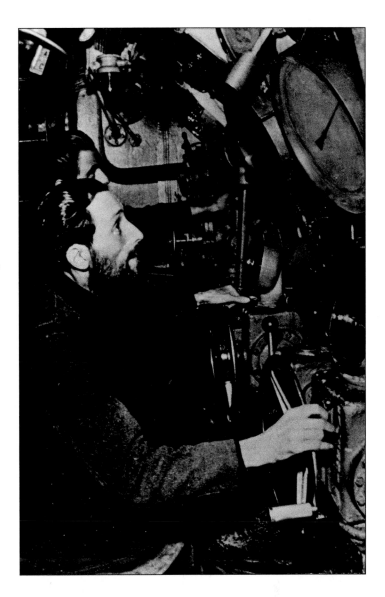

Above: U-boat crew members monitor the instrumentation above their positions. The U-boats offered a cramped and unpleasant working environment for their crews, who either baked in tropical conditions or froze in arctic temperatures, depending upon where their vessels were operating.

Aconit obtained an ASDIC contact, and depth-charged *U-432*. The submarine surfaced, and was finished off by ramming. On 12 March, *Bogue* was able to launch aircraft, and the U-boats stayed submerged. The arrival of aircraft from RAF Coastal Command to cover the convoy made it too dangerous for further attacks, and the U-boats withdrew. The battle ended with four merchantmen and one destroyer lost, with two U-boats sunk and two seriously damaged.

The Climax

While SC121 and HX228 were fierce battles, they were relatively minor compared to those involving SC122 and HX229. SC122 left New York on 5 March, covered by a US Navy destroyer, a frigate, five corvettes and an armed trawler. HX229 left on 8 March, accompanied by Escort Group B4.

Eight U-boats were deployed against SC122, followed by a newly formed pack of 18 more. Another 11 boats were sent after HX229. After problems caused by the weather, the eight-boat pack (Group Raubgraf) was guided in by *U-653* on 16 March, not against SC122, which had been driven past the group by a gale, but HX229. Three ships were

Above: A U-boat crew bring a torpedo aboard. After reliability problems at the start of the war, German torpedoes were improved and the U-boats swiftly became a serious threat to Allied shipping.

sunk that night; the following morning, five more were sent to the bottom. The 18-boat group (Stürmer) arrived on the scene on the 17th, by which point SC122 had arrived in the area, providing the wolf packs with a host of targets. This caused considerable confusion at U-boat HQ, but gave the submarines unprecedented opportunities. *U-338* sank four ships from SC122, then accounted for a fifth later in the day. Two more of HX229's ships went down at lunchtime, and it appeared that the convoy was absolutely at the mercy of the pack. The losses already sustained were serious enough, but complete disaster was prevented by the intervention of RAF Coastal Command.

Two Liberators, flying from Northern Ireland, arrived over SC122 on 17 March, and kept the U-boats underwater for the course of the day. Another Liberator covered HX229, and had a busy time, depth-charging *U-221* and *U-608*, then attacking another, unidentified, boat with machine guns and cannon once its depth charges had been expended.

Two merchantmen were lost from HX229 while air cover changed over, and during the night SC122 lost two more ships. After this, though, the two convoys lost just three more ships. Heavy air escort forced a dozen U-boats to break off.

On the afternoon of the 18th, the destroyer HMS *Highlander* found HX229. By the morning of 19 March, no U-boat had been accounted for by the escorts or air cover, but by this stage the convoys had entered the Western Approaches, where the shorter-range aircraft of Coastal Command were able to join in the fray, sinking *U-384* which was still tailing the convoys.

The arrival of the convoys was met with some gloom, since it appeared that the Germans were winning in the Atlantic. In fact, the provision of air cover had demonstrated the way forward once resources were available to bring enough aircraft to bear.

Finding the Answers

It appeared that, despite all the efforts of the long-range aircraft, convoys and escort groups, the Germans were about to disrupt the vital ocean link between Britain and America. In the first 20 days of March 1943, 95 ships were sunk. These apparently devastating losses all took place against the backdrop of a conference where Allied military leaders discussed their next step. If they could not find the answer, they feared, they might lose the war.

The conference began badly, when Admiral King made clear that he was going to withdraw all US Navy forces from the transatlantic convoy routes (this was just one of the reasons why Churchill later argued that the war at sea would have been simplified if someone had shot the admiral). The solution that arose to this problem was to create a Canadian operational command in the Northwest Atlantic, which would come into operation in May. While King's news was unwelcome, it was in fact less important than it might have been. The conference was presented with evidence from Professor Patrick Blackett of Coastal Command's Operational Research Section that analysis showed that a force of 200 very long-range (VLR) aircraft might be expected to save at least 400 ships. At this point, Coastal Command had just two operational squadrons of Liberators, with a third forming. The Canadians had formed squadrons of crews that had no aircraft, while every single American Liberator not in the Pacific Theatre was employed on bombing duties. King had subverted the Casablanca agreement that 80 VLR aircraft should be assigned to the Atlantic by keeping his VLR aircraft in the Pacific. An irritated Roosevelt overruled King and ordered that 60 US Navy Liberators would be used to cover the North Atlantic; the Army Air Force would deploy another 75 for anti-submarine duties. In addition deliveries to the RAF would be expedited, so that 120 Liberators would be available.

The first 20 aircraft from this massive increase in resources arrived in the last 10 days of March. The Atlantic air gap, where convoys had been forced to brave the mid-Atlantic beyond the range of any friendly aircraft, had finally been plugged.

Raised Spirits

The British Admiralty also began to understand the reason for the apparent failure of convoys at about this time as well, and realized that matters were not as bad as they first appeared. With the introduction of convoys, sailings by individual merchantmen had been reduced to such a low level that the U-boats had very few targets to attack. This meant that they were bound to attack convoys; given that there were so few German submarines engaged on independent operations, the size of the attacking packs was bound to be larger, enabling them to cause serious problems for the escorts.

The answer to the problem was air cover. U-boats had to submerge or risk being depth-bombed – thus imposing all the difficulties of trying to operate underwater for long periods that faced submarines of that era. The Admiralty began to appreciate that increasing numbers of VLR aircraft helped but using escort carriers was also of considerable assistance. On reflection, the view that the great German victory against SC122 and HX229 was the harbinger of doom was quite misleading. Pessimism was misplaced, and it was the jubilation of the Germans at the apparent breakthrough achieved against the four unfortunate convoys that was premature.

These suspicions were confirmed in April 1943. Between 4 and 7 April, an attack was mounted against HX231, a convoy of 61 merchant ships. The escort group beat off a

'[The Tirpitz*] exercises a vague general fear, and menaces all parts at once. It appears and disappears, causing immediate reactions and perturbation on the other side. If she were only crippled and rendered unseaworthy the entire naval situation throughout the world would be altered...'*

Winston Churchill, January 1943

'The submarine weapon has not been broken by the setbacks of 1943. On the contrary, it has become stronger. In 1944 ... we shall smash Britain's supply.'

Admiral Karl Dönitz, December 1943

concerted attack. *U-635* was sunk by a frigate, while an RAF Liberator accounted for *U-632*. Between them, the air and sea escorts damaged another four boats so badly that they had to head for home. For three ships sunk, this was hardly a decent return for the Germans. By May the U-boats found that the situation had turned dramatically for the worse.

ONS5

On 29 April, convoy ONS5 was sighted by the U-boats, and ran into the largest pack of the war, made up of 40 submarines. A ship was sunk that night, but the battle was truly joined on 4 May. Six ships were sent to the bottom. The next day, a Royal Canadian Air Force Canso (the Canadian version of the Catalina flying boat) sank *U-630*. That evening, the U-boats sank seven ships, but the escorts damaged an equal number of submarines. Then, on 5 May, *U-192* was sunk by HMS *Pink* and all attacks attempted on the convoy were driven off. After dark, four merchantmen were sunk, but now the escorts gained the upper hand. HMS *Loosestrife* pounded *U-638* with depth charges and destroyed it. HMS *Vidette* located *U-125*, and used her Hedgehog anti-submarine mortar to good effect, blowing the submarine to pieces. *U-531* was sunk by HMS *Oribi* after ramming. Fog descended, but the sloop HMS *Pelican* used her radar to find *U-438* and sank that as well. At 09:15 on 6 May, U-boat HQ called off the attack. Twelve merchant ships had been sunk, but crucially, the U-boats had suffered a devastating blow. No escorts were lost or seriously damaged, but eight U-boats had been sunk in the course of the action – two having collided – while another five were so seriously damaged that they limped home in a sorry state.

On 16 May, another convoy, HX237, made port having lost just three merchantmen, with the escorts having accounted for *U-89*, *U-186* and *U-456*, while *U-402* and *U-223* were seriously damaged. A pack had been decimated for little return.

Victory

The next convoy of note was SC130. The convoy ran into fog, and might have collided with an iceberg but for the alertness and quick thinking of the crew of the destroyer *Vidette*, which warned the shipping away. The next problem came in the form of a pack of 33 U-boats, which were detected by signals intercepts. Nothing was found on 18 May, but next evening HMS *Duncan* ran down a radio bearing just in time to see a U-boat submerging. At first light, RAF Liberators arrived and reported submarines all around the convoy. In the course of the next 12 hours, the U-boats made repeated attempts to force their way into the convoy, but ran into the escorts. *U-381* made one too many attempts, and was pounced upon by the *Duncan* and HMS *Snowflake*, which sank the submarine with a fusillade of Hedgehog bombs. Later that day, the 1st Escort Group joined the convoy, adding a cutter and three frigates to the convoy's strength. This did not deter the U-boats, which attacked again. *U-954* was despatched by a Liberator, *U-209* was sunk by the escorts, and an RAF Lockheed Hudson joined the fray to sink *U-273*. On the 20th, *U-258* was surprised on the surface by another Liberator, and went to the bottom as a result of the attack. On 21 May, the pack was called off. The submarines had not sunk a single ship from SC130; indeed they had not fired a single torpedo. In return five U-boats had been lost. The blow struck against the U-boats had been immense, not least because as well as their reduced success in convoy operations, the Germans had found their submarines under attack elsewhere.

Left: Standing on the bridge of his ship, HMS Starling, *Captain F.J. 'Johnny' Walker urges on other ships in his 2nd Escort Group. On the patrol during which the picture was taken, the escort group sank six U-boats, sending three to the bottom in less than 24 hours.*

While VLR aircraft were enjoying successes, shorter-range ones operating in the Bay of Biscay were gaining the upper hand there as well. The introduction of centrimetric radar meant that it was impossible for the radar warning equipment fitted to U-boats to warn of the approach of an aircraft, and U-boats had to cross the bay submerged both by day and at night. However, they also needed to charge their batteries. This meant surfacing, and Dönitz's answer to the air threat was to order U-boats to shoot it out with attacking aircraft with their anti-aircraft guns. However, while this increased the problems for the attacking aircraft, it left the submarines dangerously exposed.

Seven U-boats fell to Coastal Command in May as a result of operations in the bay, and it was clear that the tide of battle had turned. Despite the gloomy predictions of early March 1943, the Admiralty had in fact managed to acquire almost all the tools it needed to defeat the U-boats by this time. The only element missing was air power. When they became available in sufficient numbers, aircraft completed the 'tool kit' needed. The balance turned in favour of the Allies. By 22 May 1943, 31 U-boats had been lost. On 24 May, Dönitz radioed his surviving commanders, and commented on how difficult their struggle had become. He told them that only U-boats could fight the enemy offensively, and that the hopes of the Third Reich rested upon them. The same day, Dönitz ordered his U-boats out of the North Atlantic to the easier waters south of the Azores. Despite his exhortations, he knew something that his determined crews did not. They had lost.

The End of the U-Boats

The victory against the U-boats was the result of three years and nine months of incessant struggle, but although the Germans had to all intents and purposes lost the Battle of the Atlantic, this could not be taken for granted. The Allies now had to maintain their dominance over the U-boats until the end of the war, recognizing that the Germans would continue to try to regain the upper hand.

Right: By April 1943, it became clear that the tide was turning against the U-boats, despite heavy Allied losses suffered in the preceding months. Convoy escorts, aided by land-based air power, enjoyed considerable success in protecting convoys, while air operations against U-boats in the Bay of Biscay caused serious difficulties for German operations. By the autumn, it was clear to the Germans that they had lost the battle.

Battle of the Atlantic II
May–September 1943

——	Extent of air escort cover
☐	Major convoy routes
•	Allied merchant ships sunk by U-boats
⚓	U-boats sunk
▨	Territory under Allied control
▨	Territory under Axis control
☐	Neutral territory

The technological war between submarine and aircraft therefore intensified, as the Germans endeavoured to produce submarines that could operate effectively underwater, and as the Allies attempted to make sure that their technology was adequate to prevent such boats from becoming a serious threat. The Germans succeeded in developing the first true submarine – one that could operate effectively while submerged – but it was already too late. Continuing attacks by Allied forces meant that the U-boats were always at a disadvantage, no matter how innovative the technology employed.

Designs for Type XXI and Type XXIII submarines, able to use new engine technology that allowed underwater operations for a considerable time, appeared in June 1943. Earlier U-boat types had often been limited to single-figure speeds underwater, the Type XXI and Type XXIII could offer submerged performance of 18 knots for 90 minutes, or 12–14 knots for anything up to 10 hours. This was a promising development, but there was a major problem. Production of the new designs would be slow, and it meant that the first two Type XXIs would only be ready at the end of 1944, with mass production beginning in 1945, for full service entry in 1946. Naval production was reorganized by placing it under Albert Speer, the head of the Ministry of Arms and Munitions. Innovative solutions to production problems, such as building the submarines in sections and then assembling them at the coast, were introduced, and these methods meant that the first Type XXI was able to enter full service in 1944, with sufficient numbers in service by the autumn of that year for a proper campaign to be mounted.

While this was a good plan, in practice things were different. Disruption caused by Allied bombing had a profound impact. Production was delayed by at least four weeks after the air raids on Hamburg during August, and it was obvious that further attacks would destroy the submarine-building plan before it had even begun. A new factory near was built near Bremen but this took time to construct. In addition, getting the submarines from the factory to

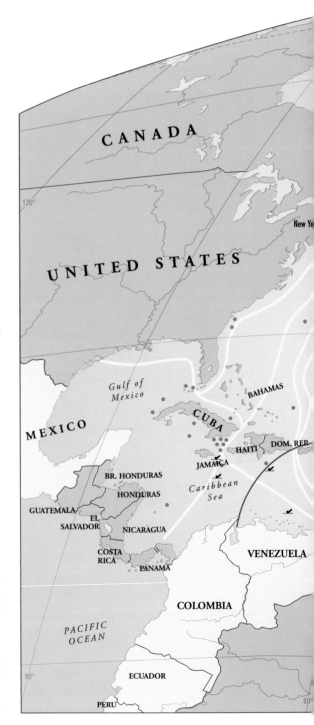

the coast demanded the use of the canal network, which was under severe attack by late 1944. On 23 September 1944, an RAF attack on the Dortmund–Ems canal aqueduct caused such damage that traffic was brought to a complete standstill, and it was not repaired until November, whereupon the RAF came back and destroyed it again. The submarine plan would have been a cause of considerable concern had it been

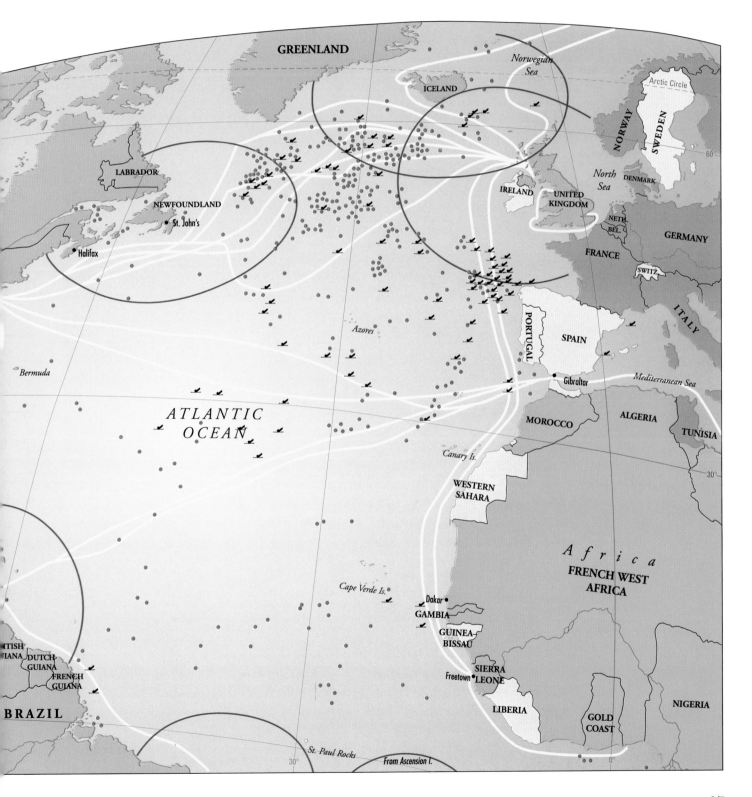

implemented by a nation not facing the sort of difficulties confronting the Germans in 1943 and 1944, but would in fact never be able to deliver the boats required to achieve the effect needed. Once the Allies had the lead over the German submarine arm, they were never to surrender it.

Surface Action

In stark contrast to the U-boat arm, the German surface fleet came nowhere near to influencing the outcome of the war, and after the sinking of the *Bismarck* in 1941, Germany's ships posed little threat to the overall superiority of the Allies. However, the threat posed by the remaining surface ships was a concern to the British, particularly in the shape of the battleship *Tirpitz* and the battlecruiser *Scharnhorst*. The two ships remained a nuisance, since although safely bottled up in harbour, it was clear that they could attack both North Atlantic and Arctic convoys.

The *Tirpitz* problem exercised the Admiralty for some time, until it was decided that the way to deal with the threat was through an attack by midget submarines, known as

X-craft. These carried two large charges of explosive that could be placed on the sea bed directly beneath their targets. Six X-craft were towed towards their target by full-sized submarines on 11 September 1943, but two slipped their tow lines *en route,* and another broke down when the time came to part company with the towing submarine. The remaining three entered the fjord in which *Tirpitz* lay on 20 September, and after a difficult journey in past obstacles and torpedo nets, two laid their charges beneath the battleship. The two craft to make it through (the fate of the third is uncertain) may have managed to lay their charges, but they could not escape. The crews were forced to scuttle their craft and were taken prisoner; both submarine commanders (Lieutenant Godfrey Place and Lieutenant Donald Cameron) were awarded the Victoria Cross for their daring.

When the charges detonated, the *Tirpitz* was badly rocked by the force of the explosions. All her engines were put out of action, the rudder and steering gear were badly damaged, and several hundred tons of water poured into the ship. While this guaranteed that *Tirpitz* would be unable to put to sea for months, the fact that the ship remained afloat meant that the Allies could not be certain as to whether the attack had succeeded.

While the Admiralty worried about the threat still posed by *Scharnhorst* and *Tirpitz,* convoys to Murmansk were suspended. They were resumed in November, and within a matter of weeks, the *Scharnhorst* sought to intervene. However, this was not without design on the part of the British admiral Sir Bruce Fraser, the Commander-in-Chief Home Fleet. Fraser reasoned that the Germans would wish to attack a convoy on the Murmansk run, after the suspension of the summer, and would sortie in force against the next convoy to appear. Fraser therefore ensured that the convoy was unusually well protected, sending 14 destroyers, two sloops and a minesweeper to escort the chosen convoy, coded JW55B.

German reconnaissance aircraft located convoy JW55B on 22 December 1943, and *Scharnhorst* and its accompanying destroyer flotilla left harbour during the late afternoon of Christmas Eve, under the command of Rear Admiral Erich Bey. Bey was completely unaware of the fact that as well as the escort vessels, a further naval squadron was in distant support, in the form of Admiral Fraser's flagship – the battleship HMS *Duke of York* – plus the cruisers *Jamaica, Norfolk, Sheffield* and *Belfast,* along with their attending destroyers.

Although the Germans became aware that there was a possibility of heavy surface escort to the convoy, the *Scharnhorst* did not turn about and head for safety. Unfortunately for Bey, the British knew of his location, while he had no idea of where anything other than the convoy was. At about 09:20 on 26 December, *Scharnhorst* was engaged by *Norfolk, Sheffield* and *Belfast,* and Bey turned away, without exploiting the superiority of his ship's guns. The cruisers raced to cut off *Scharnhorst*'s approach to the convoy, and succeeded in forcing Bey to turn straight into the direction from which Fraser was approaching. At 16:17, the radar on *Duke of York* located *Scharnhorst,* and at 16:50, *Duke of York* and *Jamaica* opened fire, while the other cruisers closed in and attacked from the other beam.

At 18:20, *Scharnhorst* was forced to slow as the result of a shell hit, and by 19:30 she was dead in the water, with the ship's secondary armament firing defiantly at the out-of-range British ships. *Scharnhorst* was sent to the bottom by torpedoes from Fraser's destroyers at 19:45, and only 36 members of her crew were rescued.

The *Tirpitz*, meanwhile, had remained firmly in port, and the Admiralty sought to sink her by air attack. The first raid, launched by carrier aircraft in April 1944, achieved six hits on the ship in the first assault, followed by another eight in the second wave. Other raids had to be aborted because of bad weather until, on 17 July 1944, a further attack was made. All went well until the attacking formation was spotted and a smokescreen thrown over *Tirpitz*. Unable to see their target, the British aircraft could not bomb accurately, and only one bomb fell near to the ship. A further set of raids was mounted in August, under the codename Goodwood (a confusing choice, since this was the name of an operation by the Army in Normandy at around the same time). Goodwood I and II were unsuccessful, but Goodwood III succeeded in hitting *Tirpitz* with two bombs – however, one failed to explode, and the damage caused by the other was minimal.

At this point, the RAF intervened in proceedings. Lancaster bombers from 9 and 617 Squadrons launched two attacks, one from a temporary base in Russia (and which was unsuccessful) and the second from Britain. On this raid, on 12 November 1944, at least two of 28 5443kg (12,000lb) 'Tallboy' bombs found their mark, and the ship capsized, causing fearful casualties amongst her crew, many of whom were trapped in the hull. 617 Squadron later returned to finish off the *Lützow* in the same manner, although as the ship settled on the bottom of the fjord with her decks still above water, the Royal Navy (jokingly) claimed that the RAF could not claim that the ship was sunk, merely that her lower decks were awash.

The End
While still firmly on the back foot, the U-boats did not have a completely disastrous 1944, in that the number of sightings made by enemy aircraft declined. This owed much to the widespread use of the *Schnorchel*, a development that worried the Allies. The Allied anti-submarine effort had been based upon the fact that the most effective way to counter the U-boats was to locate them when surfaced and sink them, or to force them to stay underwater for long periods, with a concomitant reduction in the amount of time that the submarine could remain at sea. The use of the *Schnorchel* meant that the air threat was considerably reduced. Furthermore, the U-boats were unable to make use of their radio when submerged, which denied an array of information to Bletchley Park, and prevented location of submarines by signals interception.

From September 1944, though, the U-boats were switched towards British home waters, reducing the risk to Atlantic convoys still further. They began to make their presence felt from November. Casualties caused by the U-boats rose, and the fact that the boats were operating in inshore waters meant that it was extremely difficult to use anti-submarine detection devices properly, since these were optimized for ocean-going warfare. Fortunately for the Allies, even this offensive was a case of too little too late. The Type XXI and Type XXIII submarines caused no little concern with their underwater speed and endurance, and caused some losses; but it was too late for them to make a difference. Everywhere, the German Army was in full retreat, and the Allies were approaching the Third Reich on two fronts. The end of the war was fast approaching. While U-boat operations from Norway continued as late as April 1945, there was nothing these submarines could do to alter the outcome of the war, which had become inevitable. In British home waters, 10 merchant ships and two escort vessels were sunk, in exchange for 23 U-boats. Allied bombing reduced the U-boat bases to chaos, forcing the U-boats to head for the Baltic. There, the last five weeks of the war saw the

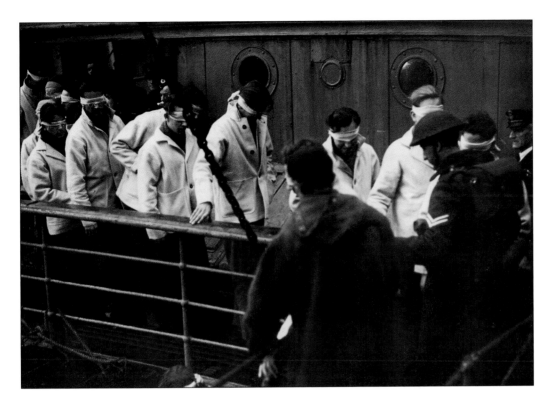

destruction of 83 U-boats by a whole variety of aircraft. Coastal Command strike wings were joined by rocket-firing Typhoons from 2nd Tactical Air Force, wreaking havoc amongst the unfortunate submarines. The last U-boat to be lost was *U-320*, so badly damaged by a Catalina on 7 May that it sank two days later.

The Final Reckoning

Despite initial hopes, the U-boats did not win the war for Germany, for a variety of reasons. Most notably, there were never enough U-boats available to make the sort of concerted effort against the convoys that was needed. The work of the large wolf packs towards the height of the campaign in later 1942 and early 1943 demonstrated what could have been achieved had enough been available to swamp the defences of the convoys. By the time sufficient U-boats were available, the British had dramatically increased the number of escort vessels and managed to combine these with long-range aircraft that kept the U-boats underwater, or attacked them as they transited the Bay of Biscay. The entry of the United States into the war meant that the shipbuilding might of the US yards would always make it impossible for the Germans to sink more ships than the Allies could build – while inflicting so much attrition on Allied shipping that Britain would be starved into submission was a possibility before American war production had geared up, once the US shipyards were at their wartime capacity, this was a forlorn hope.

Improved technology, more escorts and the combination of air and sea power meant that the task of the U-boat crews became ever more difficult, culminating in defeat when the defences became just too strong. As for the surface fleet, the Germans caused some embarrassment in the early phases of the war, but once the *Bismarck* was sunk, their surface units presented very little threat. While the key battles of the war were largely fought on land after 1943, winning the Battle of the Atlantic was a fundamental requirement for Allied victory, the value of which was fully seen in 1945.

The Air War Against Germany

World War II was marked by the rise of air power, particularly the employment of strategic bombing against the enemy homeland. Bombing did not bring the Third Reich to its knees as the interwar theorists might have suggested that it would, but was an important factor in the final defeat of Nazi Germany nonetheless.

Although much of the Royal Air Force's doctrine in the 1920s and 1930s had been based around the effectiveness of strategic bombing, when war broke out in 1939, RAF Bomber Command was ill-prepared to mount a bombing offensive against Germany. As well as the practical difficulties of sending bomber aircraft against Germany, concerns over whether attacks on towns would provoke German retaliation led to a situation where Bomber Command was used for raids against military targets. When early attacks met with disaster upon being intercepted by fighters, it was decided to move over to night raids instead. As bombers were not equipped with anything other than the most rudimentary navigation equipment, and since most RAF navigators had not been trained to navigate with any accuracy at night, it was hardly surprising that bombing raids were ineffective.

A further obstacle to effective bombing came from the fact that the bomb loads of the RAF's main aircraft of the day (the Wellington, Whitley and Hampden) were not large enough to achieve an adequate concentration of bombs to the extent required for a truly effective offensive; nor did they have the fuel supplies to carry them to the heart of the Reich. This had been appreciated in the run-up to the war, and orders for 'heavy' bombers had been placed. The first of these designs, the Short Stirling, arrived in service in August 1940, and was followed by the Avro Manchester and Handley Page Halifax. By early 1941 there were three squadrons of each type, but this was still not regarded as being a sufficient level to launch the sort of bombing offensive that could have a major impact on Germany. The older bombers had to bear the brunt of the offensive, which meant that so-called fringe targets had to be attacked. To make matters worse, the

Opposite: RAF armourers prepare a 1000lb bomb for loading onto the Lancaster bomber in the background. The Lancaster was the most versatile bomber in the European theatre of war, and the mainstay of the RAF's bombing effort from 1943 onwards.

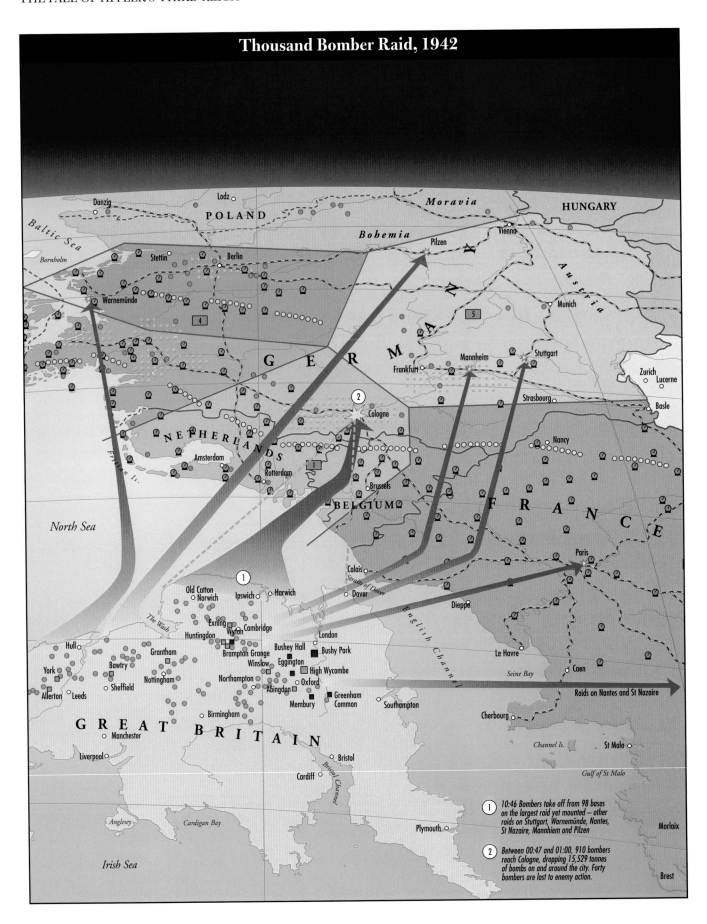

Thousand Bomber Raid, 1942

Baltic Sea

Danzig

Lodz

POLAND

Moravia

HUNGARY

Bornholm

Stettin

Berlin

Bohemia

Pilzen

Vienna

Austria

Warnemünde

4

5

Munich

G E R M A N Y

Frankfurt

Mannheim

Stuttgart

Zurich

Lucerne

Strasbourg

Basle

2

Cologne

NETHERLANDS

Amsterdam

1

Nancy

Rotterdam

Brussels

BELGIUM

F R A N C E

North Sea

Calais

Straits of Dover

Dover

Paris

1

Old Catton

Norwich

Ipswich

Harwich

Dieppe

The Wash

Exning

Wyton

Cambridge

Huntingdon

Brampton Grange

Winslow

Eggington

London

Bushey Hall

Bushey Park

Le Havre

Hull

Grantham

High Wycombe

Seine Bay

Caen

York

Bawtry

Nottingham

Northampton

Oxford

Abingdon

Sheffield

Allerton

Leeds

Membury

Greenham
Common

Southampton

Raids on Nantes and St Nazaire

Birmingham

Cherbourg

G R E A T

Manchester

B R I T A I N

Channel Is.

St Malo

Liverpool

Bristol

Gulf of St Malo

Cardiff

Bristol Channel

Anglesey

Cardigan Bay

Plymouth

Morlaix

Irish Sea

Brest

1 10:46 Bombers take off from 98 bases
on the largest raid yet mounted – other
raids on Stuttgart, Warnemünde, Nantes,
St Nazaire, Mannhiem and Pilzen

2 Between 00:47 and 01:00, 910 bombers
reach Cologne, dropping 15,529 tonnes
of bombs on and around the city. Forty
bombers are lost to enemy action.

English Channel

Manchester's Rolls Royce Vulture engines proved to be appallingly unreliable – the disaster of losing an otherwise sound airframe from the front line was solved by replacing the two Vultures with four Rolls Royce Merlins, creating the Avro Lancaster; however, the redesign meant that the first squadron was unable to re-equip until the end of 1941.

The problems of accurately striking targets at night meant that Bomber Command turned to the notion of area bombing as the means to achieve the desired effect of destroying German industry, although this inevitably meant that entire German towns would be attacked, with the associated risks to civilians. This approach was beginning to be adopted by early 1942, when Air Marshal Sir Arthur Harris was appointed as the Air Officer Commanding-in-Chief of Bomber Command. Harris was a firm believer that area bombing would win the war, and if it was carried out on a sufficient scale, the employment of ground forces would not be necessary, since the Third Reich would be driven to its knees by air attack.

The Millennium Raids

The turning point for Bomber Command, from which point it developed into a key weapon of war, might be said to have arrived in mid-1942, when Harris sent over 1000 aircraft to bomb Cologne as part of Operation Millennium on the night of 30/31 May. The raid was launched mainly for propaganda purposes, with the aim of demonstrating that Bomber Command could carry out devastating attacks against major targets. To make the tally of aircraft up to the important 1000 figure, Harris was compelled to draw upon training units, a risk that paid off when the attacking force lost just 40 aircraft. The attack on Cologne was followed up by two more on Essen and Bremen, but it was quite evident that the disruption caused to Bomber Command's training schedule by such large raids, along with the subsequent maintenance demands, outweighed the value of the attacks, even if they made for effective public relations opportunities.

Opposite: Shortly after assuming command of RAF Bomber Command, Air Chief Marshal Sir Arthur Harris launched three raids against Cologne, Essen and Bremen in which over 1000 bombers took part. To achieve this strength, Harris had to make use of aircraft from training squadrons, and it was to be some time before raids nearing this scale could be repeated.

Thousand Bomber Raid
30/31 May 1943

⟋ Main RAF night attacks

☐ Main Headquarters

☐ Group Headquarters

◉ Bomber Command airfields

✳ Targets bombed

— Fighter Division boundary

▦ Fighter Division

◉ German radar station

● German night fighter station

∞ Searchlight batteries

▭ Anti-aircraft batteries

Left: German flak gunners sprint for their 88mm anti-aircraft gun. German anti-aircraft defences were particularly strong, and took a heavy toll of bombers, particularly on daylight raids. However, it required a large number of anti-aircraft guns firing an even greater number of shells to guarantee a hit on a single bomber.

Harris was also more concerned about correcting the inaccuracy of bombing, and gave instructions that the development of navigation aids should be prioritized, to allow more aircraft to reach their intended target. Refinements to tactics so as to concentrate more aircraft over the target were also introduced, and had an almost immediate effect. However, one of the most significant contributions to improving the accuracy of bomber attacks was initially opposed by Harris. During the Blitz on Britain during the winter of 1940–41, German bombers had been guided to their destinations by a pathfinder force, which had marked the targets with special bombs. It was suggested that this would be a profitable line of approach for Bomber Command to adopt – a pathfinder force, equipped with target-marking bombs instead of conventional ordnance, could provide a clear indication of the aiming point for the main bomber stream following them. Harris was opposed to the plan on the grounds that he was not convinced that creating an elite force within Bomber Command was a good idea. However, he was overruled at a high level within the Air Staff, and on 15 August 1942, the Pathfinder Force (later to be designated as 8 Group) was formed under the command of Air Commodore Donald Bennett. By the end of 1942, the Pathfinder Force had begun to have an effect in terms of increasing the number of aircraft that located and bombed the correct target, while the a new radio navigation device for bombers, codenamed Oboe, had been installed in Mosquito light bombers, enabling them to navigate very precisely to their targets. Although Harris had improved the quality of his force immeasurably during the course of 1942, it was still not quite in a position to launch decisive attacks against Germany. However, by the end of the year, a further significant development had taken place. The US Army Air Force's first bomber units had arrived in Britain, enabling 'round-the-clock' bombing to commence. There were many trials and tribulations to be overcome in 1943, but the progressive development of the Allied bomber force into a major weapon

Right: A formation of B-17 Flying Fortresses drops its bombs over a target in Germany. The close formation was designed to allow the bombers to provide mutual fire support against enemy fighters, using their array of machine guns to stop the Germans from getting through. This proved to be an inadequate solution, however, and the provision of long-range escort fighters was needed to deal with German fighter attack.

of war gathered pace, and began to have a telling effect upon Germany, even if not quite in the manner envisaged by those who had proclaimed that victory could be brought about entirely by the application of bombing.

The 'Mighty Eighth'

With the agreement that the United States would follow a 'Germany first' policy, it was a logical step for American bombers to be sent to Britain. VIII Bomber Command was to be the UK-based bomber force, as part of the Eighth Air Force. The first elements, in the form of the command's staff, arrived in February 1942, led by Major-General Carl A. Spaatz, but it took until May before the first combat units arrived, flying in B-17 and B-24 bombers. The first operation was flown against Rouen on 17 August, escorted by RAF Spitfires, and was followed by another raid two days later. The use of escorts was contrary to American doctrine, which held that the heavy armament of the bombers would be enough to protect them from fighter attack, an idea that was to be severely tested over the next 12 months. The rest of 1942 was taken up with relatively short-range raids against targets in occupied Europe, with the intention of carrying out the first raids on Germany in 1943. By the end of the year, however, there were increasing concerns about German fighters – the German pilots had swiftly evolved tactics that enabled them to conduct highly effective frontal attacks against the bombers, exploiting the fact that the forward-firing armament of both the B-17 and B-24 was relatively light, relying upon single hand-held guns rather than power-operated gun turrets. Although it seemed that the notion of carrying out unescorted raids needed to be abandoned, the lack of fighters with sufficient range to accompany the bombers all the way to the target meant that there was no other alternative.

The Battle of the Ruhr

The policy of carrying out round-the-clock bombing of Germany was reaffirmed at the Casablanca Conference in 1943, with a directive being sent to Harris that he was to undertake a campaign that would lead to 'the progressive destruction of the German military, industrial and economic system' and which was also to reduce the morale of the German people so that 'their capacity for armed resistance is fatally weakened'. Harris chose to concentrate upon the latter aspect of the directive, which, he felt, was best served by area bombing, which as well as damaging and destroying German industrial centres had, in Harris' phrase, the effect of 'dehousing the German worker' with a concomitant reduction in his or her morale.

Harris duly set about increasing the tempo of the night offensive with an attack against the industrial cities of the Ruhr valley, in an assault that was to become known as the Battle of the Ruhr. The first operation was carried out on 5/6 March 1943 against Essen, marked by the first wide-scale use of Oboe to aid navigation. The aid was important, since the bomber crews were faced with the difficulty of finding their targets when confronted with the haze of pollution rising from the factories. The raids on the Ruhr continued for the next six weeks, culminating in one of the most famous air operations in history – Operation Chastise, which became far better known as the Dambusters raid.

The Dambusters

The choice of dams as a target for bombing had been raised prior to the war. It seemed fairly obvious that breaching the Ruhr valley dams would have several effects, both in

'It is true to say the heavy bomber did more than any other single weapon to win this War.'

Sir Arthur Harris, Despatch on War Operations, October 1945

107

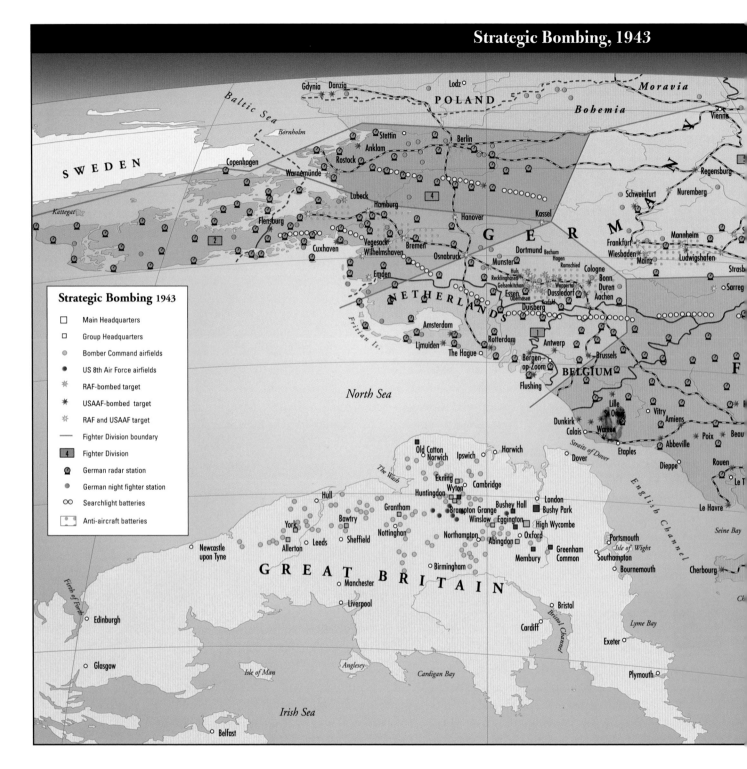

Strategic Bombing, 1943

terms of the sheer physical destruction caused by the release of millions of gallons of water, and the need to restore the dams to full working order before production in the area could restart.

The difficulty with targeting the dams lay in the fact that destroying them was far from simple. Bomb aiming was simply not accurate enough to deliver the required weight of explosive onto the dam to destroy it, while the use of torpedoes could be made impossible by installing netting that would prevent the weapons from striking the wall of

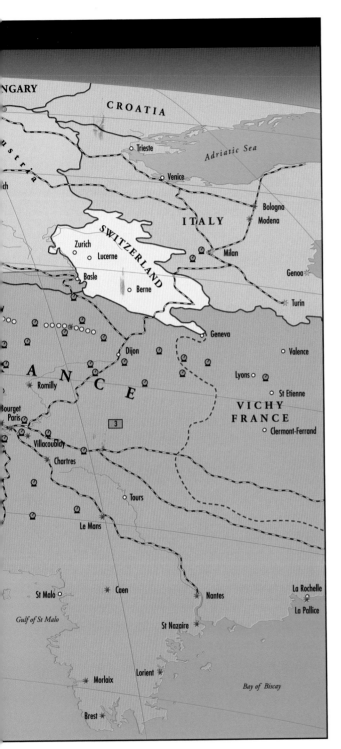

the dam. The solution came in a revolutionary idea from the scientist Barnes Wallis, who proposed a special bomb, to be dropped at low level to achieve the desired result. The idea behind the bomb was simple, but appeared at first glance to be slightly eccentric. Wallis worked out that to breach a dam, it was imperative that the bomb used detonate right against the wall, with the water held behind the dam being used to magnify the force of the explosion. To place the bomb exactly where required, Wallis hit upon the idea of bouncing the weapon across the surface of the lake; it would hit the wall, and because of the backspin applied to it, would sink to the bottom of the lake while remaining in close contact with the dam.

While Wallis was refining his design, a special RAF squadron, number 617, was formed under the command of Wing Commander Guy Gibson. Gibson's squadron undertook a great deal of low-level flying, and improvised a solution to both maintaining the required height of 60 feet above the water and dropping the bomb at the correct distance from the dams. The first problem was solved by using spotlights in the belly of the aircraft angled so the beams converged at 60 feet, while improvised bombsights made from nothing more advanced that a few pieces of wood with nails driven into them were devised to release the weapon accurately.

The raid was launched on the night of 16/17 May 1943, with 19 aircraft taking part. The Möhne and Eder dams were breached, and the Sorpe dam was hit. The destruction of the dams was achieved at high cost, with eight of the attacking force being lost, along with all but one of the 56 aircrew aboard. The raid caused considerable damage through flooding, but a massive German repair effort managed to minimize the effect of the attack on industrial output. Controversy over whether the raid was a success or not has been ongoing, although there is little doubt it provided a massive boost for British morale as the nature of the daring attacks became more widely known.

Left: From 1943 onwards, strategic bombing operations against Germany and targets in occupied territories were carried out by both day and night by the British and American bomber fleets. American operations were hampered by the lack of escort fighters until late in 1943, but once these were provided, they allowed effective operations against the German capital to be undertaken.

Above: German fire-fighters battle against the results of an RAF bombing raid against Cologne in 1943. In the area bombing campaign, great use was made of incendiary bombs to raze large sections of German cities to the ground, and there was often little that the German emergency services could do to quell the flames.

Hamburg

The Dambusters raid was followed by a more conventional attack as Harris turned his force against Hamburg, with the city being subjected to four attacks between 24/25 July and 3/4 August 1943. Harris chose the city as the target for a sustained attack given its importance to the German war effort, particularly submarine production. The attacks saw the use of a new device codenamed Window – which took the form of millions of thin tin-foil strips dropped from the attacking bombers, with the aim of jamming German radar sets by sending back thousands of spurious radar returns.

The first bombs began to fall on Hamburg just before 02:00 on 25 July, as the Pathfinder Force released a mixture of illuminators followed by 250lb target indicators to highlight the aiming point to the following waves of bombers. The leading aircraft unloaded incendiaries to set fires to the many timber buildings in Hamburg. As the emergency services rushed to put out the many small fires started, the next wave of aircraft dropped high explosives, bringing down buildings, shattering water mains and killing around 4000 rescue workers. The devastation caused by the first raid was immense, but was merely the start of the city's sufferings. On 27 July, Bomber Command returned, with over half of the bombs dropped being incendiaries. These quickly turned Hamburg into a vast fire, in which the air became superheated. To feed itself, the fire sucked in oxygen from around its outer edges, creating a massive and terrifying firestorm, carrying blazing timbers further into the city and causing yet more fires and beginning the process again – by the end of the raid, a massive conflagration had been started, and winds of up to 150mph ripped through the streets, causing huge casualties. Many civilians in air raid shelters were suffocated, while those who managed to escape had to brave the firestorm. Many leapt into nearby canals, the only way in which they could survive the fire raging around them. By the next morning, over 6000 acres of the city had been reduced to ashes, and still Harris was not finished. Another raid took place two days later, the bomber crews guided in by fires still alight from the previous attacks, and a second firestorm was caused. A final attack was then carried out, causing a third firestorm, despite the torrential rain that fell throughout the duration of the raid.

By the end of what came to be known as the Battle of Hamburg, over 60 per cent of the residential accommodation had been destroyed, and nearly 600 factories were knocked out. The German armaments minister, Albert Speer, feared that another six similar raids in succession would force Germany to surrender. However, despite the immense casualties caused, with over 41,000 killed and 37,000 severely wounded in the raid, Hamburg's manufacturing output recovered within six weeks. Bomber Command did not return, for the truth was that it simply could not sustain attacks of this nature, as it did not have the resources to do so. As his command recovered from its intensive efforts, Harris turned his thoughts to attacking Berlin, the most difficult target, with the aim of striking the decisive blow that would win the war.

The Daylight Offensive

While Harris was attacking Germany at night, the US Army Air Force increased the tempo of its operations, launching its first attack on Germany on 27 January 1943, attacking Wilhelmshaven. Experience in 1942 had shown the need for fighter escort, but

Left: The grisly aftermath of the raid on Dresden in 1945 – the remains of just some of the victims are piled up on a funeral pyre, ready for cremation. The scale of destruction wrought by the attack on Dresden demonstrated the level of lethal efficiency that Allied bombing could achieve, and raised serious doubts amongst some of the Allied leaders about the ethics of a campaign directed against cities.

Right: The Dambusters raid of 16/17 May 1943 was one of the most daring attacks of World War II, with the use of the famed 'bouncing bomb' to destroy two major German dams and inflict damage on two more. Losses from the raid were heavy, with eight aircraft out of nineteen failing to return.

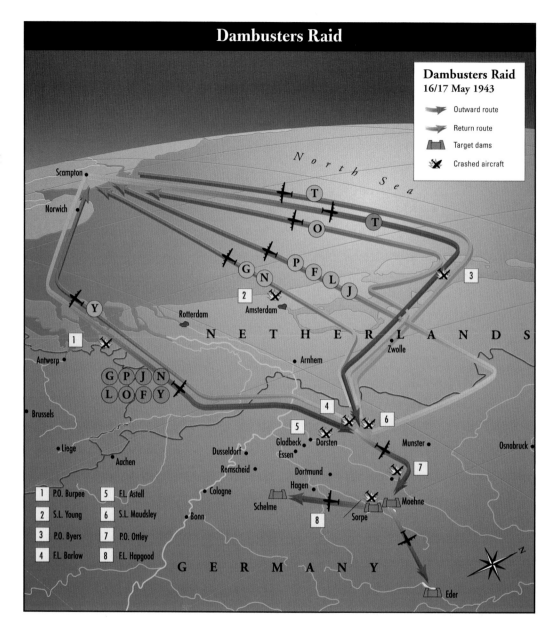

Dambusters Raid

Dambusters Raid
16/17 May 1943

Outward route
Return route
Target dams
Crashed aircraft

1	P.O. Burpee	5	F.L. Astell
2	S.L. Young	6	S.L. Maudsley
3	P.O. Byers	7	P.O. Ottley
4	F.L. Barlow	8	F.L. Hapgood

this was problematic as aircraft with adequate range to cover operations deep into Germany were not available. Although P-47 Thunderbolts carrying additional fuel in drop tanks could cover the bombers for much of their flight, the first major raid deep into Germany demonstrated how important fighter escorts were. Attacks against Regensburg and Schweinfurt on 17 August 1943 led to the loss of 59 bombers out of 200, which would be unsustainable if continued. The solution lay in the North American P-51 Mustang, a fighter originally designed for the RAF. Fitted with a Rolls Royce Merlin engine, the P-51 had a range of over 2000 miles when carrying external fuel tanks, and they made the difference almost as soon as they arrived in December 1943. The presence of escort fighters meant that it became possible to make the *Luftwaffe*'s fighter force one of the targets of the bombing campaign. By early 1944, the Eighth Air Force had begun to mount large-scale attacks against German targets, with the first visit to Berlin being made on 6 March 1944. By this point, Bomber Command's campaign against Berlin was drawing to a conclusion.

The Battle of Berlin

Harris was extremely confident that large-scale attacks against Berlin would paralyse the German war effort, and bring about a swift end to the war. As a result, Harris launched 16 major attacks against Berlin, beginning on the night of 18/19 November 1943. The city was an extremely difficult target, and the Battle of Berlin did not produce the results Harris had predicted. In the course of 9111 sorties against the capital, 587 aircraft were lost along with over 3500 aircrew killed or missing. Harris was forced to end the assault, but not before a disastrous raid on Nuremberg on 30/31 March 1944, in which over 100 bombers were lost as the *Luftwaffe* night-fighter force set about them. To Harris' intense irritation, he was ordered to turn his attention to bombing transportation targets in both Germany and France in support of the forthcoming invasion. His arguments that his crews would not be capable of attacking such targets were disproved when trial attacks ordered by the Air Staff demonstrated that his bombers were more than able to destroy railway lines and key transport nodes. Attention thus turned away from the bombing of German cities and to French and Belgian targets; before this occurred, the Americans attempted to inflict large-scale attrition on the *Luftwaffe* as part of its bombing campaign.

The Final Raids

From August 1944, the Americans began to carry out heavy attacks against the German oil industry, and a host of industrial targets across the Third Reich. The potency of the escort fighters meant that the Germans found it extremely difficult to inflict damaging levels of attrition on the bomber forces, while they sustained notable losses themselves as the battle escaped them. Although night fighters had more success at dealing with the RAF's attacks, these were increasing in efficacy – by early 1945, Bomber Command's level of accuracy was such that it was able to drop its bombs at night more accurately than the Americans could in daytime – a feat that no one would have thought possible just five years previously. The most controversial episode of the entire bombing campaign occurred in February 1945, with the British raid on Dresden. Huge numbers of casualties were caused by an extremely effective attack that devastated the city, and the effect of the raid was to highlight some of the serious ethical questions about targeting cities and, inevitably, their populations. Although there was never a policy of terror bombing of Germany, critics have subsequently argued that this was, in effect, what occurred. By April 1945, the number of viable targets for the bombers to strike had dwindled considerably. RAF bombers began to undertake daylight raids again, the threat of the *Luftwaffe* having all but disappeared as the German fighter force ran out of fuel. The RAF concluded its campaign with a raid on Hitler's mountain retreat at Berchtesgaden by 617 Squadron. As a sign of the dominance of the bombers over Germany, this was difficult to beat.

The bomber campaign against the Third Reich proved to be extremely costly and, after the war, controversial as the sheer scale of the casualties sustained during the course of the air assaults was appreciated. The fact that the Germans did not surrender as a direct result of the attacks has been taken as a sign that the campaign was a failure, but this is too simplistic a view. The bomber campaign tied up a substantial amount of manpower and resources, while disrupting production and diverting industrial output towards defensive weapons rather than items that could have been put to use on the Eastern or Western Fronts. While a controversial campaign, the air war against the Reich played its part in bringing down Hitler's regime.

The Liberation Of France

The turn of the tide in favour of the Allied cause during late 1942 and early 1943 meant that it was inevitable that the Americans and British would have to consider an invasion of mainland Europe to drive German forces out of the occupied countries, and then to inflict a final defeat on the Third Reich. As well as the simple practical necessity of a land assault in Europe for the defeat of the Reich (despite the claims of air power proponents, strategic bombing did not appear to be about to win the war by itself), political considerations had to be taken into account.

Stalin had made no secret of the fact that he took the opening of a second front to be a sign of good faith from Britain and America, and although the assault on Italy could be said to represent just such a development, Stalin was not convinced that this demonstrated the full commitment of the Western Allies to relieving the burden on the Red Army (despite the fact that the invasion of Italy caused Hitler to withdraw units from the Battle of Kursk at a critical point to reinforce the wavering morale of his ally). In fact, there were few doubts on the Anglo-American side that an invasion of France was required to bring about the defeat of Nazi Germany. Just as in World War I, the decisive field of battle in the West would be France, not Italy or anywhere else, even if the pressure that could be applied from these areas would make a substantial contribution to the overall outcome of the war.

Early Notions
In fact, the Americans had been extremely keen on an invasion of France almost from the outset of their involvement in the war. While the United States could not present an immediate threat to the German position on mainland Europe in early 1942, this did not prevent them from making planning assumptions about how they could best assist in bringing about an early conclusion to the conflict. America was at a disadvantage to begin with, since its isolationist policy in the interwar period meant that its army was relatively small. Although the American Army was larger than those of many other nations, it would still take time to build up its strength before it could be pitted against an army the size of

Opposite: A young French woman joins the celebrations as Allied troops march through Paris, marking the liberation of the city after four years of German occupation.

COSSAC Plan

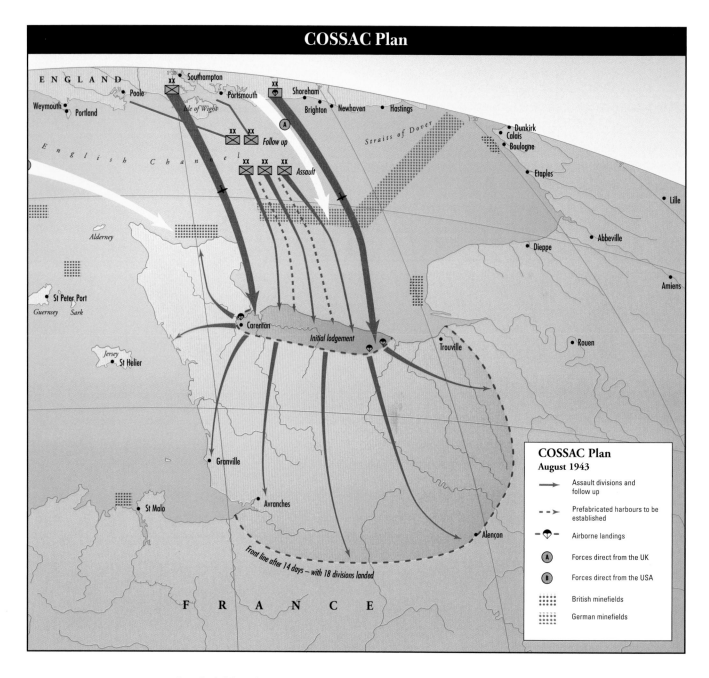

Above: Planning for the invasion of France began in 1943, well before the appointment of General Eisenhower as Supreme Allied Commander. Major-General Morgan, appointed as chief of staff to the yet-to-be named commander, oversaw the development of the plan.

that held by the Germans in Europe. In addition, it was obvious that the demands of fighting both in Europe and the Pacific Theatre would have an effect on the pace of the build-up of American capabilities for intervening in the war against Germany. The Germans were not slow to recognize this fact, and came to the conclusion that it would not be until early 1943 that American troops could arrive in Britain, the only place from which an invasion to open a second front could be launched. It was therefore logical for the main German effort to remain on the Eastern Front, particularly since the Russians were at this point (early 1942) proving more difficult to break down than had at first been anticipated – Stalingrad and Kursk were yet to come.

While the main German effort would remain in the East, Hitler appreciated that it would be necessary to establish substantial defences along the coastline of occupied Europe to deal with any invasion attempt. Hitler formally recognized this in March 1942, issuing a directive ordering construction of an immense line of fortifications stretching from the Franco-Spanish border up to the North Cape in Norway. For reasons that are not altogether clear, Hitler was convinced that the British would attempt a landing in Norway as their first priority. While his rationale that the British would want to be in a position to protect their Arctic convoys from the depredations of U-boats had some merit, the dynamics of Allied decision-making clearly escaped him. There was little chance that the British or Americans would see Norway as an obvious point for invasion, given that it was so far away from the United Kingdom, with all the logistical problems that this would present in contrast to an attack on France. Nonetheless, Hitler gave instructions that the Norwegian coastline was to be given top priority in the construction of shore defences, and his instructions were carried out to the letter – by the end of 1943, Norway's coastline was the most heavily fortified in the world. The effort placed into building the Norwegian defences meant that the French coastline received relatively little attention. Construction work began at a comparatively leisurely pace, which meant that the defences at Dieppe were only partially completed when British and Canadian troops staged a landing there on 18 August 1942.

The Impact of Dieppe

The Dieppe raid failed, although it provided a great number of valuable lessons for the future. In response to the operation, Hitler issued another directive giving greater priority to the construction of fortifications along the French coast. However, while he instructed that the work should be undertaken quickly, those responsible for implementing the order were unconvinced. A major raid had been driven off with half-completed fortifications manned by inexperienced and over-age reservists, all of which

Left: General Eisenhower talks with an American soldier on a visit to pre-invasion manoeuvres. His deputy, Air Chief Marshal Tedder, is at the left of the picture (in the fur-lined jacket), while General Montgomery can just be seen over Eisenhower's shoulder.

Above: A Churchill tank sits forlornly on the beach at Dieppe after the disastrous raid there in 1942. Many lessons were learned from Dieppe, and the planning staffs took meticulous care to ensure that such scenes would not be repeated when the invasion itself took place.

implied that the pace of building did not need to be frenetic, as even half-finished fortifications would make it problematic for an invading force to break through.

This attitude had changed by autumn 1943. The landings in Tunisia, Sicily and Salerno demonstrated that the Allies were more than capable of carrying out successful amphibious operations. Hitler was moved to order the creation of a series of fortifications that would ensure that any invasion was defeated 'before, if possible, but at the latest upon the actual landing'.

COSSAC

Anglo-American invasion planning began after the meeting between Prime Minister Churchill, President Roosevelt and their Combined Chiefs of Staff at Casablanca in January 1943. Two months later, the Trident Conference in Washington laid down that the landings should take place on 1 May 1944 under the codename Overlord. Planning responsibility was given to the Chief of Staff to the Supreme Allied Commander (COSSAC), the British general Sir Frederick Morgan. Morgan's title was rather misleading, since no supreme commander had then been appointed. Undaunted, Morgan and his Anglo-American staff set about working out the details of an invasion.

The first task for COSSAC was to work out where the invasion should take place. Three locations in France appeared to offer the best choices – the Pas de Calais, Normandy and Brittany. The Pas de Calais had several advantages, most notably that it offered the shortest route across the Channel. However, the area's topography was far from ideal, and it was such an obvious area for assault that the Germans had begun to fortify the region with some vigour, a step that had not been missed by Anglo-American intelligence. Also, the exits from the beaches around the Pas de Calais were restricted, making it difficult to move armour and heavy equipment forward – landings would also have to be made on the Belgian coast or at the Seine estuary ports to allow such material to be landed. Finally, the Kentish ports were simply not big enough to accommodate the whole landing fleet, which would demand that some vessels sail from Portsmouth and Southampton – a journey of over 100 miles within range of German shore batteries.

Brittany enjoyed a brief period of favour amongst the American planners, on the grounds that it had good beaches for landing. As with the Pas de Calais, though, Brittany was rejected. First, it was clear that logistical difficulties presented by its being far to the west of the Low Countries, extending the supply lines as the Allies broke out and headed for Germany, were far from encouraging. In addition, the Royal Navy representatives on COSSAC were aghast at the thought of landing in Brittany. They pointed out that the weather on the Atlantic coast was often appalling (and when it was not appalling it was bad), and then went on to highlight the hazardous nature of the waters. Such strong reasons against using Brittany as the landing site meant that only Normandy was left.

That is not to say that Normandy was chosen by default – rather that the disadvantages of a Normandy landing were far less than those presented by the other choices. Once the location for the landings had been decided upon, more detailed preparations could be undertaken. The number of American troops arriving in England increased, and the training regime for all Allied soldiers in the United Kingdom became more intense as the men were prepared for the invasion. Landing craft were built, maps prepared and specialist tanks that could swim, clear mines or fire heavy demolition charges were constructed. By May 1944, there were over three million soldiers, sailors and airmen from Britain, America, Canada, New Zealand, Australia, Poland, France, Belgium, Norway, Holland and Czechoslovakia in England waiting for the instruction to launch an invasion.

By this time, COSSAC had a supreme commander to work for. On 7 December 1943, General Dwight D. Eisenhower was appointed Supreme Allied Commander for the invasion. One of his first tasks was to deal with the clashing egos of his subordinate commanders. As they included Bernard Montgomery and George S. Patton, this was a far from easy task. Montgomery in particular was to prove a regular source of anguish to Eisenhower, since it was quite evident that the British general thought that he should be in command of all operations in Europe after the landing (rather than just for the first phase) and made little effort to disguise this fact.

BRITISH VERSUS GERMAN TANKS

One of the most notable features of the war was the superiority enjoyed by German tanks on the Western Front, particularly over British tanks. While the Germans saw tanks as being ideal for fast, mobile all-arms warfare, the British showed signs of confusion over how to employ theirs. This meant that while the Germans developed a range of fast, heavily armed and well-protected tanks, the British went through a process which provided either relatively slow, heavily armoured but inadequately armed tanks or fast, lightly armed and lightly armoured vehicles that were no match for their opponents. By 1944, the main British tanks were the Cromwell and Churchill, joined by large numbers of American M4 Shermans.

Although the German Panther, Tiger and upgraded Panzer IV tanks were able to defeat their opponents in a one-on-one engagement, the numerical supremacy enjoyed by the Allies meant that they were often able to overwhelm the Germans by sheer weight of numbers.

Finally, by early June 1944, everything was ready. The invasion was planned to be launched on 5 June, but poor weather forced a postponement of 24 hours. Despite only slightly better weather the next day, Eisenhower issued the orders for the invasion. During the night of 5/6 June 1944, over 250,000 men launched one of the largest and most complex military operations the world has ever seen – securing a foothold in Normandy as the first element in bringing about the defeat of Hitler's forces in the West.

The Other Side of the Hill

Hitler's rising concern about the defences in France led to him sending Field Marshal Erwin Rommel (one of his favourite generals) to inspect the so-called Atlantic Wall.

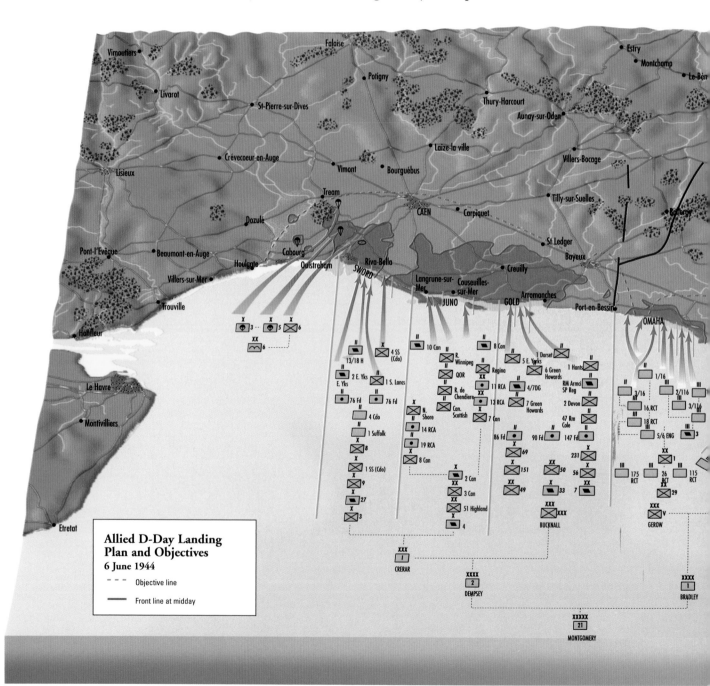

Allied D-Day Landing Plan and Objectives

6 June 1944

--- Objective line

— Front line at midday

Rommel was also appointed commander of Army Group B, with operational command over the German forces in northern France, on 1 January 1944. By this point, it was clear that the Allies would be in a position to launch an invasion in the near future, although no one knew exactly when, or even more importantly just where, it would be.

Rommel was immediately in dispute with the Commander-in-Chief West, Field Marshal Gerd von Rundstedt, over the way in which the coast should be defended against an invasion. Von Rundstedt wished to allow the Allies to land before attacking them with six panzer divisions as they were establishing their beachhead. Rommel was unconvinced – having experienced the effect of air attack on armoured columns in his time commanding the *Afrika Korps*, he was convinced that the panzers would be

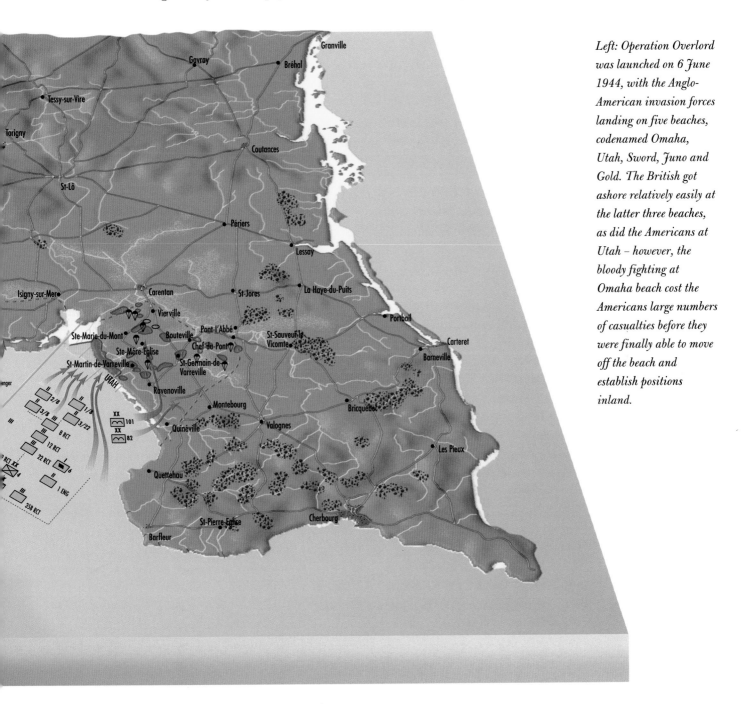

Left: Operation Overlord was launched on 6 June 1944, with the Anglo-American invasion forces landing on five beaches, codenamed Omaha, Utah, Sword, Juno and Gold. The British got ashore relatively easily at the latter three beaches, as did the Americans at Utah – however, the bloody fighting at Omaha beach cost the Americans large numbers of casualties before they were finally able to move off the beach and establish positions inland.

destroyed by bombing (and naval gunfire) as they headed for the beachhead. They might not even manage to make it into battle with the enemy. Rommel argued that the only way of defeating the invasion was to destroy the landing forces as they came ashore.

This bitter dispute between von Rundstedt and Rommel led to Hitler suggesting a compromise – the panzers would be placed under his direct control, and he would give the order to move them in the light of events. While this was accepted, it meant that operational control in the face of an Allied landing became more rigid than it needed to be, and opened the possibility that the panzer reserve might not be able to be deployed in time. Although Rommel did not prevail in regard to the armoured reserve, his views on the need for strong fortifications were accepted. By spring 1944, the defences were at last beginning to be built.

D-Day

The first major actions in the invasion were not carried out by troops from the seaborne invasion force, but by members of the French Resistance and the men landed shortly after midnight on 6 June by an aerial armada of transport aircraft and gliders. The air drop was marked by confusion as paratroopers landed miles from their drop zones (and often miles from other elements of their units), but displaying the initiative expected from airborne troops, they set about attacking the Germans anyway. The air drops were followed by the actual landing of the amphibious force. The landings went relatively smoothly, with the exception of that at Omaha beach. For a while, it appeared as though the landing would have to be suspended, but Brigadier-General Norman Cota, the assistant divisional commander of 29th Division, managed to make sense of the confusion on the beach. Cota brought together a company-sized force of men on the beach, made up of Rangers, engineers and infantrymen. Cota led them from the beach to a fold in the bluffs, which protected them from machine-gun fire.

Cota next sent his men to attack German positions. By 11:00, they had captured the Vierville exit to the beach, and within half an hour of this, more determined attacks had captured the St Laurent exit and the Americans could finally begin moving off the beach in strength. Elsewhere, the British and Canadians had moved forwards from Sword, Juno and Gold beaches, while American forces at Utah beach had endured a far less torrid time than their comrades at Omaha.

The German reaction proved to be confused. The first parachute landings were interpreted as supply drops to the Resistance, and only appreciated for what they were some time later, when it became clear that the Resistance appeared to be receiving enough equipment to arm every man, woman and child in France twice over. The appearance of the invasion fleet was at first assessed as a diversionary move. Von Rundstedt could not be shaken from his view that the Pas de Calais was the real landing area, and nor could Hitler. There appeared to be evidence of an invasion force approaching the Pas de Calais, and it was not until some time later that it was realized that this was a deception – in fact, the radar contacts that suggested ships approaching had been caused by RAF aircraft dropping bundles of aluminium foil to produce spurious signals on German radar screens.

Hitler was reluctant to order the release of the armoured units, although 21st Panzer Division's commander had begun to engage the airborne troops around the Orne bridges on his own initiative. By nightfall on 6 June, the German response was more coordinated, but the Allies were firmly ashore.

Break-out

Establishing a beachhead was just the first step. Once ashore, the Allies then had to break out into the countryside beyond. This proved difficult. A major reason for this lay in the topography of the Normandy countryside. Between Capriquet and the Cotentin peninsula lay *bocage* – narrow, sunken lanes surrounded by tall, thick hedges that led to small, well-built villages or individual stone farmhouses. All of these features meant that *bocage* was an almost perfect terrain to defend.

Allied first attempts to exploit the success of their landings met hard resistance all along the line as the Germans began to recover their poise. The experience of the British 7th Armoured Division at Villers-Bocage served to demonstrate the nature of the bitter struggle that would follow. Montgomery wished to use the 7th Armoured Division (the famed Desert Rats) to punch through the gap in the area of Villers-Bocage, enabling it to link up with the 51st Highland Division, and then encircle the key city of Caen. On 10 June, 7th Armoured moved from Tilly towards Villers-Bocage, which was defended by the Panzer Lehr Division – understrength, but still a formidable opponent. The attack

Above: American troops head for the shore in a landing craft. Hours of practice went into the amphibious assault, which paid off on D-Day itself as the landings went ahead successfully, allowing the Allies to establish a lodgement on the coast of France.

123

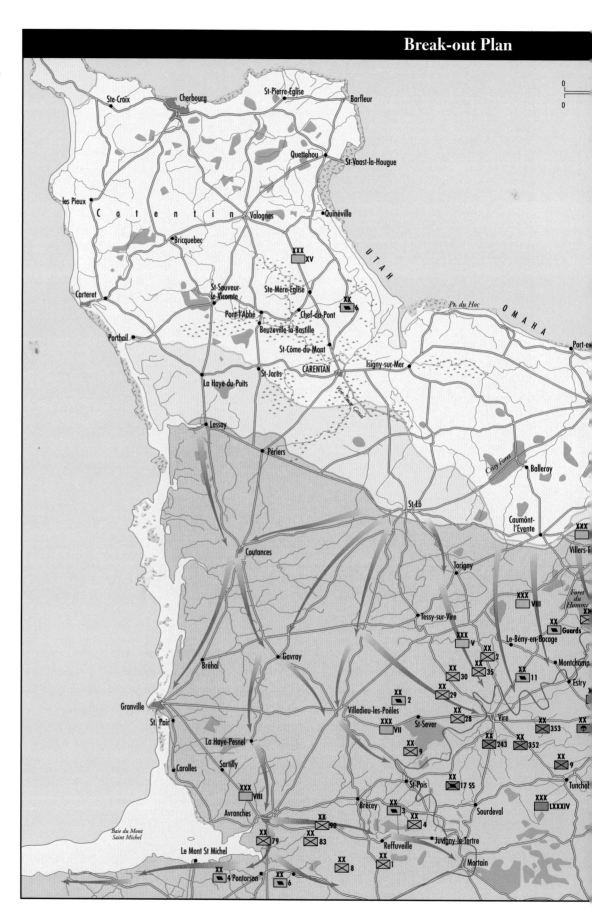

Break-out Plan

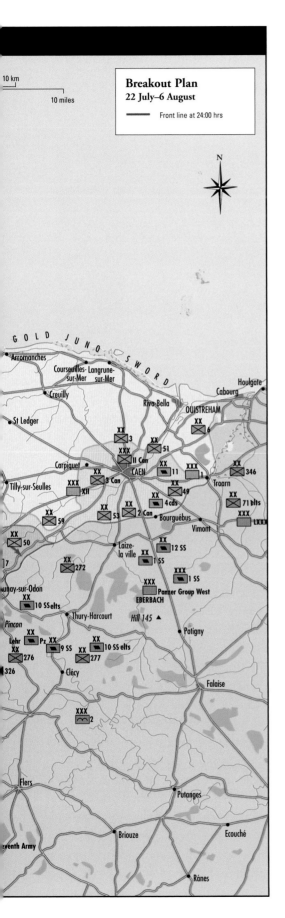

Breakout Plan
22 July–6 August

—— Front line at 24:00 hrs

10 km

10 miles

was conducted on a narrow front, which aided the Germans, who might not have been able to resist an attack all along their overextended line. A bitter battle developed. It took three days for the lead elements of 7th Armoured to enter Villers-Bocage, and shortly after they passed through the town, they were ambushed by a lone Tiger tank commanded by Michael Wittmann, a panzer 'ace' from the Eastern Front. Wittmann destroyed the lead tank, cut off an easy escape route for the column by also destroying the rear tank, and began to move along the column picking off the British tanks as he went. A rescue force in the form of tanks from the 8th Hussars was mauled before a shot from an anti-tank gun knocked a track from Wittmann's vehicle, rendering it immobile. He escaped on foot (later succumbing in the battle when an air strike delivered by RAF fighter-bombers destroyed his tank), but left carnage behind him. A counter-attack that afternoon by the Panzer Lehr Division drove 7th Armoured Division back to Tilly; in the fighting, the British lost 25 tanks, 28 other vehicles and a large number of men. The pattern was to be repeated as the Germans fought doggedly over every inch of French soil. The British forces faced a considerable proportion of the German Army, making their advance difficult and costly. By the start of July, neither the Allied nor German high commands were content – the Allies were not progressing as quickly as they had hoped, while German efforts at a counter-offensive had failed. On 3 July, Hitler removed von Rundstedt from his command, replacing him with Field Marshal Gunther von Kluge. Von Kluge had an unfortunate reputation as a 'yes man', possibly one of the reasons for Hitler's choice. Most generals found Hitler's increasingly unrealistic demands to hold fast in the face the Allied advance impossible.

20 July

On 20 July 1944, Hitler held a planning meeting at his headquarters in East Prussia. Hitler's bunker was being strengthened, so the meeting was held in a large wooden hut instead.

Above: RAF groundcrew load 60lb rocket projectiles onto a Hawker Typhoon fighter-bomber. The Typhoon became famous for carrying out rocket attacks on German tanks and transport, and was one of the most effective weapons platforms available in Normandy, the notorious inaccuracy of rockets notwithstanding.

The meeting began without Field Marshal Wilhelm Keitel, the head of the German high command – the *Oberkommando der Wehrmacht* (OKW). Keitel's absence was explained when he arrived a few moments later with Colonel Count Claus von Stauffenberg, the representative of the Training and Replacement Command, who was scheduled to provide a report on the raising of new divisions. Keitel introduced von Stauffenberg, and he took his place at the conference table, placing his distinctive yellow leather briefcase beneath it. After a few moments, he muttered an apology to the man next to him, explaining that he had to go and make a telephone call. A few minutes later, as Keitel began wonder where von Stauffenberg had gone, there was a huge explosion.

Men came running. The first survivors began to emerge, and finally Keitel appeared, supporting Hitler as the two men left the wreckage. Hitler was bleeding from wounds on his face, his arm was temporarily paralysed and his legs contained hundreds of fragments of the conference table. It was clear that there had been assassination attempt, and Hitler sent officers to look for evidence of a bomb. The search party deduced that the explosion must have occurred under the map table around which the conference was being held.

Suspicion was already falling on von Stauffenberg. He had disappeared, apparently to a nearby airfield, and pieces of his distinctive briefcase were retrieved from all over the remains of the conference room. In the middle of the afternoon, copies of signals from

Berlin reached Hitler. He was incredulous to learn that an unscrupulous group of officers and politicians had assassinated the *Führer*, and that the government had declared a state of emergency. For a few hours it appeared as though the coup might succeed – Hitler was at an isolated location, and all those commanders loyal to Hitler were, naturally, at the battlefront.

Fortunately for Hitler, his run of luck had not ended with his survival. Just after 18:30, the *Führer* received a telephone call from Josef Goebbels, the propaganda minister. With some difficulty, Goebbels explained to the still-deafened Hitler that he had a Major Renner with him. Renner was the leader of the only combat unit then in Berlin, the Grossdeutschland Battalion. Goebbels explained that Renner was confused – he had received one set of orders instructing him to place members of the government under house arrest and another telling him to arrest Field Marshal Witzleben (who had taken authority in Berlin under the terms of the signal announcing Hitler's death) and von Stauffenberg. Goebbels wondered if Hitler would like to talk to Renner. Hitler said he would. He told Renner that he was to restore order in Berlin, and to shoot anyone who stood in his way. By midnight, von Stauffenberg and three other conspirators were dead. A wave of arrests and executions followed. Rommel, now implicated in the plot, was given the choice of suicide, followed by a state funeral, or a public trial, execution and a similar fate for his family. Rommel chose a capsule of fast-acting poison. The bomb plot thus cost Germany one of its most capable commanders, and had one further important effect – it reinvigorated Adolf Hitler.

Only an hour or so after the blast, Hitler was entertaining Mussolini to lunch. He spoke excitedly about how his survival clearly demonstrated his true destiny and that of Germany. Divine providence meant that whatever the current unfavourable circumstances facing Germany, the Third Reich would triumph in the end. A further effect of the bomb was that Hitler no longer trusted his generals, with one or two notable exceptions, and took an ever greater degree of control over military operations. He began to accept even less advice from the Army, and displayed an unwillingness to listen to any suggestions that contradicted his own perceptions of the situation on the battlefield. This was to have important repercussions for the future conduct of the war. The current situation, though, was bad enough, and the Allies finally started to make the breakthrough they had been looking for after weeks of bitter fighting.

Goodwood and Cobra

By early July, the invasion forces were no more than 15 miles inland at any point. Although few people were commenting openly about it, fears of a stalemate increased. By the second week in July it seemed as though Montgomery was the only commander

ALLIED AIR SUPPORT

The importance of air support had been fully recognized in the desert war, and this had prompted the Allied air arms to develop extremely effective cooperation methods with the surface forces. These predominantly used fighter-bombers to attack targets on the battlefield, or supply columns. The most famous of the aircraft employed in this role were the Hawker Typhoon and Republic P-47 Thunderbolt. Robust and well armed, these two types caused havoc amongst German ground units, with the Typhoon gaining a particular reputation for destroying tanks with rockets. The domination of Allied air power over France meant that it was extremely difficult for the Germans to counter the effect of enemy air attack, and this caused them no little difficulty in their attempts to stop the Allied advance across France.

with any sense of optimism left, as he planned to make the decisive breakthrough. On 10 July, he issued instructions for the break-out from Normandy. General Omar Bradley's US First Army would attack towards Avranches, after which the lead element of US Third Army (VIII Corps) would strike into Brittany. To assist this general advance, General Sir Miles Dempsey's British Second Army would attack through the open countryside to the east of Caen. This attack, Operation Goodwood, was to start on 18 July, with Bradley's offensive, Operation Cobra, starting the next day. However, until St Lô was captured, it was impossible for Bradley to start his attack, and this was only achieved on the morning of 19 July. As a result, it was necessary to put Cobra back until 24 July.

On the afternoon of 19 July, just as it appeared that success had been achieved, Goodwood's armoured element ran into heavy resistance, and was halted short of Bourguébus Ridge. Heavy rain the next day brought the attack to a total standstill. Although it appeared that Goodwood had failed it had in fact achieved Montgomery's aim of drawing in German armour away from the Americans. Thirteen German divisions now faced the British, while nine were opposite the Americans; only two of these nine divisions were armoured, giving the Americans a notable superiority.

Although it began later than intended, Operation Cobra was conducted according to the original plan. This was that the attack was to start with the carpet-bombing of the German forces in front of the US VII Corps, who would advance towards the Germans' main line of resistance and seek to break through. At the end of the first phase of Cobra it was hoped that the Americans would be in a position push into Brittany to seize the ports.

Cobra was meant to begin at 13:00 on 24 July with the bombing attacks, but a heavy overcast sky above the battlefield prompted the decision to call the attack off. Some bombers did not receive the recall message; over 300 dropped their bombs, and one unit released theirs on elements of the 30th Division. Bradley was furious, not just because of the casualties, but because he feared that it would alert the Germans to the offensive. As it happened, the Germans did not change their plans. The commander of the German Seventh Army, General Paul Hausser, did not appear concerned when he reported the events of the day to von Kluge.

A Second Attempt

Cobra began again the next day with an air attack just after 09:30, fighter-bombers being followed by 1500 bombers. These dropped over 3048 tonnes (3000 tons) of bombs, and were in turn followed by 380 B-26 medium bombers that added another 1422 tonnes (1400 tons) of high explosive to the fray. The German defences were shattered. Over 1000 defenders were killed, and a similar number wounded or so badly dazed that they were incapable of resistance. Many of the German troops nearest to the American positions were not affected by the bombs, however, and once again, bombs fell short, killing 111 men, including Lieutenant-General Lesley McNair, the head of US Army Ground Forces, and wounding 490.

The ground assault started at 11:00, running into stiff resistance in areas where bombing had not inflicted much damage. This meant that the first day proved to be disappointing for the Americans, who gained about a mile rather than the three that were anticipated. The advance continued, at which point Hitler intervened with orders for a counter-attack.

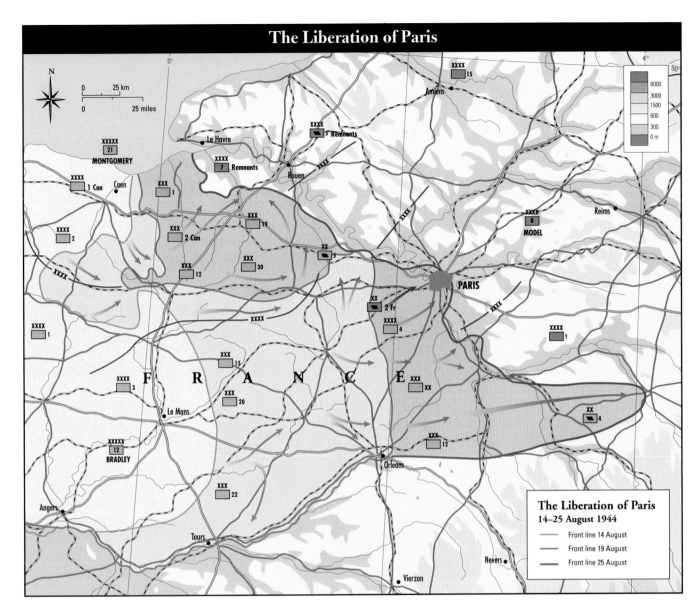

The Liberation of Paris

The Mortain Counter-attack

The attack was to be launched around Mortain, striking at Avranches. Avranches was the key to the American advance, since it was the supply hub for Patton's Third Army. Hitler believed that an attack here would dislocate the entire American effort, and allowed himself to imagine that the forward American divisions would be cut off, and then could be destroyed. The counter-attack began on 7 August and penetrated almost 10 miles into American lines. Some American units were indeed cut off, and for a while it seemed as though Hitler's plan might work. However, a more tangible form of intervention from above came the next morning. As dawn broke on 8 August, the weather was fine. By the middle of the morning, the sky was filled with British and American fighter-bombers. The advance had to stop as the Germans sought cover, and for the next three days they would only attack at night. Bitter fighting followed, but the Germans made no significant gains. The attack had failed.

On 8 August, the first elements of Patton's Third Army reached Le Mans. Eisenhower ordered them to turn north and head towards the British sector. Meanwhile, the

Above: The liberation of Paris proved controversial amongst the Allies, since it was not a primary objective for General Eisenhower. Political pressure from General de Gaulle, and the generally favourable situation, persuaded Eisenhower that he could afford to divert forces to retake the city, a task that was completed by the end of August 1944.

129

Above: Weary but satisfied American troops have a cigarette while awaiting transport to take them to the rear for a few days' rest. The picture was taken in October 1944, and the three soldiers in question had been at the front line since 12 June. The ferocity of the combat in Normandy took its toll on both sides, and it was necessary to give troops some time for rest and recuperation.

Canadian II Corps was planning to make a thrust towards Falaise. If this succeeded, they would be able to link up with the Americans and cut the Germans off. Consequently, just after nightfall on 8 August, 1000 heavy bombers attacked the flanks of the Falaise corridor. The Canadians then advanced along the corridor, marking the start of Operation Totalise.

The Germans counter-attacked just before midday on 9 August. They were stopped by 14:00, but just as the Canadians and the Polish forces accompanying them were about to resume their advance, the sky was filled with 500 B-17 Flying Fortresses from the USAAF. The intention was to repeat the bombardment of the night before, but this went disastrously wrong. Many bombs fell short, killing friendly forces and damaging or destroying many tanks. The next day, a Canadian battle group managed to lose its way and blundered into two panzer groups. To make matters worse, the Poles were engaging the panzers, and took the Canadians under fire as well. Although Totalise was still making ground, it was in serious danger of grinding to a halt as opposition became stiffer. The Americans, on the other hand, were having a better time, and were pushing on towards Argentan. The prospect of linking up with them added new impetus to the British forces, and a development of Totalise was swiftly put in train.

THE LIBERATION OF FRANCE

Operation Tractable

The new plan, Tractable, was intended to strike a decisive blow against the Germans. It began with a massive artillery bombardment closely followed up by 300 tanks and four infantry brigades. At this point, disaster struck, when many of the 800 heavy bombers called upon to provide air support began dropping short of the Germans and onto the advancing Allied forces. Although the troops pressed on, the dust and smoke kicked up by the bombing and the artillery was intense and visibility was almost nil. Inevitably, tanks and armoured personnel carriers collided with one another in the confusion and the advance fell into disarray. The debacle was compounded when the armour encountered a narrow stream in its way. While the stream itself was too narrow to cause the tanks difficulty in fording it, the problem lay in the fact that the banks were too steep for tanks to even attempt to traverse it. Eventually, armoured engineers dropped fascine bundles into the stream and the armour moved on – but the advance had slowed irreversibly. Once again, the Canadians found themselves making a slow, hard advance, eventually entering Falaise on 15 August.

Although the Allies were now gaining the upper hand, Hitler was totally convinced that they could still be defeated by launching a series of counter-attacks. Von Kluge was ordered to maintain pressure on Avranches. It was at this point that von Kluge's predominant characteristic of obeying Hitler's every order deserted him. He decided that Hitler's orders were completely ridiculous, and informed Berlin that his forces were no longer strong enough to defeat the Allies. Without waiting for a reply, von Kluge ordered the troops in the pocket to begin a withdrawal.

The End in Normandy

Hitler was furious, and sacked von Kluge immediately. The unfortunate field marshal poisoned himself rather than make the journey home to face Hitler's wrath and probable execution. On 17 August Field Marshal Walther Model, a loyal Nazi who would obey orders, was appointed in von Kluge's stead. Model's loyalty may not have been in doubt, but nor was his intelligence. As soon as he took over, he appreciated that the position was hopeless, and that von Kluge had been right. However, Model was clever enough to withdraw while using the remnants of his armour to make thrusts against both Falaise and Argentan. He knew that these would fail, but he could claim to have carried out Hitler's instructions to the letter. By 19 August, the Germans were in a dire state – artillery and air strikes were decimating their retreating columns; two days later, those forces remaining in the pocket were trapped as the jaws of the trap closed. Free French forces raced for Paris. The city fell to the French forces, and by 29 August, American troops were marching down the Champs Elysées as part of the liberation celebrations.

Operation Dragoon

While the fighting in Normandy was going on, the Allies sought to open a second front in France, by landing in the south of the country. The plan had been endorsed at the Tehran Conference, but no firm date was given for the operation (codenamed Anvil) since it swiftly became clear that providing enough shipping for both it and the Normandy landings was impossible. Eisenhower, who was not convinced about the wisdom of the operation taking place alongside the Normandy landings, secured agreement that it should take place after Overlord, and as late as 11 June, Churchill was pressing for the landings to be abandoned in favour of landings in the Balkans.

'The battlefield at Falaise was unquestionably one of the greatest "killing grounds" of any of the war areas ... Forty-eight hours after the closing of the gap, I was conducted through it on foot, to encounter scenes that could be described only by Dante. It was literally possible to walk for hundreds of yards at a time, stepping on nothing but dead and decaying flesh.'

General Dwight D. Eisenhower, Crusade in Europe

131

Roosevelt rejected this suggestion, telling Churchill a landing in the Balkans would be deeply unpopular in the United States. The message was quite clear – it was an election year in America, and Roosevelt was politely informing the prime minister that he had no intention of doing anything unpopular. Churchill made desperate attempts to convince Eisenhower to modify the plan; Eisenhower refused. Churchill joked bitterly that as he had been dragooned into accepting, the plan should be renamed Operation Dragoon. Oddly, the joke was taken as being an expression of seriousness, and the landings were given the codename of Anvil/Dragoon as a recognition of Churchill's offhand remark.

The invasion fleet assembled in a variety of locations in the Mediterranean and the landings began with commandos coming ashore on the night of 14 August. They were followed by parachute and glider-borne assaults which aimed to seize the vital intersection at Le Muy. Some of the paratroopers were dropped outside their intended landing zone, right on top of the headquarters of the German LXII Corps. As was now common with paratroops who found themselves miles from where they ought to be, the soldiers made a quick assessment of the situation, worked out how best to inconvenience the opposition and set about doing it. They attacked the headquarters, preventing it from coordinating the defences on the beaches against the seaborne attack. Le Muy fell the next day. The main landings took place at 05:50 on 15 August, and made good progress. On 17 August, orders for the abandonment of southern France (apart from the ports) were issued by the German high command, and the forces there began to retreat.

Below: A motley collection of members of the French Resistance pose for the camera in a town somewhere in France. The men are mainly equipped with British rifles, and a Bren light machine gun can be seen on its bipod to the bottom right of the photograph. These weapons had almost certainly been dropped to the Resistance by British aircraft.

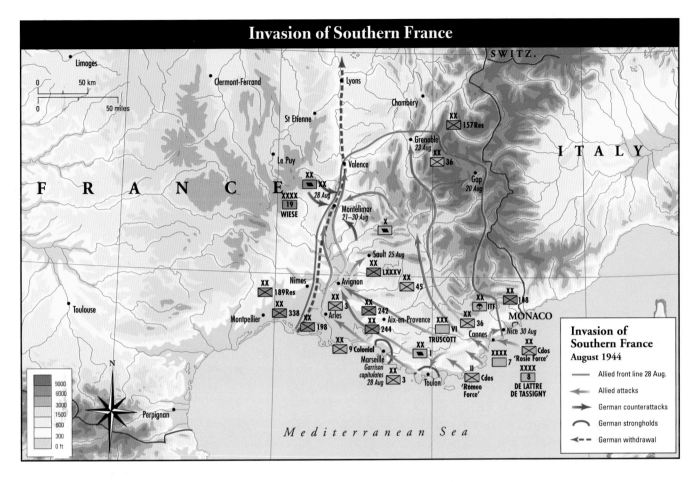

Invasion of Southern France

The Franco-American advance proceeded smoothly; Marseilles surrendered on 28 August, and leading elements of General Lucian K. Truscott's VI Corps entered Lyon on 3 September to the acclaim of the population, overjoyed that the Germans had been forced out. By the time Truscott had reached Lyon, the Allied forces in the north had rapidly exploited their breakthrough. Montgomery launched Operation Kitten, an advance to the Seine on 16 August, forcing the Germans to carry out a phased withdrawal across the river to escape complete destruction. As the Germans fell back, heading for the Belgian and German frontiers, they were pursued by the Allies. By the first week of September, the Allies began to outrun their logistics, so they halted along a line from the Meuse to Maastricht and then south from Aachen to the Swiss border. While plans for the next stage of operations were being drawn up, Truscott's forces linked up with Patton on 11 September, trapping the last 20,000 men of the German rearguard, who surrendered. While the operation in the south of France actually increased logistical problems, Anvil/Dragoon succeeded in ensuring political stability in the south of France, which had been one of the key concerns for the Americans when they had insisted upon the operation over Churchill's objections.

By the end of August 1944, the Allies had succeeded in their aim of driving the Germans back. Most of France was liberated, and once the logistic system had been restored, the advance would continue into Germany. Although the Germans had been compelled to pull back, their resistance remained fierce. It was quite obvious that they would remain a formidable enemy as the Western Front was pushed ever closer to the German border as the final reckoning between the Allies and the Axis powers drew near.

Above: The controversial invasion of southern France (Operation Anvil/ Dragoon) was carried out despite British opposition. Originally planned as a means of dividing the efforts of the Germans, the operation went ahead even after they had begun to withdraw north, since it was deemed necessary by the Americans as a means of ensuring the maintenance of order and the restoration of government in the south of the country.

Northwest Europe, August 1944 – April 1945

The Allied armies arrived on the banks of the River Seine after only 80 days, and while Paris was being retaken, the bulk of Allied forces started to cross the river, aiming to keep in touch with the retreating Germans. There was concern that if the pursuit fell some distance behind, the Germans could use the time to prepare strong defensive positions that would inevitably hamper the drive towards Germany. Memories of the defences along the Somme, the Marne, the Aisne and the Meuse from World War I returned to the minds of the senior officers, many of whom had experienced the effectiveness of these positions at first hand.

US First Army (Lieutenant-General Courtney Hodges) was the first to drive on after crossing the Seine, and fought a series of sharp engagements as they pursued the Germans, taking St Quentin by the end of August, and then Mons and Tournai. Patton's Third Army conducted a similarly rapid advance to the Meuse, but was forced to halt on 31 August when it ran out of petrol. Montgomery's 21st Army Group, meanwhile, moved in preparation for the capture of Le Havre, Dieppe, Boulogne and Calais, before heading into Belgium. XII and XXX Corps from the British Second Army crossed the Seine and after overcoming stiff resistance began a drive to Amiens, gathering momentum as they went. At dawn on 31 August, the leading tanks of the 11th Armoured Division were in Amiens, and by the end of the morning had secured the river crossings over the Somme. The next day saw units from XXX Corps in Arras and Aubigny on the River Scarpe, followed the next day by Lens and Douai. Although the British had to fight their way into all these locations, German resistance was relatively light. A rest was ordered on 1 September, so as to allow an airborne operation to seize Tournai prior to the arrival of Hodges' US First Army. In fact, First Army moved so quickly that Tournai fell before the parachute drop could take place, and the British were now instructed to drive on Brussels. The Guards Armoured and 11th Armoured Divisions were tasked with

Opposite: An American infantryman shows off a variety of captured German weapons that he has collected. He has three MP40 sub-machine guns slung over his right arm, and is carrying two MG42 machine guns in his left hand. The MG42 later formed the basis for the American M60 machine gun.

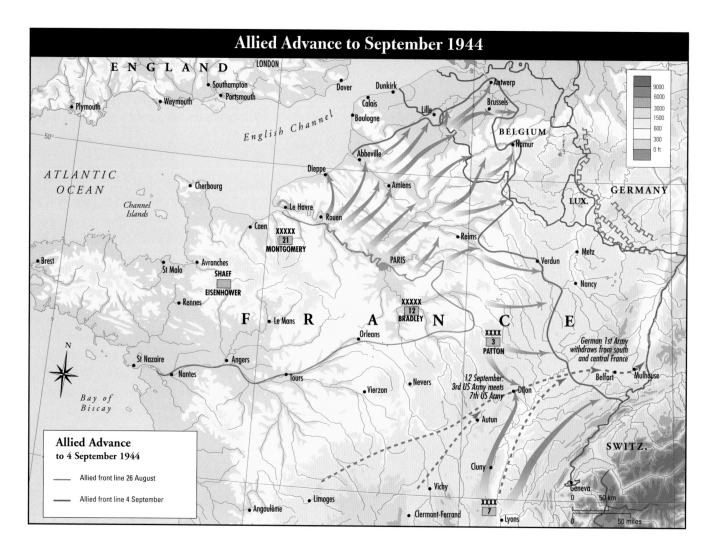

Allied Advance to September 1944

Above: After the difficult task of breaking out from Normandy was complete, the Allies enjoyed considerable success in their advance, virtually clearing France of German troops by the end of August, and entering Belgium.

liberating the Belgian capital and Antwerp respectively. The Guards entered Brussels on the evening of 3 September to great jubilation, while 11th Armoured received a similar welcome in Antwerp.

Le Havre

The battle for Le Havre, undertaken by the British I Corps, was a far more difficult prospect than the advances undertaken by XII and XXX Corps. The port was well defended, and the commander, Colonel Eberhard Wildermuth, was faced with a dilemma. He was anxious to avoid heavy casualties, but could not simply surrender because of the inevitable consequences this would have for his family. As a result, the city had to be taken by force. RAF Bomber Command bombed the port for 10 consecutive days, and naval gunfire was added to the maelstrom of the preparatory bombardment. The infantry of the 49th and 51st Divisions carried out offensive patrolling as they moved into place for the attack, which was launched at dusk on 10 September.

The preliminary bombardment of Le Havre was immense, and rivalled the massive preparatory fire directed against German positions by the Red Army in the East. Bombers dropped 5080 tonnes (5000 tons) of bombs onto the port, and as the last one left the area, the artillery opened fire. Armour moved forward, closely followed by the infantry, and the British fought their way into the city. Despite the bombardment, it took all night and most of the following day before the outer defences were captured, and then another 24 hours passed before British troops entered the city centre, where Colonel Wildermuth was captured. Le Havre was in British hands, but at the cost of many more lives than would have been necessary had Hitler not given such stringent orders backed up by the threat of dire consequences for officers' families if they capitulated, and considerable damage to the port facilities, which meant that it took several weeks before Le Havre could be brought into use to aid the Allied advance.

Overall, the last two weeks of August 1944 saw the British and Americans covering up to 500 miles, taking thousands of Germans prisoner as they went. However, the logistics system supporting the advance was becoming increasingly strained as the Allies moved on. The situation was not helped by the fact that there was rampant inefficiency and corruption amongst the logistics organization under General J.C.H. Lee. An unpopular, flamboyant man (critics said his initials stood for 'Jesus Christ Himself'), Lee oversaw an organization that was drastically overstaffed, and which encompassed the brilliant creation of the 'Red Ball Express' to keep troops supplied, to wild profligacy in the form of Lee diverting resources to move his staff into opulent headquarters in Paris (in the form of no fewer than 290 hotels) when they were required at the front, and to straightforward black-marketeering, which is alleged to have encouraged around 10 per cent of Lee's command to desert and set up in business in Paris with their ill-gotten supplies. Coupled with this inefficiency, the Allies faced the simple problem that they needed to begin operating from ports closer to the front line, a difficult task given that some (such as Le Havre) needed weeks of repair, while Antwerp was not operational

Below: A dead German Waffen-SS soldier lies at the side of a track somewhere in France. By the end of August 1944, this scene had been repeated countless times throughout France, with the Germans sustaining thousands of casualties as they were pushed back towards Germany.

even after its capture, since the Germans controlled the approaches. This all meant that the Allies would not be able to sustain thrusts across a broad front, and resources would have to be carefully husbanded. This meant that trying to satisfy the demands of Patton and Montgomery would be a particularly difficult task for Eisenhower. Both his subordinates wished to be at the head of the Allied advance, and neither took kindly to the idea that they might have to take second place to the other as a result of supply problems.

Operation Market Garden

Montgomery wished to use 21st Army Group as the main offensive force, and developed a daring plan which, if it worked, would place his men across the River Rhine and in a position to sweep towards Berlin, possibly before the year was over.

Montgomery's plan contrasted dramatically with the more cautious approach he usually adopted for offensives, and when he proposed it to Eisenhower, the Supreme Commander was almost mesmerized by the audacity of the proposition before him.

The plan was to land some 30,000 British and American airborne troops at key river bridges while General Sir Brian Horrocks' XXX Corps drove north through Holland along the 60-mile-long corridor created by the landing. Montgomery suggested that such an operation could cause the Germans to collapse, shattering their will to continue fighting. Even if it did not, he contended, the Allies would still benefit since they would have gained a bridgehead across the Rhine. The major German defensive position on the West Wall (or Siegfried Line) would be outflanked by the move. The furthest bridge to be seized would be that at Arnhem, which the British 1st Airborne Division was to hold until relieved by XXX Corps. The plan was codenamed Market Garden with 'Market' covering the airborne component and 'Garden' the ground element. Eisenhower's amazement at Montgomery's suggestion did not prevent him from seeing the logic that lay behind it. He agreed to the plan, with the date of the operation being set for 17 September 1944.

While the plan was recognized as being particularly bold, it was not without difficulties. One of the key problems was that the Allied First Airborne Army was bedevilled by the poor relationship between its commander, General Lewis Brereton, and his deputy, Lieutenant-General Sir Frederick 'Boy' Browning. Browning had been involved with airborne operations since he had overseen the creation of the Parachute Regiment in 1940, and had harboured hopes that he would be given command of the Airborne Army. However, Brereton had been given the position, much to Browning's irritation. Brereton was an officer in the US Army Air Force, specializing in transport aircraft; since the bulk of the air transport strength available to the Allies was American, his appointment was not unreasonable.

Regrettably, Browning and Brereton disliked each other intensely, and the two barely spoke to one another. This culminated in the utter farce that ensued when it transpired that the two men had planned two completely different operations for the airborne troops on 6 September. Both had to be cancelled when Browning refused to cancel his plan, and threatened to resign if Brereton overruled him. Relations between the two could not have been worse, and to compound matters, their breakdown in relations occurred at a time when strong, unified leadership was required, given that the bulk of their staff was inexperienced and needed clear guidance. Of equal concern was the problem of aircraft availability. Although the USAAF and RAF had the largest air

transport fleet ever assembled, this was still not enough to transport more than a third of the army at a time, making additional air drops essential. The problem here lay in the danger that one element of the Airborne Army could land, vastly outnumbered, but be left cut off if the second and/or third part of the army could not be dropped as the result of bad weather obscuring the landing zone. On the positive side, the men were highly trained and amongst the most determined and professional on the Allied side. The forces included Lieutenant-General Matthew Ridgeway's XVIII Airborne Corps, consisting of the American 82nd and 101st Airborne Divisions, and the British 1st Airborne Division, supported by a brigade of Polish paratroopers.

The plans for Market Garden were complete by 15 September, and envisaged the seizure of bridges at Eindhoven, Nijmegen and Arnhem. Browning passed the now immortal comment 'I think we may be going a bridge too far', but it was too late to modify the plan. The precursor to the airborne assault came in the form of a heavy bombardment of German fighter airfields in Holland, beginning in the early hours of 16 September with an attack by RAF Bomber Command, and then a 1000-aircraft raid by

Above: Men of the 82nd Airborne Division aboard a C-47 transport aircraft as they await take-off as part of Operation Market Garden. The 82nd Airborne was assigned the task of seizing the bridge at Nijmegen, which was seized after some sharp fighting.

139

*Right: The airlift in
support of Operation
Market Garden was
enormous in its scale.
When the operation began
on 17 September, a
stream of aircraft and
gliders left England,
carrying some 20,000
men and their equipment.
By 14:00, the first phase
of the airlift was
complete, and 20,000
troops had been landed
successfully, and were
heading for their
objectives.*

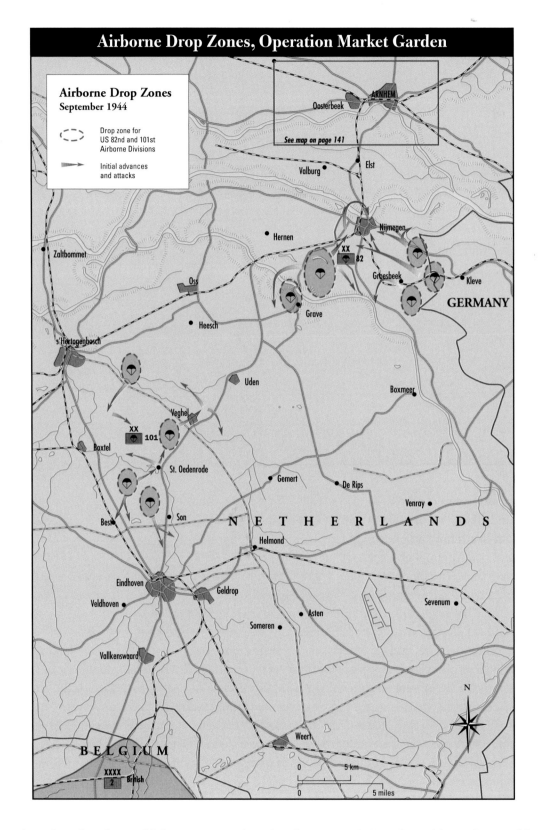

American bombers which was targeted against known anti-aircraft positions that could interfere with the transport aircraft.

On 17 September, no fewer than airbases in England were alive to the sound of the massed transport fleet taking off to carry the airborne component into battle. The

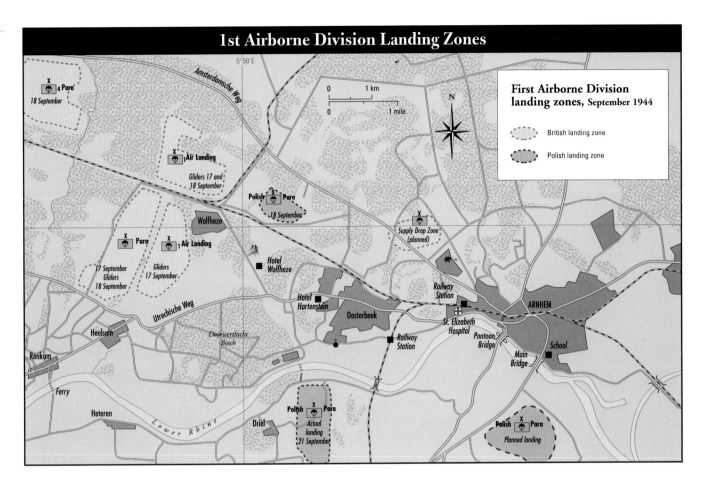

1st Airborne Division Landing Zones

First Airborne Division landing zones, September 1944

British landing zone

Polish landing zone

X 4 Para
18 September

X 1 Air Landing
Gliders 17 and 18 September

Polish X Para
18 September

X Para

X 1 Air Landing

17 September Gliders
18 September

Gliders 17 September

Wolfheze

Hotel Wolfheze

Supply Drop Zone (planned)

Hotel Hartenstein

Oosterbeek

Railway Station

ARNHEM

St. Elizabeth Hospital

Railway Station

Pontoon Bridge

Main Bridge

School

Heelsum

Doorwerthsche Bosch

Renkum

Ferry

Heteren

Driel

Polish X Para
Actual landing 21 September

Polish X Para
Planned landing

Amsterdamsche Weg

Utrechtsche Weg

Lower Rhine

transports roared across southern England, bringing considerable excitement on the ground below as onlookers gaped in astonishment at the sheer scale of the airlift. A stream of aircraft and gliders carrying some 20,000 men and their equipment to Holland passed over them, with each aircraft heading on one of two routes – the northern route carried the 82nd Airborne and British 1st Airborne Divisions to their objectives at Nijmegen and Arnhem, while the southern track was made up of the aircraft carrying the US 101st Airborne. The southern stream suffered some losses from German flak, but reached the drop zone, where 7000 men were dropped. By 14:00, the first phase of the airlift was complete, and all 20,000 troops had been landed successfully.

The airborne troops enjoyed initial success, taking most of their objectives with ease (although 101st Airborne suffered the mortification of seeing one of the bridges they were meant to capture being destroyed as they approached it). The 82nd and 101st Airborne seized their objectives, and were ready to receive XXX Corps some time before that formation was able to break through increasingly stiff German defences.

The British troops ran into more difficulties than their American counterparts. German forces around Arnhem proved to be stronger than predicted. Worse still, as the 1st Airborne Division landed, Field Marshal Walther Model had broken off from his lunch to report the landings to Hitler. II SS Panzer Corps was instantly alerted for action, while 9th SS Panzer Division was immediately sent to Arnhem, and 10th SS Panzer Division told to make all haste towards Nijmegen.

Once the Americans succeeded in capturing the bridges at Eindhoven, they had to wait for XXX Corps to arrive. XXX Corps' tanks had to move along a single-track road,

Above: The landings by 1st Airborne Division were complicated by the fact that they occurred some distance away from Arnhem, presenting the division with the need to move swiftly into the town to secure the bridge. While this was achieved, problems with resupply meant that the division's position was tenuous, and made worse by the fact that the 9th SS Panzer Division was nearby and able to rush to the scene to engage them.

Above: Two German prisoners prepare firewood, under the watchful eye of one of their captors. The German in the camouflage suit is a Waffen-SS trooper.

which meant that even a small German force could block their path and disrupt the timing of the operation. Inevitably, they ran into German opposition. German anti-tank guns had inflicted some damage upon the lead elements of the advance before they were dealt with by air strikes and artillery fire. This skirmish delayed XXX Corps, a portent of things to come. Once past this obstacle, XXX Corps then ran into more German opposition, which again took time to overcome. By the afternoon of 19 September, XXX Corps had reached Nijmegen, and crossed the River Wahl. This left them only 10 miles south of Arnhem, the final objective – but German resistance was such that the advance ground to a complete halt, leaving 1st Airborne Division cut off.

1st Airborne had been fighting in and around Arnhem for three days, and things had not gone well. The bridge in the town was meant to be captured by a surprise attack by armed jeeps, but the gliders carrying these had failed to arrive intact. Although the 2nd Battalion of the 1st Parachute Brigade reached the northern end of the bridge, the reinforcements they anticipated coming to join them did not arrive. One of the reasons for this lay in the fact that Major-General Roy Urquhart, the commander of 1st Airborne Division, became detached from his headquarters and spent 36 hours hiding from German patrols until he was able to make his way back. In his absence, his subordinates disagreed over what course of action to take, and devoted their attention to securing high ground outside the town instead of sending reinforcements to the bridge. As a result, 2nd Battalion was completely isolated, and after beating off one attack, was subjected to a massive assault designed to literally blast them from their positions. An epic stand resulted, but the paratroopers' task was impossible, and the Germans retook the bridge on 21 September.

As the fighting in Arnhem continued, efforts to fly in supplies and reinforcements were made, but failed as a result of bad weather. XXX Corps battled on towards Arnhem, and finally broke through German resistance to reach the south side of the Rhine on 23 September. An attempt to cross the river failed, and Montgomery came to the conclusion that the airborne division had to be withdrawn, since there was no chance of success. Montgomery's plan had been predicated on the belief popular among the Allied high command that the German troops had lost their will to fight; Market Garden demonstrated that this was a fallacy. As a result, the remaining troops were evacuated from Arnhem across the river during the night of 25/26 September. Although Allied propaganda claims that the operation was 90 per cent successful were an exaggeration, the capture of the bridge over the Waal was to be of great utility in 1945 as a base from which to launch future operations.

Back to Attrition

With the failure at Arnhem it was clear the Germans were still a considerable way from being totally defeated in the West, even if their position was grave. The Germans might have been forced back onto their frontier, but they were falling back to prepared defensive positions that would be difficult to break through. In addition, the Germans had far shorter lines of communication than the Allies, who were beginning to notice the failings of their logistics organization. Until the supply situation improved, it was clear

'I would say the German as a military force on the Western front ... is a whipped enemy.'

General Eisenhower, press conference, 28 March 1945

FIELD MARSHAL WALTHER MODEL

Walther Model was commissioned into the German Army in 1909. He served in staff positions during World War I, and remained in the Army after it was slashed in size after the Versailles treaties. Impressed with Hitler (as a politician, if not as a military commander), Model joined the Nazi Party, and remained loyal to Hitler for the rest of his life. He commanded IV Corps in Poland, the 3rd Panzer Division in France and then XXXI Panzer Corps in the early fighting in the USSR. Model was then given command of Ninth Army between 1942 and 1944, when he took over as commander of Army Group North in the Ukraine. He briefly commanded Army Group Centre from June 1944, before taking over Army Group B in August. Hitler had high regard for Model, and his constant use of him to deal with difficult situations, such as in Normandy and then at Arnhem, led to Model's nickname of 'the *Führer*'s Firefighter'.

Model realized that arguing with Hitler over some of his less sensible decisions never worked, and instead carried out the *Führer*'s instructions, but interpreting these orders in the loosest possible sense, which meant that he could go some way towards reconciling Hitler's ideas with reality. Model opposed the Ardennes offensive, but carried it out to the best of his ability, and commanded his army group until it was surrounded in the Ruhr pocket in April 1945. While he allowed his troops to surrender, Model decided that he would not, and he shot himself on 21 April 1945.

THE FALL OF HITLER'S THIRD REICH

that the Allied advance would be slow, with the risk of increased attrition as the war dragged on. The question of how to improve the supply problem was of key concern to the Allies, and attention turned to Antwerp.

Although Antwerp was in Allied hands, it was of little use. The German Fifteenth Army controlled the entrance to the port, and their presence meant that the Allies would be unable to bring anything into Antwerp until they had dislodged the enemy from the banks of the Scheldt estuary. Quite understandably, Montgomery had given little priority to Antwerp while Market Garden was under way, and had left the task of clearing the estuary in the hands of the Canadian First Army. On 8 October, Admiral Sir Bertram Ramsay, commanding naval operations for Northwest Europe, reported to Eisenhower that the Scheldt would not be cleared until at least 1 November, since the Canadians had encountered stiff opposition and were now running short of supplies, particularly ammunition. The report alarmed Eisenhower, prompting him to order Montgomery to clear the Scheldt estuary with all haste. He made clear that unless Antwerp was brought into use, operations would come to a standstill. He concluded his signal to Montgomery by explaining that he considered Antwerp to be of the utmost importance to the Allied war effort. Unfortunately, Montgomery refused to accept that this task was anything more than an attempt to consign him to a quiet area, enabling the Americans to 'steal' the glory that was, in Montgomery's opinion, rightfully his. Being Montgomery, he could not keep these thoughts to himself, and added that the only reason that Arnhem had failed was because Eisenhower had an unsatisfactory campaign plan.

Eisenhower found it necessary to remind Montgomery as to who was in command of the Allied forces in Europe – whether or not Montgomery liked the fact, it was not him. To rein in Montgomery, Eisenhower explained that if he had no confidence in his handling of the matter, then they must 'refer the matter to higher authority' for arbitration. Montgomery knew all too well that such a course of action would be disastrous for him, since it was impossible to conceive of a situation where Roosevelt would side with Montgomery and remove Eisenhower. It was election year in the United States, and it would be politically impossible for an aspirant president, even one who had already served three terms in office, to side with a foreign general against an American hero. It was equally certain that Churchill would concur with Roosevelt, and despite his status, Montgomery would have to be sacrificed to protect the alliance. Montgomery carefully extricated himself from his apparently intractable position and issued orders that made clearing the Scheldt the main priority for his forces.

Clearing the Scheldt
Operations along the Scheldt were well under way even before Montgomery's about-turn. The Canadians, supported by the Polish Armoured Division, had removed the Germans from about 20 miles of the southern bank of the river, but this was still less than half the amount that needed to be cleared. The Germans, meanwhile, were fully aware of the significance of the Scheldt to the Allies, and maintained formidable defences in the mouth of the river, notably on Walcheren Island, where 12,000 men occupied well-fortified positions supported by heavy guns. The town of Flushing had been turned into a fortress, with individual houses converted into strongpoints.

The British and Canadian forces assaulted the enemy positions in terrible weather, which prevented air support from being called in to support the advance. Canadian 3rd Division fought its way along the Scheldt, employing amphibious armoured fighting

vehicles to convey them to their objective, until they finally captured the last strongpoint at Knocke-sur-Mer on 2 November. Canadian 2nd Division attacked along the Beveland peninsula on 24 October, while the British 52nd Division crossed the Scheldt with the aim of driving the Germans into the arms of the Canadians. By the end of October, the Germans had been pushed back onto Walcheren Island, which now had to be taken.

The plan for the operation addressed the formidable defences by taking the view that the best way of dealing with the island was to flood it by breaching the Westkapelle dyke. On 3, 7, 11 and 17 October, Mosquito and Lancaster bombers from the RAF carried out heavy raids on the dyke.

By the time the bombers had finished, most of the island was underwater, with the exception of the coastal dunes, and Middleberg and Flushing. Two more days of bombing and naval gunfire softened the defences of the remaining areas, and on 1 November, British commandos went ashore at Flushing and Westkapelle. A Canadian

Above: American M24 Chaffee tanks prepare to move out for another day's work. The M24 was designed to fulfil the light tank role, replacing the M3/M5 series. It was well armed, mounting a 75mm gun, and fast. The vehicle entered service in late 1944, and remained in American service after the war.

attack across the causeway was beaten back, and over the course of the next 48 hours there was fierce fighting, the advantage swinging back and forth between the warring sides. The commandos had a slightly easier task as a consequence of the flooding – a series of small islands created by the inundation stood in their way, and they took them one at a time. Flushing was far more difficult, but after yet more intense fighting, the Germans were induced to surrender on 4 November. That day, the Royal Navy began sweeping the Scheldt of mines, marking the start of a three-week-long operation. On 28 November, the first convoy of ships arrived safely, and by early December, the port was fully operational. This meant that Allied logistics were greatly improved. From a position of having far too little port capacity for months, they now had a surplus, which meant that forthcoming battles would be much easier to sustain.

American Advances

While the British cleared the Scheldt, the American First Army assaulted Aachen on 12 September. Bitter fighting ensued, and the defenders determined to follow Hitler's orders to fight to the last man. Six days of intensive street fighting saw the German perimeter pushed back into the city by 22 October, until the advance left the Germans in possession of just a four-storey air raid shelter. After 12 hours of artillery bombardment, the now rather battered and deafened Germans surrendered. The battle for Aachen was particularly bloody, but was totally surpassed by the sanguinary affair that followed in the Hürtgen Forest.

The Hürtgen Forest stretched over an area of 12 miles, intersected by elements of the West Wall. A series of American assaults between September and November cost them 33,000 casualties. Finally, on 8 December 1944, the Americans reached the banks of the River Roer; while First Army had fought its way through the Hürtgen Forest, Patton had led Third Army against Metz, which surrendered on 21 November. By the start of December, Third Army stood overlooking the West Wall – it had suffered 55,182 casualties in the process. As December began, the Allied armies appeared to have lost momentum following the bitter fighting of the previous two months. The attritional nature of the struggle concerned the Allies, particularly Montgomery, who was aware of the situation regarding the number of British reserves that could be called upon. He sought to persuade Eisenhower that finding some means of forcing the Germans into mobile warfare again was essential. As Eisenhower pondered the problem, the solution was provided by Hitler, in the form of a massive offensive in the Ardennes.

The Battle of the Bulge

Hitler's response to Allied success in the early summer of 1944 was to begin planning for a huge counter-offensive that would regain the initiative on the Western Front. Hitler decided that the target of his offensive should be Antwerp. There were many sound reasons for this, not least its importance to the Allies' logistics. A drive on the city would also have the major benefit of splitting the British and Canadian armies from the Americans, and they could then be destroyed. There were major difficulties in achieving the goal of Antwerp, but Hitler chose to ignore them.

The shortest distance to Antwerp was along the boundary between the American and British forces north of Aachen, but the terrain around the city made a quick advance impossible. Bisected by rivers and canals, the terrain presented too many obstacles to the tanks that were to drive through the Allied positions and bring victory. This forced the

Ardennes upon Hitler, but since this had been the scene of his success in 1940, this was not a concern to the *Führer*. Although the terrain was restrictive for manoeuvring forces, the campaign against France had proved that armour could move through the area. Other characteristics of the Ardennes commended the area. The forests in the German Eifel region would provide a useful means of disguising the build-up of an attacking force from aerial reconnaissance, and the distance to Antwerp was little more than 100 miles. Also, if the attack was successful, it would cut off the British and Canadians and trap the American armies around Aachen too. Hitler concluded that he could obtain a victory so decisive that the Anglo-American forces would be forced to sue for peace. The offensive would trap over half of the Allied forces, eliminate the threat to the Ruhr and its industry,

Below: An SS NCO signals to his men to advance during the Battle of the Bulge. This is a propaganda shot taken alongside a burning American column from which the survivors had been removed before the photographer arrived.

and allow Hitler to turn his attention to the Eastern Front by withdrawing troops from the West. All of this, Hitler decided, could be achieved within a week.

There remained one major problem with this plan, which was evident to almost everyone in the German high command (when they were let in on the secret) – it took absolutely no account of reality.

Hitler simply refused to accept that the situation was very different from 1940. Germany did not have air superiority and the proposed timing for the offensive sought to enlist that most unpredictable ally (unless one is Russian), namely the weather. The forces needed for the offensive would have to be created, and this would require removing troops and tanks from the Eastern Front, where they were desperately needed. Hitler intended to make the task for his troops slightly easier by using English-speaking commandos dressed in American uniform to spread confusion in rear areas by misdirecting traffic, spreading rumours and carrying out acts of sabotage, and by using an airborne assault to support the attack. Even these ideas failed to appreciate reality – the German parachute force had not conducted a combat drop since 1941, and many of the men now assigned to the formation did not even know how to use a parachute. The sacrifice of

Opposite: The German offensive in the Ardennes was designed to change the strategic situation on the Western Front. Hitler planned to seize the port of Antwerp, driving a wedge between the British and American armies and using the advantage gained to negotiate a separate peace with the Western powers. The plan was hopelessly optimistic, but the initial stages went well, with the Germans driving the Americans back and besieging Bastogne. By Christmas 1944, it was clear that the Germans were not going to achieve their objectives, and a series of Allied counter-attacks were under way.

Right, inset: From 23 December 1944, an Allied counter-attack in the Ardennes drove the Germans back, until by the end of January, their defeat was confirmed. The Germans lost over 120,000 men and 600 armoured vehicles in the offensive, weakening the forces available to defend against the crossing of the Rhine, and placing them in a far less favourable position than Hitler had intended.

transport crews on the Eastern Front meant that most of the pilots for the aircraft that would carry the paratroopers to their destination had never dropped paratroopers before, and to complete the farce, they were not allowed to carry out sufficient training to at least try to prevent the drop from turning into a disaster.

The idea of using undercover commandos was flawed as well, since there were too few English-speaking men prepared to volunteer for the mysterious mission offered them; and the majority of those who could speak the language fluently had an English accent rather than the required American one. Finally, there was not enough captured American equipment available to enable them to maintain their cover story.

When they learned of his plan, Hitler's generals were astounded at the fact that the goal set for them was virtually impossible. Outnumbered, short of fuel, men, transport, tanks and equipment, the idea seemed preposterous, but all attempts to tell Hitler fell on deaf ears. The only thing that suggested that the offensive would have any chance of success was the one obvious advantage the Germans had – surprise.

The attack started on 16 December 1944, and although the Americans were driven back, the pace of advance was nowhere near swift enough to allow for the goal of Antwerp to be achieved, a fact that was clear almost as early as the end of the third day. While the Germans inflicted serious reverses on the Americans in a number of places, dogged defence meant that the situation was kept under reasonable control, even if the response at SHAEF verged on panic at times. The Germans were delayed at St Vith and a host of other places, and found that Bastogne was far from easy to take. The 101st Airborne Division held out in the town, despite being totally surrounded – a German offer of surrender was presented to the temporary commander of the division, Brigadier-General Anthony McAuliffe, who responded with a pithy 'Nuts!' and left his staff officers to explain the sentiment behind it to the confused German officers who had been sent to parley.

After the shock of the first few days of the attack, Eisenhower ordered a counter-attack. The Germans were first slowed down even more, and then driven back in the face of a determined thrust by Patton. Bastogne was kept supplied from the air when the weather permitted, until it was relieved on 26 December, marking a turning point in the campaign. Although fighting continued until January 1945, and included another German offensive against American troops in Alsace, the Battle of the Bulge had been won by the New Year. Twenty-six American divisions were now in the Ardennes, and set about destroying the remaining German forces.

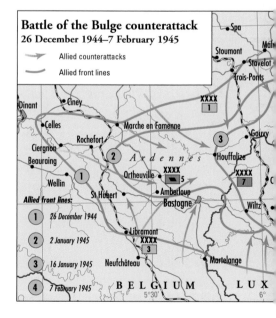

Exactly six weeks after the offensive began, the Americans were back in the positions they had occupied at the start, leaving the Germans facing the fact that they had suffered heavy casualties and gained no ground for little in return other than the psychological effect caused by the attack. With the end of the battle, optimism was returning quickly, and the Allies looked forward to making the final push against the Germans in the spring of 1945, aiming to drive into the heart of Germany itself.

Invasion of the Low Countries

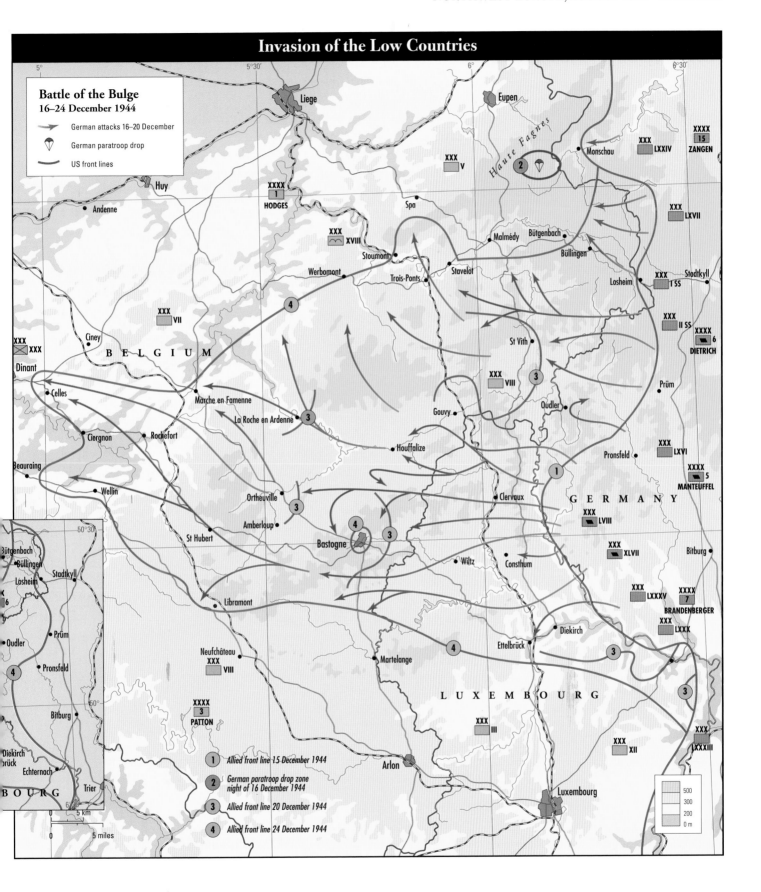

Battle of the Bulge
16–24 December 1944

German attacks 16–20 December
German paratroop drop
US front lines

Liege
Eupen
Huy
Andenne
Monschau
Spa
Malmédy
Bütgenbach
Büllingen
Stoumont
Werbomont
Trois-Ponts
Stavelot
Losheim
Stadtkyll
Ciney
BELGIUM
St Vith
Prüm
Dinant
Celles
Marche en Famenne
La Roche en Ardenne
Ciergnon
Rockefort
Houffalize
Gouvy
Oudler
Pronsfeld
Beauraing
Wellin
Ortheuville
Clervaux
GERMANY
Amberloup
St Hubert
Bastogne
Wiltz
Consthum
Bitburg
Libramont
Diekirch
Neufchâteau
Ettelbrück
Martelange
LUXEMBOURG
Arlon
Luxembourg

XXXX 15 ZANGEN
XXX LXXIV
XXX V
XXXX 1 HODGES
XXX LXVII
XXX XVIII
XXX 1 SS
XXX II SS
XXXX 6 DIETRICH
XXX VII
XXX VIII
XXX LXVI
XXXX 5 MANTEUFFEL
XXX LVIII
XXX XLVII
XXX LXXXV
XXXX 7 BRANDENBERGER
XXX LXXX
XXX VIII
XXXX 3 PATTON
XXX III
XXX XII
XXX LXXXIII

1 Allied front line 15 December 1944
2 German paratroop drop zone night of 16 December 1944
3 Allied front line 20 December 1944
4 Allied front line 24 December 1944

Bütgenbach
Büllingen
Losheim
Stadtkyll
Oudler
Prüm
Pronsfeld
Bitburg
Diekirch
Echternach
Trier

500
300
200
0 m

5 km
5 miles

149

The Red Storm, 1944–45

German expectations that the 1943 offensives would end in December as a result of fatigue amongst Soviet forces were to be rudely shattered, since the Soviets had no intention of stopping – they in fact intended to begin the reconquest of western Ukraine before the year was out.

As a result, early on the morning of 24 December, 1st Ukrainian Front launched a massive preparatory bombardment against Army Group South's positions to the west of Kiev. Once this had finished, the assault divisions were thrown into battle, and made particularly short work of their opposition. As the day drew to a close, the Russians had advanced to a depth of 20 miles, and the Germans were in complete disarray. For once, though, luck was on their side, for it began to rain on Christmas Day. The rain was heavy and prolonged, and the downpour turned the countryside into a quagmire, through which movement was either difficult or, in places, impossible.

Despite this, the advance continued, albeit at a slower pace. The Germans were forced back, with the rail link between Army Group Centre and Army Group South being cut by Soviet troops on 5 January 1944. As a result of the offensive, a hole 150 miles wide and 50 miles deep was punched into the German front before the attack began to lose momentum. This was a temporary respite for the Germans, however, since 2nd Ukrainian Front launched an offensive of its own, which reached the outskirts of Kirovograd. After two weeks' preparation, both 1st and 2nd Ukrainian Fronts attacked, trapping 50,000 Germans in the Korsun-Shevchenkovsky salient.

Following on from previous orders given to troops trapped in near hopeless situations, Hitler refused to allow any effort to break out, ordering a counter-offensive. This was initially successful, but this time the weather worked against the Germans. Temperatures were unseasonably warm, and the thawing snow and ice turned the ground into a muddy, impassable mess – German armour was literally bogged down.

Orders permitting a retreat from the Korsun-Shevchenkovsky pocket were at last given, but although the withdrawal went well at the beginning, once the Russians realized what was happening, they intervened with some well-directed artillery fire. The withdrawal collapsed into a rout as command and control disappeared as officers were killed, wounded or otherwise separated from their men. Thousands of soldiers were

Opposite: Sitting in his foxhole, an SS soldier waits for the inevitable arrival of the Red Army. He is armed with the standard German service rifle, the Kar 98 bolt-action rifle.

151

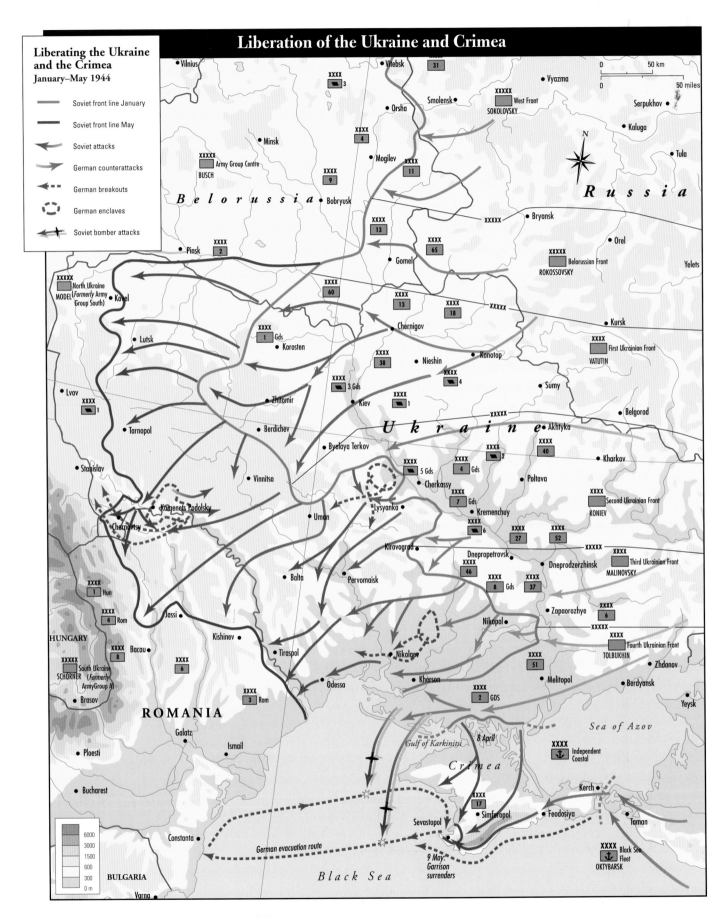

Liberation of the Ukraine and Crimea

Liberating the Ukraine and the Crimea
January–May 1944

- Soviet front line January
- Soviet front line May
- Soviet attacks
- German counterattacks
- German breakouts
- German enclaves
- Soviet bomber attacks

0   50 km
0   50 miles

• Vilnius
• Vitebsk
31
XXXX 3
• Orsha
Smolensk
• Vyazma
• Serpukhov
XXXXX West Front
SOKOLOVSKY
• Kaluga
• Minsk
XXXX 4
• Mogilev
XXXXX Army Group Centre
BUSCH
XXXX 11
XXXX 9
R u s s i a
• Tula
B e l o r u s s i a
• Bobryusk
XXXX 13
XXXXX
• Bryansk
• Orel
• Pinsk
XXXX 2
• Gomel
XXXX 65
XXXXX Belorussian Front
ROKOSSOVSKY
• Yelets
XXXXX North Ukraine
MODEL (Formerly Army Group South)
• Kovel
XXXX 60
XXXX 13
XXXX 18
XXXXX
• Kursk
• Chernigov
XXXX 1 Gds
• Lutsk
• Korosten
XXXX 38
• Nieshin
• Konotop
XXXX 4
XXXXX First Ukrainian Front
VATUTIN
• Lvov
XXXX 3 Gds
• Zhitomir
XXXX 1
• Kiev
• Sumy
XXXX 1
• Berdichev
• Belgorod
XXXX 1
• Tarnopol
U k r a i n e • Akhtyka
XXXXX
• Kharkov
• Byelaya Terkov
XXXX 2
XXXX 40
• Stanislav
XXXX 5 Gds
XXXX 4 Gds
• Cherkassy
• Poltava
XXXX 7 Gds
XXXXX Second Ukrainian Front
KONIEV
• Vinnitsa
• Lysyanka
• Kremenchuy
• Chernovtsy
Kamenets Podolsky
• Uman
XXXX 6
XXXX 27
XXXX 52
• Kirovograd
• Dnepropetrovsk
XXXXX
• Balta
• Pervomaisk
XXXX 46
• Dneprodzerzhinsk
XXXXX Third Ukrainian Front
MALINOVSKY
XXXX 1 Hun
XXXX 8 Gds
XXXX 37
XXXX 4 Rom
• Jassi
• Nikopol
• Zapaorozhye
XXXX 6
HUNGARY
• Kishinev
XXXX 8 Bacau
XXXXX South Ukraine
SCHÖRNER (Formerly ArmyGroup A)
XXXX 6
• Tiraspol
XXXX 51
XXXXX Fourth Ukrainian Front
TOLBUKHIN
• Zhdanov
• Brasov
ROMANIA
XXXX 3 Rom
• Odessa
• Kherson
• Melitopol
• Berdyansk
• Yeysk
• Galatz
XXXX 2 GDS
Sea of Azov
• Ismail
8 April
XXXX Independent Coastal
Gulf of Karkinitsi
C r i m e a
• Kerch
• Ploesti
XXXX 17
• Simferopol
• Feodosiya
• Bucharest
• Taman
Sevastopol
German evacuation route
9 May: Garrison surrenders
XXXX Black Sea Fleet
OKTYBARSK
• Constanta
Black Sea
BULGARIA
6000
3000
1500
600
300
0 m
• Varna

killed trying to cross the Gniloi Tikitsch river, which was in full spate as a result of the thaw. Despite this, some 30,000 German troops escaped out of the 50,000 trapped, but they were in little condition to be returned to the front line in the near future. Stalin's initial anger at the escape of so many Germans was alleviated when he noted the parallels with Alexander Nevsky's destruction of the Teutonic Knights in 1200.

Soviet momentum did not slacken, and on 4 March, a new attack forced the Germans back across the Dniestr. In the course of these operations, the last rail link connecting the German forces in Poland and those in the southern USSR was captured when Chernovsty fell into Russian hands. General Malinovsky's 3rd Ukrainian Front and General Tolbukhin's 4th Ukrainian Front then opened offensives of their own, each enjoying notable success. Malinovsky succeeded in recapturing Odessa, while Tolbukhin launched an attack from Sicash-Perekop. The Independent Primorsk Army joined in the assault from the Kerch peninsula, and left the German Seventeenth Army facing serious difficulties as it fought desperately to maintain its positions. This was a hopeless task. By 12 April, the Germans were withdrawing from the Crimean peninsula, with the Red Army in pursuit. Just four days later, the Germans had been driven back into Sevastopol, where they received strict instructions from Hitler that they were not to leave the Crimea.

Sevastopol was assaulted on 6 May. Although the Germans put up stiff resistance, it was abundantly clear that they would be unable to hold out. While it had taken the Germans no less than 250 days to take the city from the Russians, the Soviet high command made clear that it expected success rather more swiftly, and preferably in a matter of hours. Two days of bloody fighting marked the opening of the battle, but by noon on 7 May, the way into Sevastopol lay open. The Germans began to fall back towards the centre of the city, as Russian troops made probing attacks. By the evening of 9 May, Sevastopol was entirely in Soviet hands. Stalin demanded that the rest of the Crimea be cleared as soon as possible, and definitely within 24 hours, and his troops did not disappoint him. A massive Soviet assault forced the Germans back into the Kherson spit, a finger of land at the water's edge, from where they began an evacuation under heavy bombardment and air attack. The end followed swiftly, and by midday on 12 May, the remnants of the Seventeenth Army surrendered, some 25,000 men in all out of an army that had once been 110,000 strong.

Liberating Leningrad

While operations against the Crimea were under way, the Soviets set about dealing with the siege of Leningrad. The city had been besieged for nearly three years and raising the encirclement was a key goal for the Soviets. Although a corridor had been opened into the city in 1943, this was well within range of German artillery fire, and did not represent a permanent solution to Leningrad's suffering. In addition, Stalin was anxious to deal with the problem posed by the Finns, who were fighting as co-belligerents with the Germans, with the intention of overturning the peace treaty that had been signed after the bitter Winter War between the two nations. The early days of 1944 represented the ideal time for the Russians to focus on Leningrad, since the Germans were distracted by the disasters befalling them in the south, while Army Group North's attention was increasingly focused on the possibility of a Russian offensive in Belorussia.

As a result, General Govorov's Leningrad Front and General Meretskov's Volkhov Front were told to combine for offensive operations in the Novgorod-Luga sector,

Opposite: On 24 January 1944, the Soviets began their offensive to liberate the Ukraine, swiftly driving back the Germans. The speed of the advance left German forces trapped in the Korsun-Shevchenkovsky pocket, and their attempt to break-out was accompanied by massive casualties. The Crimea was little different. By 16 April 1944, German forces had been driven back to Sevastopol, which fell on 10 May. Under 40,000 of the 150,000 Germans originally holding the Crimea escaped.

Above: Russian troops in winter camouflage make their way past a Red Army light tank as they head towards German positions. 'General Winter' played a large part in saving the USSR in 1941, and winter conditions (snow, ice and the thaws that followed) played a major part in the fighting on the Eastern Front.

beginning on 14 January 1944. The attack was preceded by a raid by heavy bombers on German artillery at Bezzabotny overnight, then, at 09:35, an artillery bombardment against the German positions began. One hundred thousand shells were fired in a barrage lasting for an hour and five minutes. Second Shock Army moved forward as soon as the bombardment ended, gaining 3000 yards along a five-mile frontage, with some units reaching the German second line of defence.

Although the advance went reasonably well on the first day, it was hampered by mist, followed by the fall of snow in the Soviet Forty-Second Army's area. Forty-Second Army made progress, but this was slow. Govorov's chief of staff was sent to investigate, and found that the infantry were advancing without support from artillery or tanks, not least since the latter had become stuck in the snow. Nevertheless, the Russians continued to advance until by 19 January the Second Shock and Forty-Second Armies linked up near Ropsha. In the process of doing this, Russian troops captured the German heavy gun batteries that had been used to shell Leningrad, with over 100 of these weapons being taken.

The Germans managed to withdraw unmolested from around Mga on 20/21 January, much to Govorov's irritation, but it was quite clear that they would not be in a position where they could threaten Leningrad for much longer. By 20 January, the Soviet breakthrough had been completed, and the Russians moved into a pursuit phase, chasing the Germans as they pulled back. However, as at Mga, the pursuit was slow, not least because of tactical deficiencies on the part of formation commanders. Having been based in the Leningrad area for most of the war, these senior officers had not been exposed to the learning process that generals engaged in fighting elsewhere in the USSR had faced. As a result, the Leningrad operation was characterized by a penchant for using infantry for almost everything, while armoured and artillery units were left kicking their heels since they had no tasks assigned to them. By 23 January, Govorov could no longer stand the ineptitude being demonstrated, and issued orders making it clear that linear tactics were to be abandoned in favour of the use of firepower and manoeuvre. Commanders were to ensure that they conducted all-arms operations, employing the full weight of heavy weaponry available to them.

These instructions came a little too late, however, and the Germans were able to avoid encirclement. Nonetheless, Leningrad's encirclement was brought to an end on 26 January, when the Moscow–Leningrad railway line was cleared of all enemy troops and returned to Soviet control. The Germans continued fighting as they pulled back in good order as town after town fell to the Russians; once again, the slowness of the Soviet pursuit meant that the Germans were able to avoid disaster. However, despite this disappointment, the Russians had achieved their aim. By 30 January, German forces had been driven back between 50 and 60 miles. Operations continued into February, but shortages of ammunition for the artillery made the Russians' task rather more difficult than it might have been. While it was not until August that all German units were driven from the Leningrad region, the battle had been won by the end of January. The main objective, namely freeing the city, had been achieved, and most of the Leningrad and Kalinin districts had been cleared of German troops. Army Group North's hold on Russian territory was distinctly weaker than it had been, with many of its formations having taken a savage mauling.

Below: A long column of German prisoners is guarded by a young Soviet soldier armed with a PPSh sub-machine gun. German prisoners were subjected to a brutal and long captivity, with the last of the few survivors being released from Soviet camps in the mid-1950s.

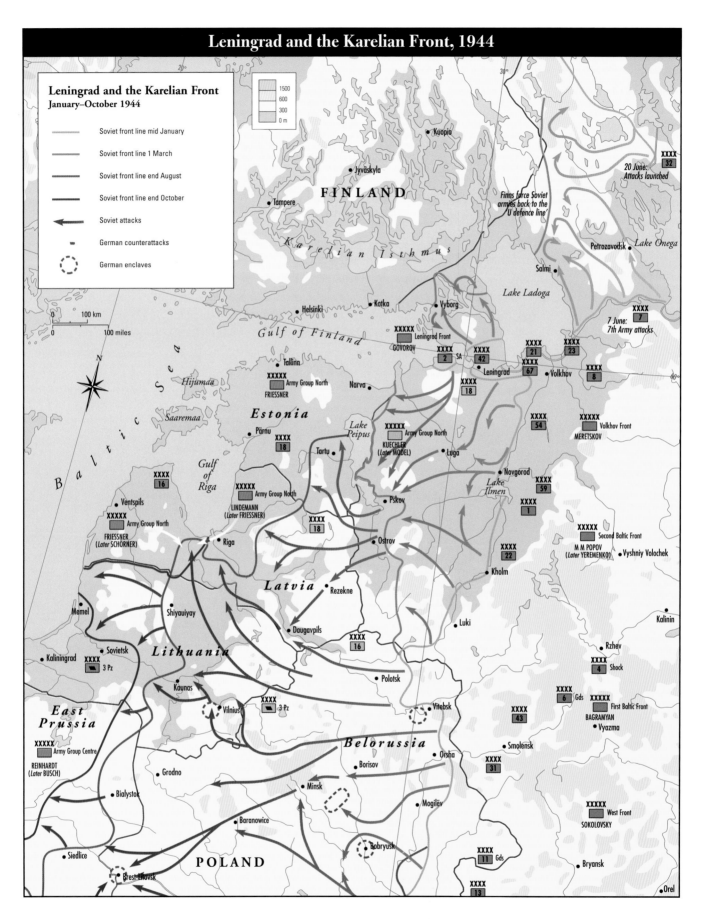

Leningrad and the Karelian Front, 1944

Leningrad and the Karelian Front
January–October 1944

Soviet front line mid January

Soviet front line 1 March

Soviet front line end August

Soviet front line end October

Soviet attacks

German counterattacks

German enclaves

1500
600
300
0 m

0   100 km
0   100 miles

FINLAND

Kuopio

Jyväskylä

Tampere

K a r e l i a n   I s t h m u s

Helsinki   *Kotka*   *Vyborg*

Finns force Soviet
armies back to the
'U defence line'

Lake Ladoga

Petrozavodsk   Lake Onega

Salmi

20 June:
Attacks launched
XXXX 32

7 June:
7th Army attacks
XXXX 7

Gulf of Finland

XXXXX Leningrad Front
GOVOROV

Tallinn

XXXX 2 SA   XXXX 42   Leningrad

XXXXX Army Group North
FRIESSNER

Narva

XXXX 18

XXXX 21   XXXX 23
XXXX 67   *Volkhov*
XXXX 8

Baltic Sea

Hijumaa

Saaremaa

Estonia

Pärnu

XXXX 18

Lake
Peipus

Tartu

XXXXX Army Group North
KUECHLER
(Later MODEL)

Luga

XXXX 54

XXXXX Volkhov Front
MERETSKOV

Novgorod

Lake
Ilmen

XXXX 59

XXXX 1

Gulf
of
Riga

XXXX 16

Ventspils

XXXXX Army Group North
LINDEMANN
(Later FRIESSNER)

XXXX 18

Pskov

Ostrov

XXXXX Second Baltic Front
M M POPOV
(Later YEREMENKO)   *Vyshniy Volochek*

XXXXX Army Group North
FRIESSNER
(Later SCHORNER)

Riga

Latvia   *Rezekne*

XXXX 22

Kholm

Luki

Kalinin

Memel

Shiyauiyay

Daugavpils

XXXX 16

Rzhev

XXXX 4 Shock

Kaliningrad   *Sovietsk*
XXXX 3 Pz

Lithuania

Kaunas

Vilnius

XXXX 3 Pz

Polotsk

Vitebsk

XXXX 6 Gds   XXXXX First Baltic Front
BAGRAMYAN

XXXX 43   *Vyazma*

East
Prussia

XXXXX Army Group Centre
REINHARDT
(Later BUSCH)

Grodno

Bialystok

Baranowice

Siedlice

Brest-Litovsk

POLAND

Belorussia

Borisov

Minsk

Mogilëv

Orsha

Smolensk

XXXX 31

XXXXX West Front
SOKOLOVSKY

XXXX 11 Gds

Bobryusk

XXXX 13

Bryansk

Orel

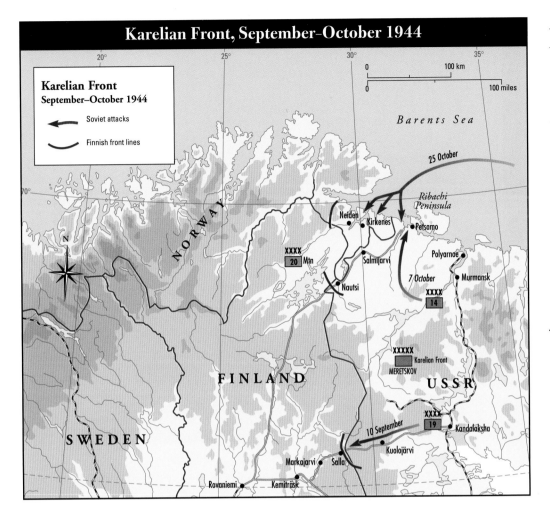

Karelian Front, September–October 1944

Karelian Front
September–October 1944

⟵ Soviet attacks

⌒ Finnish front lines

0 ————— 100 km
0 ————— 100 miles

20° 25° 30° 35°

Barents Sea

25 October

NORWAY

Neiden Kirkenes *Ribachi Peninsula* Petsamo

N

70°

XXXX 20 Mtn

Salmijarvi Polyarnoe

Nautsi 7 October Murmansk

XXXX 14

XXXXX Karelian Front MERETSKOV

FINLAND USSR

XXXX 19 Kandalaksha

10 September Kuolojärvi

SWEDEN Markajarvi Salla

Rovaniemi Kemiträsk

Left: Operations in the Karelian Isthmus were intended to bring the conflict with Finland to an end; outnumbered by Soviet forces that were far more adept than those who had been routed in the earlier Winter War between the two countries, it came as no surprise that the Finns had to fall back as the Russians retook territory that had been theirs until 1941. An armistice soon followed, allowing the Russians to focus upon driving the Germans out of the USSR completely.

All that remained was to remove Finnish forces from the territory that they had occupied since 1941. The Finns could see that the success against Army Group North rendered their position increasingly difficult, and they began to attempt to make contact with the Soviet government through diplomatic contacts. As it was, General Meretskov's Volkhov Front was disbanded in February 1944 as the operations around Leningrad developed, and he was instead given command of the Karelian Front. On 10 June Meretskov launched the Svir-Petrozavodsk offensive, while the Leningrad Front attacked the Karelian Isthmus near Vyborg. Operations lasted until 9 August, when the Finns were driven back to the line of the 1939 Finnish-Soviet border; aware that there was nothing more that they could do, the Finns sought peace, an armistice being signed on 4 September.

Operation Bagration

Even as the Spring 1944 offensives drew to a close, the Soviet high command had begun planning for the next offensive. An extensive analysis of the possible options was undertaken. An operation in the Balkans was considered, but swiftly rejected on the grounds that such an attack would overextend supply lines across difficult terrain, with possibly dangerous consequences. Other options were debated, until it was agreed that the best course of action would be an attack against Army Group Centre's positions in Belorussia, with the initial aim of recapturing Minsk. The offensive, codenamed

Opposite: On 14 January 1944, an offensive was launched to lift the siege of Leningrad. While the conduct of operations was not as skilful as seen in the offensives in the Ukraine and Crimea as a result of Soviet commanders in the area being unfamiliar with the latest tactical methods, the siege was lifted by the end of the month, although the last German units were not ejected from the Leningrad region until the summer of 1944.

Above: The corpses of three German soldiers lie in the gutter, while soldiers and civilians walk by without giving them a second glance. By the later stages of the war, the civilian population in Russia and Germany had come to regard death and destruction as being largely unremarkable, and three dead soldiers lying in the gutter was certainly not something particularly shocking.

Operation Bagration after a famed Russian commander of the nineteenth century, aimed to encircle the German army groups in the Minsk–Vitebsk–Rogachev triangle, and to completely destroy them.

The Soviets enjoyed overwhelming air superiority, which meant that their troops were able to operate with little threat of interference from the Luftwaffe. They also held a considerable advantage in manpower, for despite the massive losses sustained in the war so far, the Soviets had demonstrated an unerring ability to draw upon the population of the USSR to provide more men for the front line, a feat that the Germans were simply unable to match. The Russians had 19 all-arms and two tank armies totalling 1.4 million men, supported by 5200 tanks and assault guns and 31,000 artillery pieces and mortars. The Germans had 1.2 million men, but while their manpower was nearly equal to that of the Soviets, they had just 9500 artillery pieces, and around 900 tanks and assault guns.

The goal of destroying Army Group Centre was agreed at a conference on 22/23 May 1944, and to achieve this a breakthrough in six sectors was envisaged, with the three Belorussian fronts aiming for the first objective, Minsk.

The Germans gained some intimation of the forthcoming offensive as a result of signals intelligence that revealed that the Soviets had sent instructions to partisan groups that they should destroy as much of the German logistic system as possible in the area behind the battlefront, while air attacks on airfields and railway lines suggested that the Russians were on the verge of launching an assault.

Operation Bagration began on 23 June 1944, and within three days the 1st Belorussian Front had broken into the German positions around Bobruysk, while 3rd Belorussian Front had punched its way into Army Group Centre's defences between

Vitebsk and Orsha. The Russians drove forward remorselessly, encircling first German LIII Corps, then the German Fourth Army. In each case, it was clear that a timely withdrawal could save the German formations, but when permission to withdraw was sought, Hitler refused. He remained stubborn in the belief that defending to the last round was in some way preferable to safely evacuating the bulk of his forces so that they could be used again.

On other occasions, the *Führer*'s approval for a retreat only came when it was far too late to achieve anything. The Germans faced a series of disasters as a result. First, IX Corps was destroyed at Vitebsk, which it was only allowed to abandon long after the time for doing this had passed. Then 70,000 men of Ninth Army were trapped in the Bobruysk pocket. On 29 June the city was stormed and the remainder of the German forces there were wiped out. Their commander had been sacked two days earlier, and had been ordered to report to Germany. While this ensured that he was not captured, it meant that his men were left generally leaderless, and chaos ensued in the final stages of the battle.

This was not all. A Soviet breakthrough at Orsha left the German Fourth Army in a completely untenable position. This was obvious, yet once again Hitler issued strict orders that the army was forbidden to withdraw and should fight to the death. General Tippelskirch found this too much to bear and disobeyed his orders and withdrew.

Below: German troops prepare to leave their trench for an attack against nearby Red Army positions. The soldier in the background is carrying a rifle with bayonet fixed, suggesting that he is expecting to be involved in close-quarter fighting at some point. He also has a grenade at the ready.

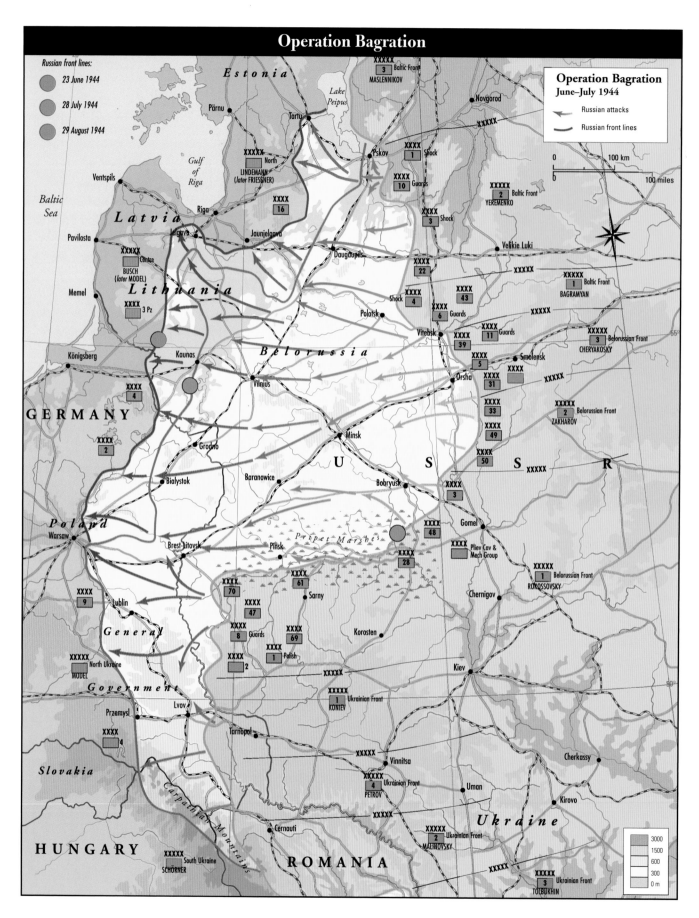

Operation Bagration

Russian front lines:
- 23 June 1944
- 28 July 1944
- 29 August 1944

Operation Bagration
June–July 1944

← Russian attacks
↖ Russian front lines

0   100 km
0   100 miles

Estonia

Pärnu
Lake Peipus
Novgorod
Tartu

XXXXX 3 Baltic Front
MASLENNIKOV

Gulf of Riga

Ventspils

Pskov
XXXX 1 Shock
XXXX 10 Guards

XXXXX 2 Baltic Front
YEREMENKO

Latvia

Riga
XXXX 16
Jaunjelgava
Jelgava
Daugavpils

XXXX 3 Shock

Velikie Luki

Baltic Sea

Pavilosta

XXXXX Centre
BUSCH (later MODEL)

XXXX 22

XXXXX 1 Baltic Front
BAGRAMYAN

Memel

Lithuania
XXXX 3 Pz

Shock XXXX 4
Polotsk

XXXX 43
XXXX 6 Guards

Belorussia

Vitebsk
XXXX 11 Guards
XXXX 39

XXXXX 3 Belorussian Front
CHERYAKOVSKY

Königsberg
Kaunas
Vilnius

Smolensk
Orsha
XXXX 5
XXXX 31

XXXX 4
XXXX 33

XXXXX 2 Belorussian Front
ZAKHAROV

GERMANY

XXXX 2
Grodno

Minsk

U   S   S   R

XXXX 49
XXXX 50

XXXX 3

Baranowice
Bobruysk

Pripet Marshes

XXXX 48
Gomel

XXXX Pliev Cav & Mech Group

XXXXX 1 Belorussian Front
ROKOSSOVSKY

Bialystok

Poland
Warsaw
Brest-Litovsk
Pinsk

XXXX 28

Chernigov

XXXX 70
XXXX 61
Sarny
Korosten

XXXX 9
Lublin

XXXX 47
XXXX 8 Guards
XXXX 69

Kiev

General

XXXX 1 Polish
XXXX 2

XXXXX

Government

XXXXX North Ukraine
MODEL

Lvov

XXXXX 1 Ukrainian Front
KONIEV

Przemysl
Tarnopol

Cherkassy

XXXX 4

Vinnitsa

Slovakia

XXXXX 4 Ukrainian Front
PETROV

Uman
Kirovo

Cernauti

Ukraine

HUNGARY

XXXXX South Ukraine
SCHÖRNER

ROMANIA

XXXXX 2 Ukrainian Front
MALINOVSKY

XXXXX 3 Ukrainian Front
TOLBUKHIN

3000
1500
600
300
0 m

Tippelskirch began a trend amongst German generals, by carefully fabricating situation reports, which, when examined closely, justified his actions to the high command. He completed the deception by forging sets of orders, one set of which was sent to Hitler to show that his orders were being followed to the letter, while the real orders given to his troops outlined the way in which they were going to pull back. Despite this subterfuge, by 30 June the bulk of Tippelskirch's forces were trapped to the east of the River Berezina, where they were killed or captured *en masse*.

It was clear that Army Group Centre would be destroyed without rapid withdrawals, but Hitler's only response seemed to be ludicrous orders preventing timely retreats, and to sack Field Marshal Busch as commander of the army group, even though it is hard to see exactly what more Busch could have done in the circumstances.

Army Group North endured an equally torrid time as the Soviets advanced. The Soviets succeeded in trapping the German forces around Minsk by 3 July, and set about destroying them. The city itself fell on 4 July, and some 43,000 Germans were killed in fierce fighting that followed over the next week as they tried to extricate themselves from a desperate situation. Having taken Minsk, the Russians pushed on into Lithuania, heading for Vilnius. They arrived there on 8 July, and encircled the city, although about half the garrison was able to escape before it fell five days later. Second Belorussian Front pushed on to within 50 miles of East Prussia, while 1st Belorussian punched its way into Poland and crossed the Vistula. Finally, after 68 days, Operation Bagration ended on 29

Above: A graphic piece of Soviet propaganda shows Hitler being crushed by the pincers of the Red Army. By 1944, this was an extremely accurate description of the German position in the East, yet Hitler seemed unable to see that he was facing disaster.

*Map, page 160:
Operation Bagration
began shortly after the
Allied invasion of
Normandy, with the
deliberate aim of
stretching the Germans to
breaking point. On 23
June 1944, the offensive
began, with four fronts
attacking the Germans in
the central sector of the
Russian front. By the end
of August, Soviet forces
were in the Baltic States,
Poland, and on the
borders of Romania.
Operation Bagration
marked the heaviest
German defeat of the
war. Nearly half a
million men had been
lost, and it would not be
long before the Red Army
entered Germany itself.*

August. Soviet forces had advanced between 340 and 375 miles along a 700-mile frontage, inflicting massive and near irreparable damage on Army Group Centre, and battering the other German formations that stood against the advance. The offensive placed the Soviets in an ideal position to advance on towards Germany itself.

The Advance to the Oder

The German position in the East became increasingly awkward, since from June 1944, Allied armies had been in France. After some hard fighting in June, July and early August, German resistance seemed to crumble momentarily, and the Allies were able to drive into the Low Countries. By September, they were in close proximity to the River Rhine, with the obvious implication that Germany would be invaded in the not too distant future. This meant that the situation everywhere was becoming dangerous for the Germans, but Hitler refused to see this. After surviving an assassination attempt on 20 July, the *Führer* had become convinced that some form of supernatural providence was protecting him; he also became even less trusting of his generals after a number of senior officers (including Rommel) were implicated in the plot.

As a result, by late 1944, Hitler's attention had turned from the Eastern Front to the West. He aimed to launch a daring (but over-optimistic) offensive in the Ardennes region, seeking to recreate the success of 1940. Hitler aimed to split the British and American forces from one another, and, by taking the port of Antwerp, place himself in a favourable position from which peace could be negotiated. This completely failed to appreciate the resolution of the Western Allies, but Hitler could not be dissuaded. Despite firm protestations from his generals, he refused to accept their observations that removing troops from the East to support the Ardennes operation left Germany vulnerable to another Soviet attack. Hitler dismissed these concerns with the assertion that the Soviets were not in a position to begin another offensive as they had been fighting

STURMOVIK

The most prolifically-produced aircraft of World War II was not a fighter or heavy bomber, but a robust and rather crude ground-attack aircraft, the Il-2 'Sturmovik' (armoured assault aircraft). The first aircraft were single-seaters, armed with a mix of cannon, machine guns, bombs and rockets, but they proved to be disappointing. Modifications were made, adding a second crew member with a machine gun to provide rear defence, while the wing-mounted 20mm (0.78in) cannons were replaced with high-velocity 23mm (0.9in) cannon instead. The new Sturmoviks began to enter service in 1942, and were a revelation. Their heavy armour meant that they were able to sustain a considerable battering from ground fire with little ill effect, and their success led to massive production output. Constant development saw even heavier cannon being added to later aircraft, along with more bombs or rockets. The Germans had little answer to the depredations of the Sturmoviks, and the aircraft proved extremely popular with both its crews and the ground forces that it supported. When production ended shortly after the war, no fewer than 36,183 Il-2s had been produced, more than any other aircraft before or since.

Left: Armourers load bombs onto a Red Air Force seaplane. In a practice common to air forces the world over, the bombs have been marked with a variety of pithy messages for the enemy, although these would not, of course, be seen unless the weapons failed to explode.

constantly for four months. In fact, the Ardennes offensive worked in favour of the Russians, just as the German generals feared. As they had pointed out, committing troops to operations in the West meant that they were not available to act as a reserve against a Russian attack. To deal with the developing crisis in Hungary, Hitler had been forced to denude the Vistula of forces to send them into the fray against the Russians there. This simply assisted the Soviets, who had, in fact, started planning for their 1945 offensives in October 1944, at about the time that Hitler had thought that all they would

Right: By the end of August 1944 as Operation Bagration came to an end, Soviet forces were in the Baltic States, Poland, and on the borders of Romania. 1st Belorussian Front punched its way into Poland and crossed the Vistula, leaving the Germans facing the clear threat of further advances through Poland. Bagration ended to allow the Soviets to regroup, thus giving the Germans the opportunity to crush the Warsaw Rising.

Opposite: The Polish Home Army's efforts to liberate Warsaw were ultimately thwarted by the lack of support provided from nearby Russian forces. Stalin's determination to ensure that the exiled government could not return to power meant that he was quite content to leave the Poles to their fate as the Germans sought to suppress the rising. When the fighting ended on 2 October, at least 75 per cent (perhaps over 90 per cent) of the city's buildings had been destroyed, while estimates of casualties range from between 150,000 and 200,000 Poles killed, along with some 17,000 Germans.

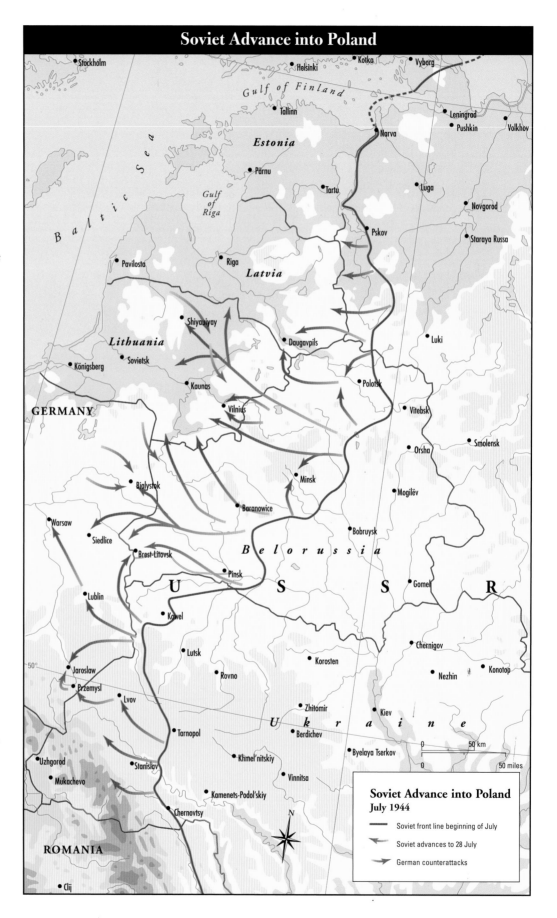

Soviet Advance into Poland

Soviet Advance into Poland
July 1944

— Soviet front line beginning of July

← Soviet advances to 28 July

→ German counterattacks

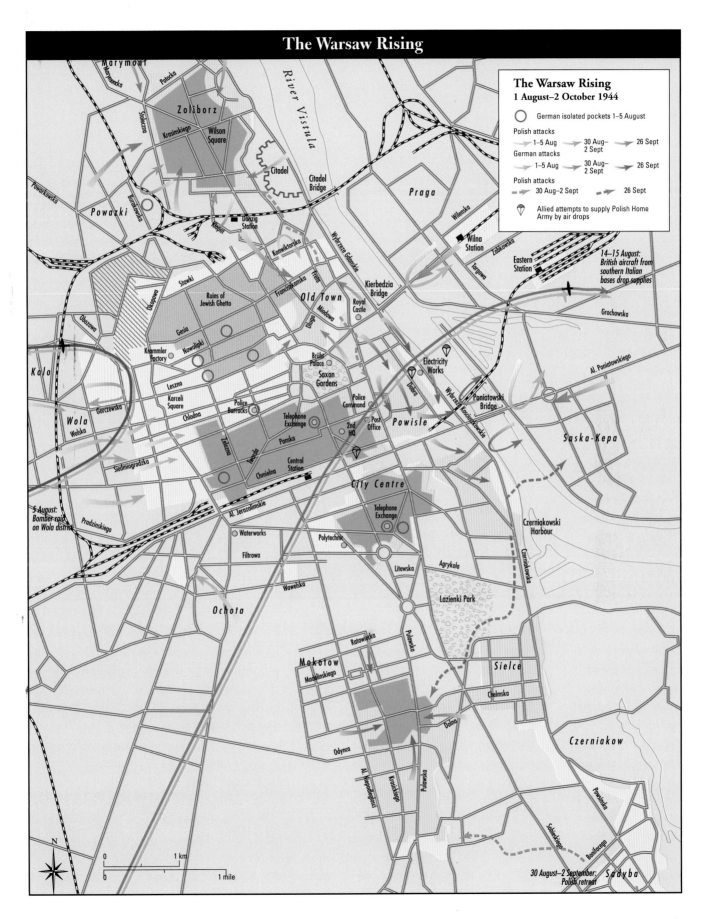

The Warsaw Rising

The Warsaw Rising
1 August–2 October 1944

○ German isolated pockets 1–5 August

Polish attacks
— 1–5 Aug
— 30 Aug–2 Sept
— 26 Sept

German attacks
— 1–5 Aug
— 30 Aug–2 Sept
— 26 Sept

Polish attacks
- - - 30 Aug–2 Sept
- - - 26 Sept

Allied attempts to supply Polish Home Army by air drops

Marymont

Zoliborz
Krasinskiego
Wilson Square

River Vistula

Citadel
Citadel Bridge

Praga

Witenska

Wilna Station

Eastern Station

Labkowska

Targowa

14–15 August:
British aircraft from southern Italian bases drop supplies

Powazki

Smolecza

Klopot

Donzig Station

Konwiktorska

Wybrzeze Gdanskie

Grochowska

Powarkowska

Burakowska

Stawki

Dkopowa

Ruins of Jewish Ghetto

Franciszkanska

Freta

Old Town

Dluga

Miodowa

Royal Castle

Kierbedzia Bridge

Obazowa

Gesia

Krammler Factory

Nowolipki

Leszno

Karceli Square

Police Barracks

Brühl Palace

Saxon Gardens

Police Command

Electricity Works

Al. Poniatowskiego

Kalo

Wola
Wolska

Gorczewska

Chlodna

Zelazna

Twarda

Panska

2nd HQ

Post Office

Dabra

Powisle

Wybrzeze Kosciuszkowskie

Paniatowski Bridge

Saska-Kepa

Siedmiogrodzka

Chmielna

Central Station

Telephone Exchange

City Centre

5 August:
Bomber raid on Wola district

Pradzinskiego

Al. Jerozolimskie

Telephone Exchange

Czerniakowska

Czerniakowski Harbour

Waterworks

Polytechnic

Litewska

Agrykola

Filtrowa

Wawelska

Lazienki Park

Ochota

Ratowiecka

Pulawska

Mokotow

Madelinskiego

Sielce

Chelmska

Dolna

Odynca

Al. Niepodleglosci

Krasickiego

Pulawska

Czerniakow

Powsinska

Sobieskiego

Bonifacego

30 August–2 September:
Polish retreat

Sadyba

N

0   1 km

0   1 mile

165

Above: A weary German soldier, armed with an StG 44 assault rifle, trudges westwards at some point during the fighting in 1944. Although the Germans were able to introduce new automatic rifles that provided troops with a significant increase in firepower, there were never enough to go around.

be looking to do would be to remain on the defensive for some months while they recovered from the losses they had sustained.

The Offensive

By early January, 2.2 million Russian troops had been assembled opposite the River Vistula, and contrary to Hitler's expectations were in a position to attack. In response to a request from Roosevelt and Churchill, Stalin brought the start date of the offensive forward eight days to 12 January 1945, so that his operations would assist with the final stages of what had now become known as the Battle of the Bulge as the British and Americans sought to defeat the Germans in the Ardennes. The offensive began at 04:30 in a blizzard, with a massive bombardment against German positions. German Fourth Panzer Army and its flank protection, Seventeenth Army, were pounded for 30 minutes, before the bombardment eased and Russian troops went forward. They penetrated the German lines to a depth of up to 2 miles in places before they were halted.

At 10:00, another massive bombardment, lasting for an hour and three-quarters, was laid down upon the German lines. Fourth Panzer Army's headquarters was blown to oblivion in the process, and the formation lost all ability to fight, collapsing into confusion as the Russians attacked. Some Germans remained in their trenches, literally unable to move, their will shattered by the massive bombardment. Others simply turned and ran in the face of the enemy attack. As a blizzard developed, the main bodies of the attacking Soviet formation drove forward, sweeping all before them. When Koniev received reports that his tanks had destroyed the 16th Panzer Division in its assembly area, he decided that it would be appropriate to commit his exploitation forces, a decision reinforced by more reports of a general German collapse.

The exploitation troops swiftly broke through the German lines, and by nightfall on 12 January 1945 had reached a depth of 14 miles along a 25-mile front. The next day, over 2000 Russian tanks charged across the icy countryside, cutting the lines of communication between Warsaw and Kraków. The Germans were forced to withdraw from Warsaw, leaving Kraków and Silesia as the next targets for the Russians.

Further north, Marshal Zhukhov had sent his troops into action on 14 January against the German Ninth Army. After making impressive initial gains, Zhukhov then sent his

First and Second Guards Tank Armies into the fray, punching their way into the centre of Ninth Army. The weight of assault was such that Ninth Army began to collapse, allowing Second Guards Tank Army to sweep to the northwest, to threaten Warsaw. On the night of 16 January, it became abundantly clear to the German high command that to remain in Warsaw would be suicidal; as a consequence orders were given that XLVI Panzer Corps should retire from the city. These instructions were given without reference to Hitler, who was apoplectic when he discovered that Warsaw had been given up without the fight to the death that he customarily demanded. Rather than deal with the immediate difficulties facing him, Hitler spent some time dismissing generals and imposing a rigid command structure upon them – every commander from divisional level upwards was instructed that they were to obtain approval for every move they made, on pain of death. This neatly undercut the ability of commanders to respond to events in a flexible and timely fashion just at the time when having the ability to do this was becoming of critical importance. While this reorganization was under way, Zhukhov sent the First Polish Army, a formation under his command, to retake Warsaw.

Kraków and Silesia

On 17 January, a new directive was sent to Marshal Koniev's 1st Ukrainian Front, ordering it to take Kraków and Silesia, as a precursor for an advance towards the German city of Breslau. Fifty-Ninth and Sixtieth Armies were employed for these tasks, with proceedings beginning with an advance on Kraków, Fifty-Ninth Army assaulting from the north and west, while Sixtieth Army came in from the east. The Germans, appreciating the weight of forces ranged against them, withdrew to avoid being encircled, and left the Soviets with the simple task of entering the city.

Below: An ISU-152 assault gun ploughs its way through a cornfield in the Ukraine. The relaxed attitude of the men on the top of the assault gun suggests that they are probably being given a familiarization ride, and are well away from the front line. The ISU-152's 152mm gun proved an extremely useful weapon in clearing German strongpoints, particularly in urban fighting.

Battle for Königsberg

German front line 5 April

German front line 8 April

German front line 9 April

German counter-attack

Soviet attacks

German defensive lines

Outer defences

First position

Second position

Third position

Right: As the Russians advenced through the Baltic States, they moved towards Königsberg, which they besieged after fierce fighting on the way to the city between 13 and 28 March 1945, at the end of which the German Fourth Army had all but ceased to exist. The German commander in Königsberg, General Otto Lasch, did his best to establish defensive lines, using the old nineteenth-century fortifications in the city as the basis of his positions but they were little match for the Soviet bombardment. The Germans were pushed back inexorably, and Lasch surrendered on 10 April 1945.

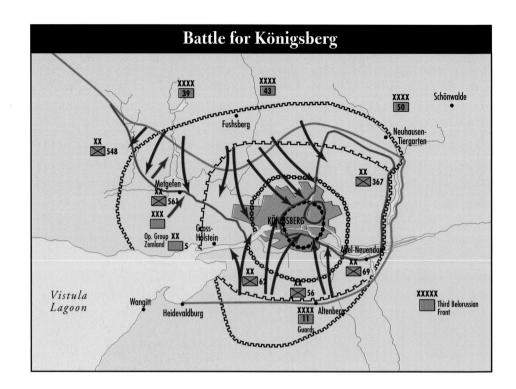

Silesia was a more difficult proposition, since it was heavily industrialized. As had been the case at Stalingrad, the nature of such an area, with large factories and urban areas, offered good defensive opportunities, but this time to the Germans. Painfully aware of this fact, Koniev decided that a slightly more innovative approach was required. He sent Third Guards Tank Army forward, and it crossed the German border on 20 January. It approached the River Oder, but when it reached the banks of the river, Koniev ordered it to turn through 90 degrees and drive along the right bank rather than cross. This technically awkward manoeuvre was conducted with aplomb, and succeeded in cracking the German defences. With Third Guards Tank Army approaching from the west, and the Fifty-Ninth and Sixtieth Armies coming from the east, it became obvious that encirclement was imminent. The decision was made for a retreat, and the Germans fell back towards the Carpathian mountains, leaving Silesia to the Russians.

Reaching the Oder

Zhukhov now issued orders for 1st Belorussian Front to drive on Poznan, the last major Polish city before the German border and the River Oder. As had been the case in Silesia, the decision to avoid urban areas was taken, and the Russians pursued the Germans across central Poland at speed. They then manoeuvred round the south side of Poznan itself on 26 January, a move that trapped 60,000 Germans there. Zhukhov then drove forward to the Oder, which Second Guards Tank Army and the forward elements of Fifth Shock Army reached on the last day of January. Units of Fifth Shock Army crossed the river and took the town of Kienitz in what was to be the last act of the offensive, which was halted on Stalin's orders on 2 February.

Stalin's decision was based on two practical reasons, both of which were eminently sensible. First, a thaw had set in, making it impossible to cross rivers until the water in them had gone down, something that would only happen in the spring. Hitler took the thaw as a sign of divine providence, and cheerfully predicted that his fortunes would

Advance to the Oder

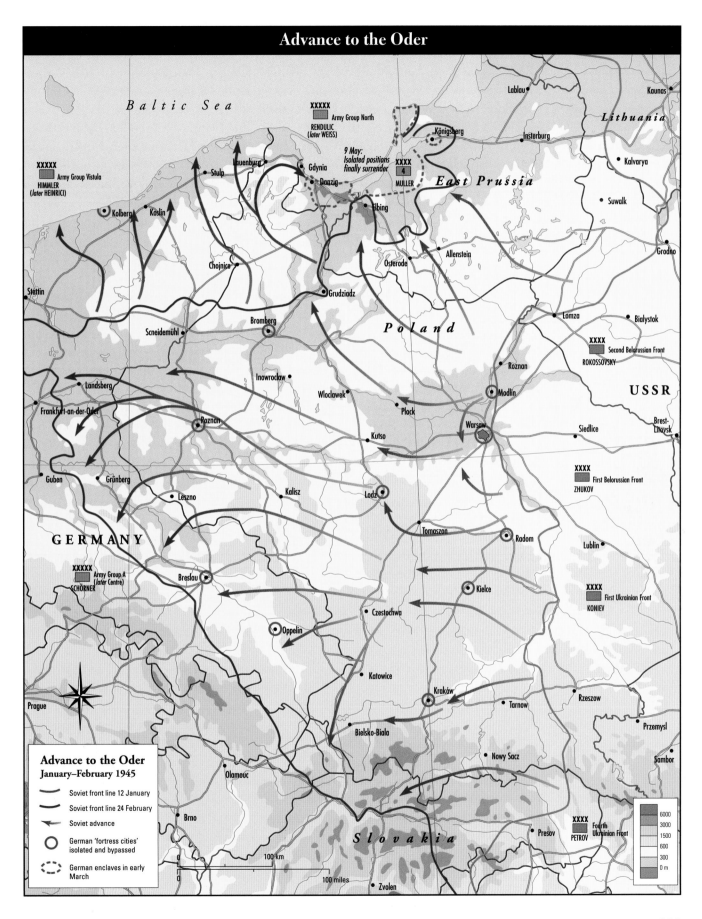

Advance to the Oder
January–February 1945

Soviet front line 12 January

Soviet front line 24 February

Soviet advance

German 'fortress cities' isolated and bypassed

German enclaves in early March

Map, page 169: The Vistula–Oder operation began on 12 January 1945. German forces crumbled in the face of a massive artillery bombardment, and withdrew from Warsaw as their position collapsed. Kraków and Silesia soon followed, and by the end of the month, the Russians were on the banks of the Oder. The advance was hugely successful, gaining over 300 miles in two weeks, and destroying Army Group Centre in the process.

soon change. Yet again, Hitler's tenuous grasp on the reality of the situation confronting him was evident – the prospect of the Germans recovering sufficiently to throw the Russians back was now non-existent. Stalin's second reason for calling a halt – again rooted in a pragmatism his opponent lacked – lay in his appreciation that his troops would need to have time to prepare for the assault against the final prize, namely Berlin itself. Unlike previous sanguinary operations, the Vistula–Oder offensive had been completed for what were relatively light casualties on the Eastern Front; 15,000 Soviet troops had been killed and four times that number wounded, but Army Group Centre had been annihilated – more importantly, Soviet forces were now within 50 miles of Berlin. The operations also saw the removal of the Germans from the Baltic States, for although they could have been left in place to wither on the vine, to have ignored them would have been dangerous.

The Baltic

The reason for this concern lay in the fact that the Germans still controlled the Baltic Sea, which allowed troops in the Baltic States to be resupplied quite easily. The possibility remained that a well-equipped force could be used to drive out from the Baltic into the Russian flank as the advance across the Oder was under way. Before any attack on Berlin could be undertaken, it was quite evident that the north flank of the advance needed to be cleared. Although the German bridgeheads at Memel and Courland were already in danger of being cut off, the Soviet high command could not take the chance.

On 13 January 1945, 3rd Belorussian Front began an attack towards Königsberg. The offensive did not go smoothly, since the Germans put up stiff resistance, leaving the attack in danger of stalling. Marshal Chernyakovsky redeployed his forces for another attempt, and broke through the German lines on 20 January, heading for Königsberg. Within a week, Russian forces had nearly surrounded the city. Their tanks almost made it into Königsberg, but the arrival of six German assault guns saved the position for the Germans, and the Soviet armour was driven back. Their chance to take the city in a swift attack gone, the Russians completed the encirclement of Königsberg on 29/30 January, and laid siege to the conurbation.

The German commander in Königsberg, General Otto Lasch, did his best to establish defensive lines, using the old nineteenth-century fortifications in the city as the basis of his positions. The outer line was based upon 12 massive forts built between 1874 and 1882, while the inner line relied upon a line of interior forts of similar vintage. Although well built, they were little match for the Soviet bombardment, and the city simply could not be held – relief was needed, and by the middle of February it was on its way. The siege was lifted on 19 February when the German 5th Panzer and 1st Infantry Divisions broke through Russian lines, joining with elements of XXVIII Corps attacking out of Samland. The result of this attack was the creation of a narrow corridor from the city to Pillau, which could be used for the evacuation of civilians. A lull in the fighting then followed, not least because Chernyakovsky was killed on the day that the siege was lifted, robbing the Russians of a commander for a short time. Chernyakovsky's replacement, General Vasilevsky, arrived with instructions to incorporate 1st Baltic Front into his new command. Installing himself in command and making the necessary arrangements to coordinate the forces now assigned to him took Vasilevsky a little time, but he was soon ready to resume the attack. General Lasch had used the lull in the fighting profitably, in an attempt to enhance the defences along city's line of fortifications but, as Lasch always knew, this was not going to be enough to hold the Soviets off. Lasch made clear to Hitler that he thought that an evacuation should begin, and was permitted to begin a limited evacuation of the city. Before this could be completed, the Soviets resumed their assault on 2 April. Eleventh Guards Army led the way, and by 6 April they had broken through the German lines. Two days later, they linked up with Forty-Third Army, cutting the last link between Königsberg and the rest of East Prussia. Lasch knew that the position was untenable, and surrendered on 10 April.

West Prussia

The final area of concern for the Russians lay in West Prussia, which also needed to be cleared to ensure that troops could not be employed in a flank attack on advancing Russian troops. Although 2nd Belorussian Front had made some progress in the area, the thaw had turned the ground into an impassable swamp, forcing Marshal Rokossovsky to call off the attack on 19 February 1945. The Soviets could not allow the Germans to remain in West Prussia, in a position to interfere with the advance on Berlin, so it was necessary for the offensive to resume. At the start of March 1945, 1st and 2nd Belorussian Fronts attacked again. The attack cut the railway to the east of Koeslin, denying communications to German Second Army, and then pushed onwards to Danzig and Gdynia, the main supply bases for Königsberg and Courland, a factor that made the defence of both areas even more difficult, and which contributed to the events in the Baltic States described above. The Soviets advanced inexorably, and by the middle of March, the Germans were reduced to holding small enclaves in West Prussia. By 18 March, Kolberg fell, followed 10 days later by Gdynia and then, on 30 March, Danzig.

At the end of March 1945, therefore, the Russians had placed themselves in position for the final push on Berlin, in the knowledge that although Berlin would be their prize, the Germans would face not only the might of the Red Army, but that of the Anglo-American forces now moving to the west of the German capital.

Below: T-34/85 tanks in woodland near Berlin wait to begin their advance. The T-34/85 was heavier and slower than earlier models of the tank, but its 85mm gun made it a match for almost all German armoured vehicles.

The Fall Of The Reich

By early 1945, the Third Reich was in a desperate state. The Ardennes offensive had failed to achieve the goals set for it by Hitler, and the Allies had resumed their approach to Germany itself. On the Eastern Front, the Red Army was sweeping all before it, and the best that German forces appeared capable of doing was to delay the advances rather than halt them.

In Italy, the German position was slightly better, but within a matter of weeks, the Allies had renewed their offensive and it was clear that it would be only a matter of time before the German position there gave way. The situation in the Balkans had collapsed, and German troops had been forced out of Greece, Yugoslavia, Hungary and Romania. The war at sea was lost, and although the Luftwaffe was still able to fly in defence of the Reich, Allied bomber formations could attack anywhere in Germany at will, bombing round the clock and supported by large fighter escorts in the daylight hours that prevented a meaningful defence against air attack. Despite all of this, Hitler remained optimistic to the last. Only when the battle reached the last remaining part of the Third Reich, its capital Berlin, did the *Führer* finally accept that his dream of a great Nazi Germany that would last for 1000 years was over. Before this situation was reached, however, there was still a great deal of fighting to be done.

The War in the West
After the shock caused by the Ardennes offensive had begun to wear off, the Allies made plans for crossing the Rhine and entering Germany itself. The Rhine provided a natural defensive feature for the Germans, and was bolstered by the West Wall, which had to be overcome before the advance into Germany could begin. To compound these challenges the appalling weather of early 1945 meant that much of the low-lying ground near the river was underwater, making forward movement utterly impractical. This situation did at least provide the Allies with time to refine their plans.

Eisenhower's scheme for crossing the Rhine involved two phases. In the first phase, Operation Veritable, Montgomery's 21st Army Group would clear the approaches to the Rhine opposite Wesel. XXX Corps was to advance from its positions in Nijmegen to the

Opposite: US and Soviet troops celebrate the link-up made between the two armies at Torgau on 25 April 1945. Relations between the two sides were soon to deteriorate, and for the next 45 years, the former allies would face each other in a tense stand-off in Germany.

Above: American anti-aircraft guns watch over the bridge at Remagen, the first Rhine crossing taken by the Allies. The weapons are quadruple Browning 0.5-inch machine guns, mounted on the rear of an M3 halftrack.

Reichswald. This was to be followed by Operation Grenade, in which Lieutenant-General William H. Simpson's US Ninth Army would push through Mönchengladbach and link up with the rest of Montgomery's forces. They would then pause to consolidate prior to the next phase of the operation. Once this was completed, 21st Army Group would then prepare to cross the Rhine, with the aim of outflanking the Ruhr from the north. Once this was completed, the army group would drive onto the North German plain. The plain offered excellent terrain for armour, and if the preceding operations succeeded, Montgomery would then be in a position to move on towards Berlin.

In the American sector, to Montgomery's south, General Bradley's 12th Army Group would carry out Operation Lumberjack. This would begin with an advance to clear the

approaches to the Rhine between Cologne and Koblenz. Patton's Third Army would head for Mainz and Mannheim, where it would link up with the US forces advancing from the Saarland as part of 6th Army Group's Operation Undertone. When all these aspects of the plan were complete, bridgeheads over the Rhine would be established.

Eisenhower's intention was that these bridgeheads would divert German attention away from Montgomery's attacks, but this was not at all popular with Bradley and Patton. They argued that American forces should play a much larger role, and that they felt that Eisenhower's plan as it stood was not acceptable. It may have been the case that had Montgomery not so irritated the American commanders with such consistency since 1942, the complaints from Patton and Bradley would not have been so uncompromising,

Opposite: Eisenhower's plan for crossing the Rhine involved two phases of operations. The first would see Montgomery's 21st Army Group clearing the approaches to the Rhine opposite Wesel, leaving him in a position to move on towards Berlin. Bradley's 12th Army Group would advance to the south of Montgomery, clearing the approaches to the Rhine between Cologne and Koblenz. Patton's Third Army would swing towards Mainz and Mannheim, linking up with the US forces advancing from the Saarland. Once this was achieved, bridgeheads across the Rhine would be established.

but as it was, Eisenhower could simply not ignore the strength of feeling. There would be no alteration to the first part of the plan, but Eisenhower decided that he would revisit his notions of allowing Montgomery to make the main Allied thrust once across the Rhine when the goals of the first phase had been achieved.

All of these plans were contingent on breaching the West Wall and traversing the difficult ground in front of the River Ruhr, which the Germans could flood if they wished by opening the dams. The possibility of movement being denied by flooding meant that the coordination of the four operations could not be guaranteed.

Operations Vertiable and Grenade

In keeping with his reputation, Montgomery's plans for Veritable and Grenade were drawn up in a thorough and methodical fashion, with almost every detail seemingly covered in the process. This was entirely appropriate for the circumstances, since the obstacles to success were formidable. The defences opposite the British were well prepared, and manned by 12,000 men. The defenders enjoyed the benefit of being on high ground, while the attackers would be forced by the waterlogged conditions in much of the region to use a series of narrow roads through the Reichswald, densely forested and difficult to fight through if properly defended.

At 05:00 on 8 February, First Canadian Army made the opening moves in Operation Veritable. A two-and-a-half hour bombardment opened proceedings. When it stopped, the Germans returned fire, and the British guns resumed the barrage, this time against the enemy positions, raining down high explosives for another three hours. Once this massive opening bombardment was over, the infantry at last moved forward.

The sodden ground made their advance difficult, and the troops were forced to advance with little in the way of artillery or air support. The advance was far slower than expected, and it took until the last week of February until all objectives were obtained, instead of the three or four days originally planned for. The Germans had also taken the opportunity to destroy all the bridges over the Rhine, and open the gates to the Ruhr dam. This prevented the launch of Operation Grenade until the waters had subsided. The operation had to be postponed until 23 February, but when the advance started Ninth Army found that the opposition was relatively weak. A link with Anglo-Canadian forces was made at Geldorn on 3 March, leaving the approaches to the Rhine from Nijmegen and Düsseldorf clear of German forces. Montgomery could now turn his attention to crossing the Rhine, which he planned to do on 23 and 24 March.

As the Germans had destroyed the bridges over the Rhine, 21st Army Group faced the problem that it would have to negotiate the Rhine via an assault crossing, rather than using bridges.

THE BUFFALO LVT

One of the key tools for crossing the Rhine was the LVT (Landing Vehicle Tracked), essentially a tracked armoured box that could 'swim' to the shore and then drive out of the water and serve as an armoured personnel carrier and supply vehicle. The LVT was known as the Buffalo in British service, and these were used with great success to cross the Rhine. The Buffaloes had a crew of three, and could carry a section of seven men.

The vehicles were equipped with a variety of weapons, and many of the Buffaloes used for the Rhine crossing were fitted with 20mm cannon in addition to their more usual machine guns, with the aim of suppressing German positions on the opposite bank should the need arise.

The American Sector

While Montgomery's troops were encountering difficulties in their operations, Bradley's attack went far more smoothly. The Germans had been forced to redeploy a significant number of units to defend against Montgomery's attack, which made the opening stages of the American advance a simpler proposition than they might have been (although to interpret this as meaning that the American advance was ludicrously easy would be grossly inaccurate). Cologne fell into American hands during the course of 6 March, German resistance being destroyed by all-arms operations. Other elements of First Army headed for Bonn, while the 9th Armoured Division made the link with Patton's forces at Sinzig. Late on 6 March, the division reached Meckenheim. To protect the division as it moved down the Ahr river valley, Combat Command B was instructed to close the Rhine at Remagen. To the astonishment of the first Americans to reach Remagen, the bridge across the Rhine was still intact.

The Americans crossed the bridge and reached the east bank of the Rhine at 16:00 on 7 March. News of the crossing spread quickly, and Eisenhower ordered that the success should be exploited immediately, even though sending forces over the Rhine at Remagen would demand that the plan for operations be recast. In fact, Eisenhower did not switch the weight of the Allied attack away from Montgomery as a result of the capture of the bridge, since the terrain around Remagen meant that the opportunities for a breakthrough would be limited. Patton's Third Army completed its part in Operation Lumberjack by ensuring that the Rhine was

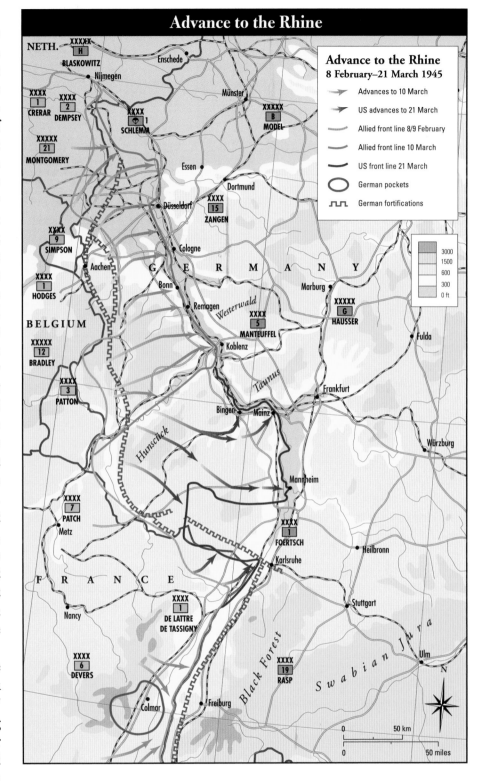

Advance to the Rhine
8 February–21 March 1945

Above: An American soldier guards members of the Hitler Youth who surrendered near Martinzelli. While the Western Allies tended to treat the Hitler Youth as children fighting because they had no choice or were misguided rather than because they were ardent Nazis, the Soviets made no such distinctions, and treated Hitler Youth members as ruthlessly as adult soldiers.

secured as far as Koblenz, but Patton was not finished. The success of First Army at Remagen irritated Patton, and he ordered that his men should cross the river by boat on 22 March. The 11th Infantry Regiment completed the task, allowing Patton to issue a barbed press release proclaiming his success and attempting to belittle Montgomery by noting that the Americans had not required aerial bombardment, artillery, the use of smoke or airborne attacks but failing to mention that the reason for this was because the opposition at the crossing point – Nierstein – had been negligible.

The British Cross the Rhine

Montgomery ignored Patton's remarks, and continued to put the finishing touches to his plan to cross the Rhine, Operation Plunder. The assault was to take place on the night of 23/24 March, preceded by a massive preparatory bombardment, to which air attacks would be added. Montgomery's caution was justified, since the Germans were expecting the attack to be launched by 21st Army Group, and a set-piece attack was the only option open to Montgomery, rather than the opportunistic use of infantry in boats that Patton had been able to exploit.

A dense smokescreen was put across the river, and at 18:00 on 23 March, over 5000 guns bombarded the opposite bank of the Rhine and beyond. The assault troops moved down to the river bank and boarded the variety of landing craft and amphibious assault vehicles that would take them across, joined by the famed Sherman DD (Duplex Drive) swimming tanks that had gained their reputation 'swimming' ashore on D-Day.

The sheer weight of fire and preponderance of numbers Montgomery had so carefully built up in preparation for the crossing told. The British gained a foothold, and waited for a pre-arranged bomber attack on Wesel before they moved forward into the town. Over 200 bombers attacked at 22:30, and the raid completed the town's destruction. Then 1st Commando Brigade moved into Wesel and brought the town under control after a sharp fight. By dawn on 24 March, it was clear that the crossings had been a major success, with five bridgeheads being established.

The momentum of the attack was then maintained by Operation Varsity, a large airborne assault by US 17th and British 6th Airborne Divisions. The airborne troops were to consolidate the ground already taken, enabling the depth of the bridgehead to be increased swiftly. The operation was launched in daylight to take advantage of air supremacy, and unlike the drop at Arnhem, all the troops were to be landed in one lift. They were also scheduled to be landed almost on top of their objectives and within range of friendly artillery (again unlike Market Garden). The landings started at 10:00 on 24 March, but there were problems. Some of the paratroops were dropped in the wrong place, and gliders were released at the wrong time. This meant that the Germans were able to inflict casualties on the airborne troops and their aircraft, with over 100 gliders and aeroplanes being destroyed. Despite the casualties, the paratroops took their objectives, and the operation was a considerable success. The village of Hamminkeln was taken along with the three bridges over the River Issel. By the end of the day, 21st Army Group had secured its position on the other side of the Rhine, and the stage was now set for the break-out.

The Final Stages in the West

At this point, Eisenhower changed his strategy, partly in light of the concerns expressed by Bradley and Patton, but also because of the changed strategic situation which meant that Berlin was no longer the goal for the Western Allies. As Montgomery started planning his advance across the North German plain towards the capital, Eisenhower changed the focus of operations towards 12th Army Group, which would attack around the Elbe and Mulde rivers, with the aim of cutting the German Army in two before linking with the Red Army. Twenty-first Army Group would move towards the Baltic coast with the aim of reaching it before the Russians, clearing Holland, seizing the north German ports and cutting off Denmark as they went. To the south of 12th Army Group, the US Sixth Army was to drive into Austria and defeat German forces remaining there.

In accordance with the new plan, the British Second Army broke out of its bridgehead on 28 March, crossed the Weser River and, despite some spirited German resistance around Hanover, gained 200 miles in three weeks. By 18 April on 21st Army Group's front, I Corps had reached the Zuider Zee, XII Corps was well on the way to Hamburg, XXX Corps had reached Bremen and VIII Corps had taken Lüneburg and was closing in on the Elbe river. Meanwhile, 12th Army Group encircled the Ruhr, and began mopping up the German forces there. US Ninth and First Armies met at Lippstadt on 1 April, and by 12 April the Americans were in Essen, the Germans totally unable to counter the advance.

German troops were now surrendering in large numbers to the extent that the Allies were having serious difficulties in processing them all. Organized resistance in the West had collapsed totally in the American sector, and the British began to encounter the same phenomenon.

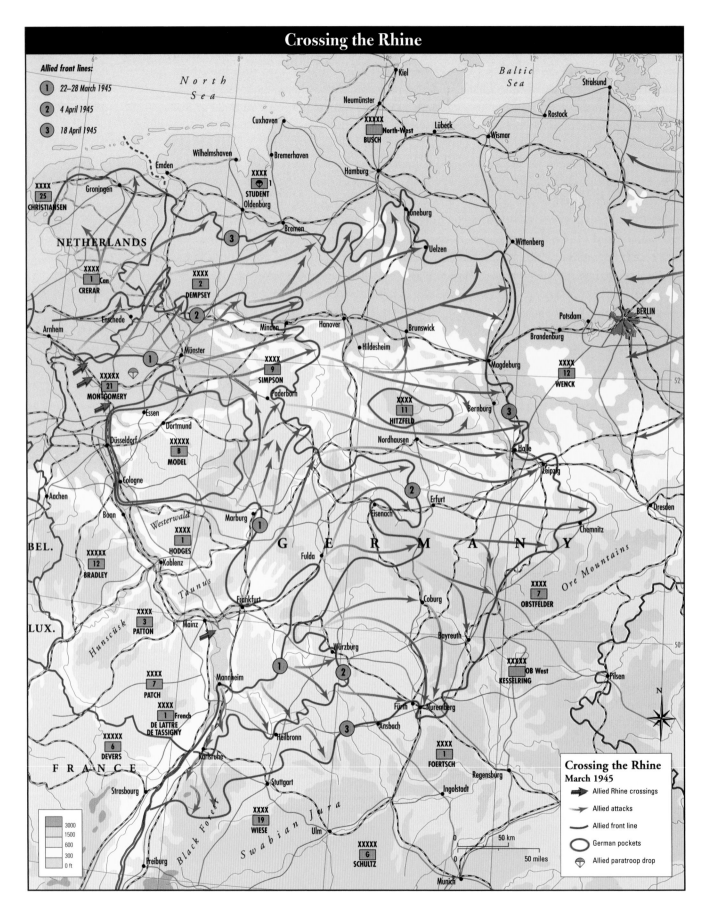

Crossing the Rhine

Allied front lines:
- **1** 22–28 March 1945
- **2** 4 April 1945
- **3** 18 April 1945

Crossing the Rhine
March 1945

- ➤ Allied Rhine crossings
- → Allied attacks
- — Allied front line
- ◯ German pockets
- ⛟ Allied paratroop drop

Twenty-first Army Group moved into the Netherlands and on towards the Baltic coast, meeting little in the way of organized opposition as it went. By 18 April 1945, the army group was on the outskirts of Bremen, and closing in on Hamburg. To their south, the only serious opposition came from the Germans defending against US Seventh and French First Armies around Würzburg and Karlsruhe respectively; even this was not enough to seriously delay the advance. By 18 April, the Western Front did not have far to advance before the final defeat of Germany would be achieved. Attention now turned to the East, where the Russians had closed in on Berlin.

The Russian Advance to Berlin

By March 1945, it was quite clear that the advancing Red Army would shortly be turning Berlin into a battleground. Hitler issued orders for the defence of the capital, but these were characterized by a great deal of ideological rhetoric and exhortations to the German people, and lacking in the precise details of what exactly was required to defend the city. To make matters worse, Hitler's overwhelming confidence that everything would eventually turn in Germany's favour meant that efforts to turn Berlin into a fortress had not been fully implemented, since the pressure to do this had been lacking. One of the key features of the battle for Berlin was that the solid defensive positions that might have been expected were notable by their absence in many parts of the city.

Despite these problems, a plan for defending Berlin was completed by the second week of April, but the reality of the German situation was clear. No matter where the German high command looked, its units were short of ammunition. The artillery units were the most seriously affected by this situation. Movement was hampered by a shortage of fuel, which in turn meant that the mobility offered by German armour was lacking, since the tanks could not move. Supplies could not be transported because there were no vehicles to move them; and the *Luftwaffe* was all but gone, grounded by lack of gasoline for its remaining aircraft. Finally, while the Berlin garrison was a million strong, a figure that encouraged Hitler, many of the soldiers defending the city were boys beneath military age, or men who had been too old or unfit to serve with the Army before. Many lacked anything other than rudimentary training, with only those who had fought between 1914 and 1918 having experienced anything like a proper programme of instruction. All, though, were determined to defend against the Russians, the stories of the treatment meted out to German civilians by Soviet troops in areas already under their control being prominent in their thinking.

Hitler had moved to the fortified bunker underneath the Chancellery building, continuing to make over-optimistic plans to throw the Russians back. His spirits rose greatly on 12 April when news arrived that President Roosevelt had died. Ever one to see omens in events, Hitler took this as a positive sign, excitedly suggesting that this was the opportunity that he had been waiting for. He might negotiate a favourable armistice now that one of the leading proponents of unconditional surrender was dead. Over the next two days, Hitler began to think that success could still be achieved when news came that German troops had inflicted a serious reverse upon American bridgeheads over the River Elbe.

This was all illusory – neither the death of their president nor a tactical setback were going to dissuade the Americans from prosecuting the war to a finish. It was most improbable that Roosevelt would have appointed a vice-president who did not agree with the policy of forcing total surrender, while neither Stalin nor Churchill were likely

Opposite: Although the capture of the bridge at Remagen provided the first crossing point, the first concerted effort to move across the river began on 22 March, when troops from Patton's army crossed the river at Nierstein and Oppenheim. Operation Plunder, Montgomery's plan for the British crossing of the Rhine, began on 23 March, and was a notable success. By 25 March, 21st Army Group had gained a firm base on the east bank of the Rhine, consolidating the position three days later. With both British and Americans across the Rhine, attention turned to the final phases of the war.

Above: A Soviet 152mm howitzer crew prepare to engage targets near the Reichstag in late April 1945. The Soviets made considerable use of their artillery to blast the Germans out of their positions, firing over open sights at targets only a few hundred yards away; the effect of the shells was devastating.

to suddenly change their position either. More importantly, speculating on gaining a peace settlement in the West ignored the fact that the Soviet armies were very near to beginning their attack, which would hardly help negotiations even if the Western Allies intended to assist Hitler in realizing his flight of fancy. The Soviets had carried out a massive build-up since February, undertaking the largest and most complex redeployment of forces in history so that they were in the most favourable position to assault the enemy capital. Over 2.5 million men, 6000 tanks and armoured fighting vehicles and 45,000 guns and rocket launchers, along with supplies ranging from food to artillery shells, were moved into place by mid-April.

On 16 April, the attack on Berlin began. The Soviet plan was brutally simple – a number of attacks along a wide front would be launched, with the intention of encircling the German forces before destroying them. Zhukhov's 1st Belorussian Front would attack from its positions near Küstrin on the west bank of the Oder, and head direct for Berlin. Koniev would use his 1st Ukranian Front to cross the Neisse and would then attack the southwest of the enemy capital. Rokossovsky and 2nd Belorussian Front, meanwhile, would attack in the area around Stettin to ensure that Third Panzer Army could not be used to reinforce the beleaguered German defenders in Berlin. This plan irritated Koniev considerably. His rivalry with Zhukhov was intense, and he was extremely jealous that he would not have the opportunity to take Berlin, even if it seemed obvious that the task should fall to Stalin's nominated deputy commander. This apparently trivial case of ego was to be of some importance in the battle that followed, but was exploited to telling effect by Stalin as he urged his subordinates on towards the capture of the enemy capital.

At 03:00 on 16 April, Zhukhov's forces attacked, aiming to take the Seelow Heights. An enormous bombardment put down one million shells on the German positions, and was accompanied by a heavy bombing raid. In the Vistula–Oder operation, such massive firepower had subdued the enemy to the point of near passivity, but this was not the case now, since many of the Germans were fighting to protect their homes and families in the face of an enemy whose reputation for treating civilians in a proper fashion was not high. Zhukhov's forces did not break through that day, but Koniev enjoyed some success. After a second day of fighting in which Koniev made more gains, Stalin told Zhukhov that he

Map, page 184: Although Berlin was the main objective of the Soviet operation, consideration had to be given to defeating all of Germany, which meant linking with the Western Allies. The British and Americans drove towards the River Elbe, while the Russians carried out several manoeuvres to encircle Berlin and move beyond it to join their allies. Caught between the two sides, the German Army stood little chance. The first meeting of American and Russian troops occurred at Torgau on the Elbe, and it was not long before only small pockets of enemy resistance remained.

Left: A Soviet soldier equipped with a PPSh 43 sub-machine gun makes his way forward, demonstrating for the camera the way in which he would move in an urban area.

Encirclement of Berlin

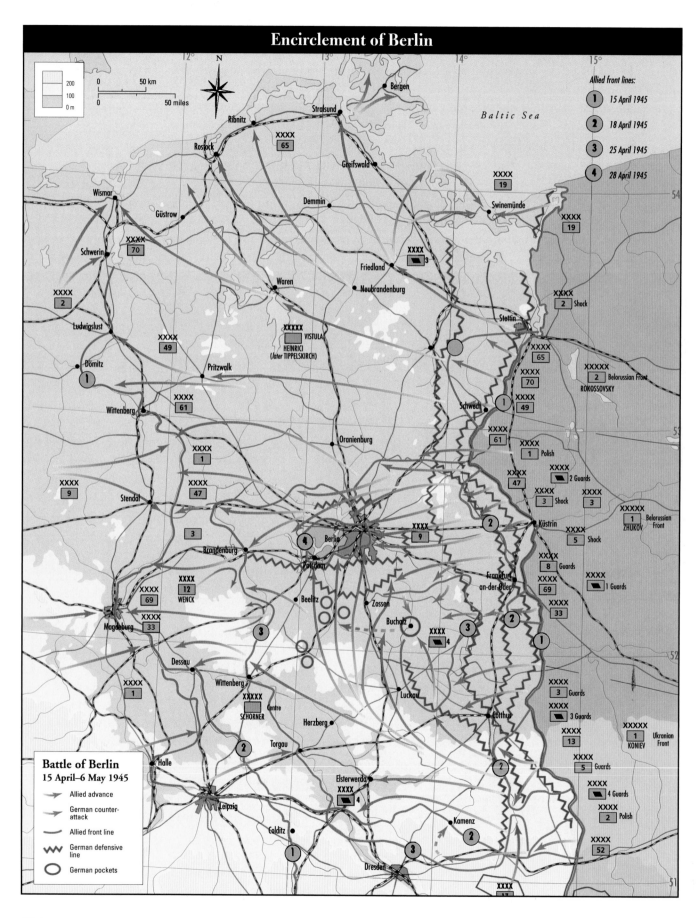

Allied front lines:
1. 15 April 1945
2. 18 April 1945
3. 25 April 1945
4. 28 April 1945

Baltic Sea

Battle of Berlin
15 April–6 May 1945

→ Allied advance

→ German counter-attack

— Allied front line

ᗱᗳᗱᗳ German defensive line

◯ German pockets

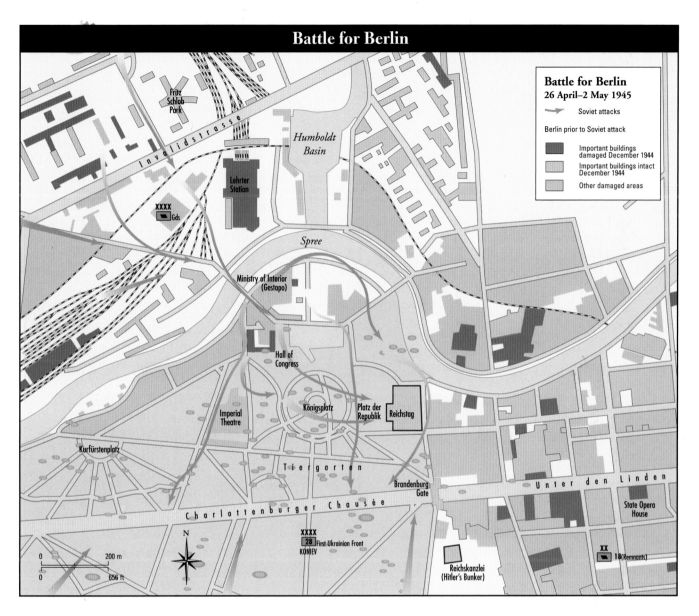

Battle for Berlin

Fritz Schlob Park

Humboldt Basin

Invalidstrasse

Lehrter Station

XXXX Gds

Spree

Ministry of Interior (Gestapo)

Hall of Congress

Königsplatz

Platz der Republik

Reichstag

Imperial Theatre

Kurfürstenplatz

T i e r g a r t e n

Brandenburg Gate

U n t e r d e n L i n d e n

State Opera House

Charlottenburger Chaussée

XXXX 28 First Ukrainian Front KONIEV

XX 18 (Remnants)

Reichskanzlei (Hitler's Bunker)

N

0   200 m
0   656 ft

Battle for Berlin
26 April–2 May 1945

Soviet attacks

Berlin prior to Soviet attack

Important buildings damaged December 1944

Important buildings intact December 1944

Other damaged areas

might allow 1st Ukrainian Front to seize Berlin if he could not capture the Seelow Heights.

This threat energized Zhukhov, who could not bear the thought of being denied the final victory. He set about encouraging, cajoling and threatening his subordinates, making clear to some of them that failure would result in them being stripped of their rank and privileges and sent to join the first wave of the next Soviet assault. Although little progress was made on 18 April, the pressure on the German lines began to tell, and Zhukhov broke through the next day, without having to demote any of his generals.

On 21 April, Zhukhov's Third and Fifth Shock Armies entered the suburbs of Berlin, and then advanced towards the centre. Koniev's troops reached the Tetlow canal by the end of 22 April, and began to push towards Zhukhov's forces. On 24 April, 1st Ukrainian and 1st Belorussian Fronts met on the River Havel, encircling Berlin in the process. The Russians now began a methodical, street-by-street battle, using tanks and artillery to blast through German positions. The Germans were pushed ever further back, their defensive position contracting almost hourly.

Above: After holding Russian forces outside Berlin for some days, the weight of attack told against the Germans. Gaps started to appear in their lines on 18 April, and the next day, a breakthrough was made. The upper floors of the Reichstag were taken on 30 April, but fighting in the cellars continued until, on 2 May, the garrison surrendered.

Above: German prisoners are marched down an autobahn near Giesen, as American tanks roll past them on their way to the front. By late April 1945, German units were surrendering en masse to the British and Americans, aware that the war was all but over, and that there was little point in fighting on.

By 27 April the Germans were left in a small corridor about 10 miles long and no more than three miles wide. The defensive perimeter was fractured on 28 April, and the last pockets of resistance were reduced to fighting isolated skirmishes with the Russians, still fighting with a determination that belied the hopelessness of their position. Two days later, Hitler committed suicide. The Reichstag itself was taken the same day, although some Germans remained in the cellars, continuing to fight. Finally, on 2 May the Berlin garrison surrendered, although mopping-up operations continued for a few more days. The final acts could now take place.

While the Russians had fought their way into Berlin, fighting around the city continued. On the Western Front, the final phase of the Allied advance continued to be met by a rapid collapse of German resistance. In 21st Army Group's area, Bremen was taken on 27 April, while Lübeck and Hamburg fell on 2 May. On 19 April, 12th Army Group captured Halle and Leipzig, and Dessau three days later. Finally, on 24 April, US First Army reached its stop line on the River Mulde. The Soviet forces not engaged in Berlin had driven on towards their advancing allies in the West, and on 25 April, made the first link-up on the Elbe.

US Third Army crossed the Danube on the same day, and moved on to take Regensburg. Patton then headed into Austria, taking Linz on 5 May. To his right, US

Seventh Army had taken Nuremberg on 20 April after a five-day battle, and then crossed the Danube along with French First Army. This finally destroyed resistance from Army Group G, and left the way open for the French to move towards the Swiss border. Hitler's suicide was now known about, and it was obvious that the end was near. By 4 May, almost all German resistance had ceased. At Montgomery's headquarters on Lüneburg Heath, the Germans surrendered all their forces in Holland, Denmark and North Germany; the next day, emissaries arrived at Eisenhower's headquarters and after some attempts to delay the process, signed on 7 May at 02:40. Eisenhower signalled London and Washington just a moment later:

'The mission of this Allied Force was fulfilled at 02:41 local time, May 7, 1945. Eisenhower.'

This was not quite true. Eisenhower and some of his deputies still had one more task to fulfil. At a ceremony in the Soviet sector of Berlin, representatives of the victorious Allies sat and signed the final act of surrender early in the morning of 8 May.

The war in Europe was over. Hitler's Reich, meant to last 1000 years, but managing just over 12, had finally fallen.

Left: Field Marshal Montgomery looks on as the German forces in Holland, Denmark and North Germany are surrendered to him at Lüneburg Heath on 4 May 1945. This was the first of three major surrender ceremonies – on 7 May, the Germans surrendered to Eisenhower, and the next day the final surrender to all three major Allies was signed.

Appendix: guide to map symbols

Below is a guide to the symbols used to designate the different types of military units featured on the maps.

XXXXX □ Army group	XX ⊠ Infantry division	III □ Regiment
XXXX □ Army	XX 〜 Airborne division	II □ Company
XXX ⊠ Corps	XX ◣ Armoured division	I □ Platoon

Bibliography

Atkinson, Rick. *An Army at Dawn: The War in North Africa 1942–43.* London: Little, Brown, 2003.

Bessonov, Evgeni. *Tank Rider: into the Reich with the Red Army.* London: Greenhill Books, 2003.

Black, Jeremy. *World War Two: a Military History.* London: Routledge, 2003.

Blumenson, Martin. *Patton: the Man Behind the Legend.* London: Cape, 1986.

Dunphie, Christopher. *The Pendulum of Battle: Operation Goodwood, July 1944.* Barnsley: Leo Cooper, 2004.

Eisenhower, Dwight D. *Crusade in Europe.* London: Heinemann, 1948.

Erickson, John. *The Road to Berlin.* London: Weidenfeld & Nicholson, 1983.

Erickson, John. *The Road to Stalingrad.* London: Weidenfeld & Nicholson, 1983.

Forty, George. *The Desert War.* Stroud: Sutton, 2002.

Graham, Dominick and Shelford Bidwell. *Tug of War: The Battle for Italy, 1943–1945.* New York: St Martins Press, 1986.

Guderian, Heinz. *Panzer Leader.* London: Arrow, 1990.

Hough, Richard. *The Longest Battle: The War at Sea 1939–45.* London: Cassell, 2001.

Jordan, David. *Battle of the Bulge: the first 24 Hours.* London: Greenhill, 2003.

Jordan, David. *Wolfpack: the U-boat War and the Allied Counter-attack 1939–1945.* Staplehurst: Spellmount, 2002.

Keegan, John. *Six Armies in Normandy: From D-Day to the Liberation of Paris.* London: Penguin, 1983.

Liddell Hart, Basil. *The Second World War.* London: Cassell, 1970.

MacDonald, Charles. *The Battle of the Bulge.* London: Phoenix, 1998.

Montgomery of Alamein, Viscount. *Memoirs.* London: Companion Book Club, 1960.

Parker, Matthew. *Monte Cassino.* London: Headline, 2003.

Stilwell, Alexander (ed). *The Second World War: a World in Flames.* Oxford: Osprey, 2004.

Sweetman, John. *The Dambusters Raid.* London: Arms & Armour Press, 1990.

Webster, Sir Charles & Frankland Noble. *The Strategic Air Offensive Against Germany 1939–1945. Volume I: Preparation, parts 1, 2 and 3.* London: HMSO, 1961.

Weeks, Albert L. *Stalin's Other War: Soviet Grand Strategy, 1939–1941.* Lanham, MD: Rowman & Littlefield, 2002.

Index